JULIAN OF
NORWICH

PAUL MOLINARI, S.J.

JULIAN OF NORWICH

The Teaching of a
14th Century English Mystic

LONGMANS, GREEN AND CO
LONDON · NEW YORK · TORONTO

LONGMANS, GREEN AND CO LTD
6 & 7 CLIFFORD STREET LONDON W I
THIBAULT HOUSE THIBAULT SQUARE CAPE TOWN
605-611 LONSDALE STREET MELBOURNE C I

LONGMANS, GREEN AND CO INC
55 FIFTH AVENUE NEW YORK 3

LONGMANS, GREEN AND CO
20 CRANFIELD ROAD TORONTO 16

ORIENT LONGMANS PRIVATE LTD
CALCUTTA BOMBAY MADRAS
DELHI HYDERABAD DACCA

First Published 1958

PRINTED IN GREAT BRITAIN AT THE UNIVERSITY PRESS ABERDEEN. NIHIL
OBSTAT JOANNES M. T. BARTON, S.T.D., L.S.S. CENSOR DEPUTATUS; IMPRIMATUR
E. MORROGH BERNARD, VIC. GEN.; WESTMONASTERII, DIE IIA JUNII, 1957

PREFACE

THE fourteenth century is generally considered the most important period for the history of spirituality in England: four great mystics lived and wrote in that century and left to us a valuable and precious teaching.

One of them, Julian of Norwich, an anchoress, seems to have enjoyed a popular esteem for her 'good counsel' in spiritual matters, an appreciation which has endured. Her writings—the *Revelations of Divine Love*—with the simplicity, freshness and inspiration proper to them, have been received with affection by succeeding generations, and this, not only in England—I have in mind particularly the Paris manuscript, and the translations into various foreign languages, besides the numerous editions in English since Cressy's version in 1670.

The book of the *Revelations* is highly valued for its literary worth since it is among the most beautiful works written in Middle English; but, more important, it was from the first used for 'spiritual reading', along with the works of Rolle, Hilton and the author of *The Cloud of Unknowing*.

Yet, in spite of the importance of the English school of mysticism and of Julian in particular, in spite of the numerous editions and articles published on Julian in recent years, no scientific study —at least so far as I know—has yet been published; no detailed attempt to analyse the spiritual doctrine contained in the *Revelations*. The time therefore seems to have come, if it is not overdue, for detailed studies on various aspects of Julian's writings.

The profundity of her book is clothed in such simplicity and directness of exposition that one may at first glance overlook its hidden value. And though short and by no means a treatise, it is most compact and touches upon a surprising variety of points of doctrine in both dogmatic and spiritual theology. All these points need to be studied in detail, before Julian's dependence on and connection with other currents of spirituality and with the other English mystics of her own time can properly be assessed.

v

Hence I have approached the *Revelations of Divine Love* with the intention of studying one particular aspect: namely, Julian's doctrine on prayer and contemplation.

In this analysis I have tried to see objectively, as far as possible, what Julian thinks and teaches on the soul's ascent towards God; the various stages of the spiritual life; the part played by both agents (God and the soul) in this process; and finally Julian's fundamental attitude with regard to God. My study is based entirely on the text: only after a thorough internal examination have I presumed to point out similarities with and possible dependence on other authors.[1]

If the present work is some slight help to the understanding of the beauty and depth of Julian's spiritual teaching, and if it serves the purpose of fostering further studies on Julian's eminently sound and encouraging doctrine, I shall feel that the time has been well spent.

---

[1] It is well known that the great mystics ' echo one another '. Hence it is hardly possible to cite all similarities, and all sources. I am concerned very largely to indicate that Julian owes much to the great spiritual figures of traditional Christian mysticism and that her teaching is in full accord with the principles which are laid down by the mystical theologians who systematized the teaching of the Fathers and the medieval positive theologians.

CONTENTS

	PAGE
PREFACE	V
ACKNOWLEDGEMENTS	vii
LIST OF ABBREVIATIONS	viii
INTRODUCTION	I

PART I

THE ACCIDENTAL ELEMENTS OF THE SPIRITUAL LIFE

CHAP. 1.	Julian's sickness	21
CHAP. 2.	Julian's ' Shewings '	32
CHAP. 3.	Julian's personal evaluation of her ' Shewings '	49
APPENDIX.	Julian's classification of her ' Shewings ' compared with the traditional scheme of mystical theology	60

PART II

THE ESSENTIAL ELEMENTS OF THE SPIRITUAL LIFE

CHAP. 1.	Preliminary methodological remarks	73
CHAP. 2.	The ' Second Conversion ': Contrition ; Compassion ; Longing for God	78
CHAP. 3.	Unitive ' Prayer '—Union of the wills	94
CHAP. 4.	From the ' union of the wills ' to ' beholding ' (contemplation): ' beholding ' which is ' special shewing '	104

PAGE

CHAP. 5.   A second type of infused contemplation: 'be-
           holding which is not special shewing'   118

CHAP. 6.   Summary of results   140

PART III

THE OBJECT OF CONTEMPLATION

CHAP. 1.   The 'homely loving of God' as the fundamental
           theme of the special shewings granted to Julian   149

CHAP. 2.   Julian's progressive realization of God's 'homely
           loving'   157

CHAP. 3.   A further aspect of God's 'homely loving': the   169
           concept of God as our Mother

CHAP. 4.   Consequences: Optimism and Trust. Detach-   177
           ment from self obtained by the perception of
           God's love

CHAP. 5.   Summary of results   187

GENERAL CONCLUSION   196

BIBLIOGRAPHY   199

LIST OF CITATIONS FROM AND REFERENCES TO THE TEXT OF THE
       SHORTER VERSION   210

LIST OF CITATIONS FROM AND REFERENCES TO THE TEXT OF
       THE LONGER VERSION   211

INDEX   213

INTRODUCTION

1. The Manuscripts.

2. The Author: general notes on Julian's life.

3. Julian's own description of her spiritual attitude before the Revelations.

THE MANUSCRIPTS

Five extant manuscripts of *Sixteen Revelations of Divine Love* are known, three in the British Museum, one in the Bibliothèque Nationale de Paris, and one in the Westminster Cathedral Library.

Chronologically they rank as follows:

(1) Brit. Mus., Additional MS. 37790, (A), fifteenth century.

(2) Westminster Cathedral Library, (W), late fifteenth or early sixteenth century.[1]

(3) Bibl. Nation., Paris, Fonds Anglais No. 40, (P), sixteenth century.

(4) Brit. Mus., Sloane MS. 2499, (S1), mid-seventeenth century.

(5) Brit. Mus., Sloane MS. 3705, (S2), late seventeenth or early eighteenth century.

It is not my intention to enter into the technical problems concerning the various manuscripts and their interdependence. Examination of them has satisfied me that the many small differences of readings do not affect the exposition of Julian's doctrine on prayer and contemplation. Further information on this question is given in the relevant studies of Sister Anna Maria Reynolds, C.P.[2]

There are, however, two points for consideration here.

---

[1] The Westminster MS. contains only extracts from the *Revelations*.

[2] I am indebted to Sister Reynolds for permission to read unpublished material embodying the results of her personal research, as well as for kind help in checking key passages against the manuscripts and in establishing the best readings in doubtful cases.

First, that the *Revelations of Divine Love* is a devotional book. It is very significant that two of the five extant manuscripts form part of devotional books: MS. (A) consists of a collection of twelve medieval spiritual works containing, among others, the *Amending of Life* by Richard Rolle; [1] MS. (W) contains extracts from *The Scale of Perfection* as well as from the *Revelations;* and the scribe has copied only those passages which concern more directly the spiritual life and the progress of the soul. This simple fact in itself emphasizes the high esteem enjoyed by Julian's book, and indicates that from the very first Julian was considered fit company for those English masters of the spiritual life, Richard Rolle and Walter Hilton.

Secondly, there is an essential difference between MS. (A) and all the other MSS. (P, S1, S2, W). The Rev. D. Harford points out that ' Comparison with the Paris and Sloane manuscripts shows the recovered version (A) to be very much shorter than the type of the text represented by them '.[2] A problem therefore arises concerning priority and dependence. I agree with the solution proposed by Mr. Harford that MS. (A) ' is what might be called the " first edition " of the Revelations, and the longer form is the outcome of the twenty years' subsequent meditation, thought and experience, referred to in the 51st and in the last chapters of the late version. It has been suggested that it was " abbreviated " from them: it is here maintained that they were " expanded " from it.' [3]   Harford was the first to suggest

[1] See Fortnightly Review, New Series, vol. 89 (1911), pp. 345-354, *The Mirror of Simple Souls*, by E. Underhill.   [2] Harford, Introd., p. 8.

[3] See Harford, Introd. p. 8. This solution might at first sight seem to create a difficulty. In fact, since the Longer Version was certainly completed before the year 1400, the question arises why the Shorter Version was still copied anew as late as 1413. Dr Charlotte Kröger suggests that on account of the general conditions of the time (the Lollard movement was rife at that period), the publication of a book containing doctrinal and theological reflections of a woman might not have been considered advisable. (See

this solution when, in 1911, he published this, the earliest known manuscript—Brit. Mus., Add. MS. 37790 (A). Since then it has been generally accepted.[1]

Both versions derive directly from Julian herself; the Longer Version therefore is not the original text of Julian augmented by commentaries, glosses, etc., of either contemporary or later authors. Both versions deal with the extraordinary experience received by Julian in ' the year of our Lord 1373, the eighth day of May '; [2] but whereas the Shorter Version is little more than a simple record of this experience, the Longer Version—written at least twenty years after 1373—is a much fuller account of the same experience. This is seen and exposed in the light of further insight and reflection, the result of twenty years of contemplation in which she was granted deeper understanding:

> Now I have told you of Fifteen Revelations, as God vouchsafed to minister them to [my] mind, *renewed by lightings and touchings*, I hope of the same Spirit that shewed them all.[3]

C. Kröger, *Die Mystikerin Lady Julian von Norwich*, p. 38.) Also the Shorter Version stresses the disadvantages of being a woman in this respect: ' But God forbid that ye should say or take it thus, that I am a teacher, for I do not mean that, nor meant I ever so. For I am a woman, unlettered, feeble and frail. But I know well this that I say—I have it on the shewing of Him who is Sovereign Teacher—and truly charity urgeth me to tell you of it. . . . Because I am a woman should I therefore believe that I ought not to tell you about the goodness of God since I saw at the same time that it is His will that it be known?' (Reynolds, ch. VI, p. 17.)

[1] See Thouless, *The Lady Julian*, p. 25; E. Underhill, *Mystics of the Church*, p. 129; Coleman, *English Mystics*, p. 132; Renaudin, *Quatre Mystiques Anglais*, p. 63; Hudleston, p. xi. This problem has been studied also by Sister Reynolds who has come to the same conclusion; the arguments in favour of this opinion are contained in her forthcoming book.

[2] Hudleston, ch. 2, p. 3. *Italics ours in all quotations from Julian.* See also ch. 65, p. 136: ' Of which Fifteen Shewings the First began early in the morn, about the hour of four; and they lasted, shewing by process full fair and steadily, each following other, till it was nine of the day, overpassed '; and ch. 66, p. 136: ' And after this the good Lord shewed the Sixteenth [Revelation] on the night following. . . .'

[3] Ibid. ch. 65, p. 136.

For, *twenty years after* the time of the Shewing, save three months, I had teaching inwardly, as I shall say.[1]

And from that time that it was shewed I desired oftentimes to witten what was our Lord's meaning. And fifteen years after, and more, I was answered in ghostly understanding, saying thus: 'Wouldst thou witten thy Lord's meaning in this thing? Wit it well: Love was his meaning.'[2]

As can be deduced from this description of the differences between the two versions, it will be necessary to make use of both in the present endeavour to establish the precise doctrine of Julian on prayer and contemplation. In fact the Shorter Version is more likely to yield a straightforward and unadorned account of the experience of the year 1373, without much commentary or reflection. But the Longer Version—as has been indicated—gives a much more complete account of the same experience augmented by further supernatural communications and Julian's reflections, and possibly also elements due to her reading, to instructions received by others, and so on.

Hence the Longer Version will here be taken as the principal but not exclusive source of investigation in the study of Julian's doctrinal developments; but in considering the accounts of the facts preceding the *Shewings*—such as Julian's spiritual attitude before the Revelations, and her sickness—use will be made of the Shorter Version.

The quotations of the Longer Version will be from Hudleston's edition (1952) and of the Shorter Version from Reynolds' edition (1958).[3]

[1] Hudleston, ch. 51, p. 94.   [2] Ibid. ch. 86, p. 169.

[3] The first definitive critical edition of the Revelations has been undertaken by Sister Reynolds. Meanwhile, as the basic printed text for my examination of Julian's book, I have adopted that of MS. Sloane 2499, rather than that of the Paris manuscript, as up to date editions deriving from the Sloane manuscript are easily obtainable; the Hudleston rather than the Warrack edition of MS. Sloane 2499 has been chosen, since the former keeps rather more closely than does the latter to the actual wording of the manuscript.

2

The Author: General Notes on Julian's Life

Little is known of Julian's life, for the external or historical evidence is scanty.

The scribe of MS. (A) refers to Julian in his introductory note as ' A deuoute woman and hir Name es Iulyan that is recluse atte Norwyche and ȝitt ys on lyfe. Anno domini millesimoccccxiij '. The scribe of the MS. (P) ends by saying: ' Explicit liber Revelationum Juliane anatorite Norwiche cuius anime propicietur Deus.'

Internal evidence shows that she was thirty and a half years old in May 1373, i.e. she was born towards the end of 1342 (cf. ch. 2 of the Longer Version); and ch. 51 (Hudleston, p. 94) records that ' Twenty years after the time of the Shewing, save three months, I had teaching inwardly, as I shall say ', i.e. Julian was still alive in February 1393.

There are references to Julian [1] in three wills dated respectively 1404, 1415, and 1416. These establish that Julian's anchorhold was at St Julian's Church, Conisford, Norwich, where she lived with a companion or servant.

It may, then, be asserted with certainty that Julian was born in 1342; that she was a recluse at least from 1404; that she was a recluse at the Church of St Julian and Edward, Conisford; that she was still living in 1416.[2]

Julian as a recluse

There is no direct information concerning the life of Julian as a recluse. The book of the Revelations does not

---

[1] See Sister Reynolds, LSE, p. 18, note 1.

[2] Was Julian a recluse at the time of the Revelations (May 1373)? The problem has been carefully dealt with and examined by Sister Reynolds; I agree fully with her conclusions, and am of the opinion that Julian was living in her mother's house at the time of the Shewings.

reveal anything on this point, but the kind of life she led
may be gathered from other sources, where this type of
consecration to God is amply described.   One of the most
useful sources is the *Ancrene Riwle*, specifically written for
certain anchoresses some two centuries before Julian's time
and still widely read in her own day.[1]

Julian and the Benedictines

It is almost impossible to ascertain whether or not Julian,
as a recluse, was a Benedictine nun; for whereas in the wills
and lists of names given in Rye's book (Appendix IX, and
ch. 1) nuns are invariably styled either Dame or Lady,[2]
Julian is simply referred to as a ' devout woman '.   On the
other hand, the fact that the anchorhold where Julian lived
—with the Church of St Julian—belonged to the Monastery
at Carrow, would seem to suggest that she was a member of
the Benedictine community at Carrow.[3]   In this connection
Dom R. Huddleston remarks that the fact that Julian once
quotes the *Life of St Benedict* might be taken as evidence of
a Benedictine background.[4]

As will be seen later, however, there is much more evidence
of Benedictine influence on Julian than a single citation
provides.   Yet this influence does not seem to be sufficient
to prove the existence of a strict connection with the Benedictines such as would be provided by formal membership

[1] See also L. Gougaud, *Etudes sur la reclusion réligieuse*, Revue Mabillon,
13 (1923), pp. 26-39; 77-102; *La vie érémitique au moyen âge;* RAM, 1 (1920),
pp. 209-240; 313-328; *Ermites et reclus*, Ligugé, 1928. H. Leclerq, *Reclus,*
DACL, XIV, cc. 2149-2159. L. Oliger, O.F.M., *Regulae tres Reclusorum et
Eremitarum Angliae saec. XIII-XIV*, Antonianum, 3 (1928), pp. 151-190, 299-
320; *Regulae Reclusorum Angliae et Quaestiones tres de vita solitaria*, Antonianum,
9 (1934), pp. 37-84, 243-268; R. M. Clay, *The Hermits and Anchorites of England.*
F. D. S. Darwin, *The Medieval Recluse.*

[2] See W. Rye, *Carrow Abbey, otherwise Carrow Priory.*

[3] It was a common practice among nuns and monks to leave their community in order to lead the more rigorous life of a recluse.

[4] See Hudleston, pp. ix-x.

of the Order; particularly in view of the widespread diffusion of Benedictine institutions and monasteries and its
radical influence on all Christian spirituality up to the
twelfth century. The period from the sixth century to the
twelfth, that is to say, from St Benedict to St Bernard, was
a monastic age. Since the greater number of religious
writers during those centuries were monks, the monastic
spirit deeply influenced the thought and practice of the
whole of Christendom.[1]

Authors like St Gregory, St Anselm, St Bernard were
considered as classical and the type of spirituality deriving
from their writings held sway in Western Europe to the
twelfth century, when ' the ideas and nomenclature of the
religious philosophy made current by the diffusion of the
Dionysiac writings in Latin ' [2] began to prevail. But even
so, as T. W. Coleman points out, ' the Western type was
not crushed out. In many places it had struck deep roots.
This was true of England. Here it found congenial soil.
It suited our temperament .' [3]

It is thus no matter for surprise that a writer of the immediately subsequent period should re-echo the fundamental
ideas of Benedictine spirituality. It may consequently be
concluded that Julian had some connection with a Benedictine community (Carrow Abbey), but that she was not a
formal member of it (there is no mention in the book of
anything strictly connected with the religious life, and this
would be unlikely if she had been a religious). She might
have been there as a girl—for the nuns had some sort of

[1] Particular attention should obviously be paid to the development and
diffusion of the monastic life in England. The Rule of St Benedict and the
consequent traditional uses common to all the West from the second half of
the seventh century were introduced into this country by Wilfrid and Benet
Biscop. See D. Knowles, *The Monastic Order in England; The Religious Orders
in England; The Religious Houses in Medieval England.*
[2] C. Butler, *Western Mysticism*, p. 125.
[3] Coleman, *English Mystics*, p. 28.

boarding school for girls at Carrow; [1] and since the anchorhold belonged to the same Abbey, she must have been to
some extent dependent on it, perhaps for spiritual help,
books, and so on.

Julian's personality

Julian introduces herself as a ' symple creature vnlettyrde ',[2]
but this assertion need not be taken literally: [3] the term
' unlettered ' may mean that she did not know *litteras
latinas*, or even that she was not a ' scholar ', though she
knew Latin.[4] Internal evidence shows that she had learnt to
read,[5] and from the whole book it appears that Julian must
have been endowed with keen intellectual powers. Her
descriptions reveal her as capable of profound emotion, but
yet without the least hint of emotional instability or inde-
cision. She appears to be strongly original, but entirely
orthodox and outstanding in her filial obedience to the

[1] F. Blomefield-Parkin Charles, *An Essay towards a Topographical History of
the County of Norfolk* (London, 1805-1810), vol. iv, p. 524: ' This nunnery
[Carrow Abbey] for many years had been a school or place of education for
the young ladies of the chief families of the diocese, who boarded with and
were educated by the nuns.'

[2] Longer Version (P), S1—Dom R. Hudleston in his modernized edition
has: ' a simple creature that could no letter ', ch. 2, p. 3.

[3] See Renaudin, *Quatre Mystiques Anglais*, pp. 55-56.

[4] It is interesting to remember that in opposition to the high degree of
culture existing in the English nunneries in the early Norman period (cf.
D. Knowles, *Monastic Order in England*, p. 318), the standard of learning had
dropped considerably in the following centuries. Eileen Power in her
Medieval English Nunneries gives the following main indications of this regress:
no evidence of copying of manuscripts, no evidence of chronicles, of rich
libraries, of general knowledge of Latin; at least some novices were unable to
write, and the acts of episcopal visitations show that some monasteries were
completely at a loss when writing had to be done and there was no clerk to
do it. I also understand from Dom D. Knowles that some bishops com-
plained that nuns were at times incapable of reading their Rule.

[5] In support of this Sister Reynolds refers to the passage: ' I had teaching
within me, as it were the beginning of an A.B.C.', ch. 51. Cf. Sister Reynolds
LSE, p. 20, note 12.

Church. Her originality, characterized by a singular freshness and simplicity, derives from a deep penetration into the mystery of the love of God for man and leads to an attitude of joyful confidence and trust in God who is ' All-Love '.

Such a person could not remain unknown to or be ignored by her contemporaries. An interesting document which testifies to this was left by Margery Kempe: she describes a visit paid by her to Julian, to receive spiritual advice, ' for the ankres was an expert in such things and good counsel could give '. The date of this meeting is not stated by Margery, but according to Hudleston it may be set down approximately as between 1400 and 1410. The account of this meeting contributes to a better understanding of Julian's personality and the esteem she enjoyed amongst her contemporaries:

And then she was bidden by Our Lord for to go to an ankress in the same city which hight Dame Jelyan. And so she did and showed her the grace that God put in her soul of compunction, contrition, sweetness and devotion, compassion with holy meditation and high contemplation, and full many holy speeches and dalliance that our Lord spake to her soul, and many wonderful revelations, which she showed to the ankress to learn if there were any deceit in them, for the ankress was expert in such things and good counsel could give.

The ankress, hearing the marvellous goodness of Our Lord, highly thanked God with all her heart for his visitation, counselling this creature to be obedient to the will of Our Lord God and fulfil with all her mights whatever he put in her soul, if it were not against the worship of God and profit of her even-Christians; for, if it were, then it were not the moving of a good Spirit but rather of an evil spirit. The Holy Ghost moveth never a thing against charity; and, if he did, he were contrarious to his own self, for he is all charity.

Also he moveth a soul to all chasteness, for chaste livers be called the temple of the Holy Ghost; and the Holy Ghost

maketh a soul stable and steadfast in the right faith and the
right belief. And a double man in soul is ever unstable and
unsteadfast in all his ways. He that is evermore doubting is
like to the flood of the sea, the which is moved and borne about
with the wind, and that man is not like to receive the gifts of
God. What creatures hath these tokens, he must steadfastly
believe that the Holy Ghost dwelleth in his soul. And much
more, when God visiteth a creature with tears of contrition,
devotion, or compassion, he may and ought to believe that the
Holy Ghost is in his soul. Saint Paul saith that the Holy
Ghost asketh for us with mournings and weepings unspeakable,
that is to say, he maketh us to ask and pray with mournings
and weepings, so plenteously that the tears may not be numbered. There may none evil spirit give these tokens, for
Jerome saith that tears torment more the devil than do the
pains of hell. God and the devil be evermore contrarious,
and they shall never dwell together in one place; and the
devil hath no power in man's soul. Holy Writ saith that the
soul of a rightful man is the seat of God; and so, I trust,
sister, that ye be. I pray God grant you perseverance. Set
all your trust in God and fear not the language of the world;
for the more despite, shame, and reproof that ye have in the
world, the more is your merit in the sight of God. Patience
is necessary unto you, for in that shall ye keep your soul.

Much was the dalliance that the ankress and this creature
had by communing in the love of Our Lord Jesus Christ many
days that they were together.[1]

This document is clear testimony of the popularity
and wide appreciation enjoyed by the recluse; an appreciation reflected in the title of 'Blessed' often given to her,[2]

---

[1] Quoted by Hudleston, Introd. pp. xxvii-xxix. This account is taken
from the edition of Margery Kempe's book published by the Early English
Text Society (Original Series, No. 212). The spelling is here modernized
and a few obsolete words are given their modern equivalents.

[2] See D. Attwater, *A Dictionary of Saints*, p. 175: ' Julian of Norwich, BD,
virg. May 13—The title " Blessed " is often given to Dame Julian, who was
a recluse at Norwich and died with a great reputation for holiness *c*. 1423.'

though this title was never officially confirmed by the Church.[1]

3

JULIAN'S OWN DESCRIPTION OF HER SPIRITUAL ATTITUDE BEFORE THE REVELATIONS

For a right appreciation of Julian's doctrine on prayer and contemplation it is useful and even necessary to consider not only the content of the Revelations but also her spiritual attitude before the time of the Shewings.

First, as will be seen later, there exists a real continuity between Julian's later doctrine on prayer and contemplation and the ideas and desires which typify her spiritual attitude before the Revelations. Secondly, and this is of great importance, knowledge of Julian's spiritual antecedents will eventually help towards formation of judgement concerning the divine origin of her Revelations.[2] Moreover, we know that in the case of authentic revelations God's Providence usually prepares and predisposes for the reception of these special graces. Finally, Julian herself seems to consider some knowledge of her spiritual state necessary for those who wish to understand the true meaning of the Revelations. She says:

I desired three graces by the gift of God. The first was to have mind of the Passion of Christ. The second was a bodily

[1] This absence of official recognition as 'Blessed' does not imply disapproval of Julian on the part of the Church. There seems now to be no question of introducing her cause of beatification on account of the lack of positive data concerning her life—as indicated above. In a certain sense one could even today speak of a *fama sanctitatis*, but there are no miracles recorded.

[2] Perhaps the most important reason for a consideration of Julian's spiritual antecedents is the fact that the divine origin of the Revelations has been impugned by certain authors precisely on account of her alleged 'mental condition' at the time of the Shewings.

sickness. The third, to have, of God's gift, three wounds. (Ch.I, p. 1.) [1]

The first grace was ' to have mind of the Passion of Christ '

For the first grace: it came to my mind with devotion. Methought I had great feeling for the Passion of Christ, but I desired to have yet more, by the grace of God. Methought I would like to have been that time with Mary Magdalen and others who were Christ's lovers, that I might have seen with bodily eyes the Passion of our Lord which He suffered for me, so that I might have suffered with Him as did others who loved Him. Notwithstanding the fact that I believed earnestly all the pains of Christ as Holy Church shews and teaches (and also the paintings of crucifixes made, by the grace of God, in conformity with the teaching of Holy Church, to the likeness of Christ's Passion as far as the skill of man may reach); notwithstanding all this true belief I desired a bodily sight, wherein I might have the more knowing of the bodily pains of our Lord, and Saviour, and of the compassion of our Lady and of all His true lovers who believed in His pains at that time and afterwards. For I would have been one of them and suffered along with them.

Other sight of God or shewing desired I never none until that my soul were gone forth from my body (for I trusted steadfastly that I should be saved). And this was my meaning: that I should afterwards, because of that shewing, have the more true mind in the Passion of Christ. (Ch. I, pp. 1-2.)

Julian says that she already had firm faith in ' all the pains of Christ, as Holy Church shews and teaches ' and even ' great feeling for the Passion of Christ ', yet she desired to have a ' *more true* mind in the Passion of Christ '. The means by which she hopes to obtain this ' more true mind in the Passion of Christ ' and which, in consequence, she desires, is a bodily sight. She wishes to see ' bodily ' the Passion

---

[1] In *this* section quotations from the Shorter Version, MS. (A), are according to Reynolds' edition 1958, unless the contrary is stated (cf. pp. 5-6 above).

of our Lord in order to be able to suffer 'with Him, as did others who loved Him'. Therefore the meaning of the first grace is to obtain *com-passion*, viz. to suffer with Christ as did those who were present at the foot of the Cross.[1]

The second grace was 'bodily sickness':

For the second grace: it came to my mind with contrition, freely, without any seeking—a wilful desire to have, of God's giving, a bodily sickness. I would that this bodily sickness might be grievous even to the point of death, so that I might in the sickness receive all the rites of Holy Church, I myself thinking that I should die; and I would that every creature that saw me might think the same. For I wished to have no comfort in fleshly or earthly living. In this sickness I desired to have all manner of pains, bodily and ghostly, such as I should have if I were to die: all the dreads, all temptings of fiends, and all manner of their pains save of the out-passing of the soul; I hoped that it might be a speed to me when I should come to die for I desired soon to be with my God. (Ch. I, p. 2.)

[1] The aim of Julian's request corresponds therefore to the classic teaching on the principal ends of the consideration of the Passion. Cf. e.g. Fr L. de la Puente, S.J.: 'First, procuring in meditation, to feele (as S. Paul saith) in our selves, that which Christ felt, with the affections of compassion, sorrow and sadness, in such manner that we become transformed into Christ, sad, and afflicted for our sakes and spirituallie crucified with him; in the same maner that the most holie virgin felt the sorrowes of his Sonne: for which cause Simeon said: that there should passe thorough his soule a sword, not corporall, but spirituall, of compassion and sorrow. . . . The second end which we ought to pretend in these meditations, is also to drinke the cup of the passion corporallie, conforming us to Christ our Lord in the selfe same sufferinges, assuming force and courage to this effect, and making effectuall purposes thereof. . . . And so after the imitation of the same Apostle, we ought to procure when we meditate the passion, 'to beare alwaies in our bodies the mortification of Jesus Christ' (2 Cor. iv. 10-Gal. vi. 17), and the markes of Jesus, which are the woundes and paines that afflict our flesh, as they afflicted his; so that in both manners everie one may say: 'Christo crucifixus sum Cruci' (Gal. ii. 19), 'I am nayled with Christ upon the Crosse', as well by compassion, as by imitation in suffering for him, as he suffered for me. Cf. Lewis de la Pueute, S.J., *Meditations upon the Mysteries of our Holie Faith*, P. IV, Introd., vol. 2, pp. 8-9.

This second grace is an illness which would be so serious as to procure for her the full detachment proper to death: ' I myself thinking that I should die, and I would that every creature that saw me might think the same '. In other words, she desires to have ' no comfort in fleshly or earthly living ', nay even to have ' all manner of pains, bodily and ghostly '.

She wants to obtain the bodily sickness in order to be entirely purified and hence to live afterwards only for God.[1]

The third grace was ' to have of God's gift three wounds '

Whereas in the two preceding cases, following Julian, it was necessary to distinguish between the immediate object of Julian's desire and the reason why it was asked, there is here no indication of the purpose of the petition, simply because it coincides with the petition itself. In this very fact there is also an explanation why the two first graces were asked

---

[1] This reason for the second desire is stated more clearly in the corresponding text of the Longer Version:

Shorter Version	Longer Version
In this sickness I desired to have all manner of pains, bodily and ghostly, such as I should have if I were to die: all the dreads, all the temptings of fiends, and all manner of their pains save of the out-passing of the soul;	In this sickness I desired to have all manner [of] pains bodily and ghostly, that I should have if I should die, with all the dreads and tempests of the fiends, except the out-passing of the soul.
	And this I meant for [that] I would be purged, by the mercy of God, and after live more to the worship of God, because of that sickness.
I hoped that it might be a speed to me when I should come to die for I desired soon to be with my God. (Ch. I, p. 2.)	And that for the more speed in my death: for I desired to be soon with my God. (Huddleston, ch. 2, p. 4.)

for conditionally, and eventually passed from her mind, whereas the third one was put unconditionally and 'dwelt with me continually'.

The text concerning the third grace reads:

For the third grace: I heard a man of Holy Church tell the story of Saint Cecilia, in which telling I understood that she had received three wounds with a sword in the neck, from the which she pined to death.

Moved by this I conceived a mighty desire, praying our Lord God that He would grant me three wounds during my lifetime, that is to say, the wound of contrition, the wound of compassion, and the wound of wilful longing for God.

Right as I asked the other two graces with a condition, so I asked the third without any condition. These two desires aforesaid passed from my mind, and the third dwelt with me continually. (Ch. I, p. 3.) [1]

This third grace evidently comprehends and sublimates the preceding ones; and hence this 'wilful longing towards God' represents the most typical element of Julian's spirituality at the time before the Revelations, a conclusion corroborated by the circumstances already mentioned, viz. that no condition was attached to it, and that whereas 'the two desires aforesaid passed from my mind', 'the third dwelt with me continually'. Only conditionally, and only in subordination to the basic desires, does Julian ask for a bodily sight and a sickness.

This conception, according to which Julian considers 'sickness' and 'sights' as concrete means for the attainment of a purely spiritual good ('to be purged . . . and after live more to the worship of God because of that sickness'—

[1] The condition referred to is spoken of by Julian thus: 'These two desires—of the Passion and of the sickness—I desired with a condition, as methought they passed the common course of prayers. Therefore I said: "Lord, Thou knowest what I would have. If it be Thy will that I have it, grant it me; and if it be not Thy will, good Lord be not displeased, for I will not but as Thou willest." ' (Ch. I, p. 3.)

to have ' mind of the Passion of Christ '), is of great importance for the appreciation of Julian's spiritual attitude before
the Revelations, and most of all for the understanding of her
doctrine on the spiritual life.   In fact Julian considers extraordinary phenomena (viz. sickness and sights) as mere
means, not to be sought with anxious desire and unsound
estimation, but only conditionally and only in so far as they
convey a deeper spiritual good.   She distinguishes them
from the substantial desire of finding God in ' contrition ',
' compassion ', ' wilful longing '.   She shows her practical
detachment from the former and her attachment to the latter:
' Right as I asked the other two graces with a condition, so
I asked the third without any condition.   These two desires
aforesaid passed from my mind, and the third dwelt with me
continually.'   (Ch. I, p. 3.)

All these qualifications give us to understand that according
to Julian's mind the essential element of the spiritual life
consists in the desire for union, in the ardent longing for
God, which sustains an effective and unitive love.

This is destined to increase with the progress of the soul
towards God because—as Julian says: ' Ever the more clearly
that the soul seeth this Blissful Cheer *by grace of loving*, the more
it longeth to see it in fulness ' (Hudleston, ch. 72, p. 146).

This ' wilful longing ' for God is the ' wound ' that
becomes more and more sweetly burning and will be healed
only in Heaven, when we shall be all ' had ' [1] in God.[2]   In
comparison with this essential element, the extraordinary
phenomena have only a subordinate accidental function.
This distinction, already clear at the very beginning of
Julian's account of her spiritual life, leads naturally to a
consideration of the accidental and of the essential elements
in the ascent to God as envisaged by Julian.

[1] See Hudleston, ch. 43, p. 78.   MS. (P) reads ' hid ' instead of ' had '.
[2] Compare this doctrine with the main theme of the *Spiritual Canticle* by
St John of the Cross.

I

THE ACCIDENTAL ELEMENTS OF
THE SPIRITUAL LIFE

I

JULIAN'S SICKNESS

And when I was thirty winters old and a half God sent me a bodily sickness, in the which I lay for three days and three nights. On the fourth night I received all the rites of Holy Church and thought not to be alive at daybreak.

After this I languished for two days and two nights more, and on the third night I thought often times to have passed away and so too thought they who were about me. But in this I was right sorry and loath to die, (though not for anything that was on earth that me liked to live for, nor for anything that I was afeared for; for I trusted in God). But it was because I would have lived on to have loved God better and for a longer time—that I might, by the grace of that living, have the more knowing and loving of God in the bliss of heaven, for methought all the time that I had lived here so little and so short in the regard of endless bliss.

I thought thus: 'Good Lord, may my living be no longer to Thy worship?' And I was answered in my reason and by the feeling of my pains that I should die; and I assented fully, with all the will of my heart, to God's will.

Thus I endured till day and by then was my body dead from the middle downwards, as to feeling. Then was I moved to be set upright, leaning back, with cloths to my head, in order to have the more freedom of heart to be one with God's will, thinking on Him whilst my life would last.

They who were with me sent for the priest, my curate, to be at my ending. He came and a child with him, and brought a cross. By that time my eyes were set in my head and I could not speak. The priest set the cross before my face and said: 'Daughter, I have brought thee the image of thy Saviour. Look thereupon and comfort thee therewith in reverencing of Him who died for thee and me.'

Methought that I was well as it was, for my eyes were set upwards, towards heaven whither I trusted to come. But nevertheless I assented to set my eyes upon the face of the crucifix if I could, to be able to endure the longer unto the time of mine ending. For methought I might longer endure to look straight forward than straight upward, After this my sight began to fail and it was all dark about me in the chamber, and murky as if it were night, except that on the image of the cross there remained the ordinary light. And, I knew not how, all that was beside the cross was as ugly to me as if it had been crowded with fiends.

After this the upper half of my body began to die as to feeling; my hands fell down on either side and also, from weakness, my head sank to one side. The most pain that I felt was shortness of breath and the failing of life. Then thought I truly that I was at the point of death.

And in this, suddenly all my pain was away from me: I was all whole as ever I was before or afterwards, and especially in the upper part of my body. I marvelled at this change, for methought it was a secret working of God and not of nature; yet, by the feeling of this ease I did not trust any the more that I should live, and the feeling of this ease was no true ease to me; for methought I had liefer been delivered of this world, and my heart was set thereon.[1]

It must be noted first of all that Julian had desired a sickness so as to ' be purged by the mercy of God, and after live more to the worship of God ': the above account relates how this desire for a sickness found fulfilment.

Julian attributes her sickness to a direct divine intervention: ' God sent me a bodily sickness '. But in the light of modern psychology, which has proved that some phenomena of sickness can be caused by neurotic dispositions stimulated and excited by the religious aspirations of the patient himself, we must consider whether Julian's inter-

---

[1] Reynolds, ch. II, pp. 4-6. In this chapter all quotations are from the Shorter Version (Reynolds' ed.) unless the contrary is explicitly stated.

pretation as to the origin of her sickness is the right one. In fact, if it were established that Julian's illness was merely the result of neurotic or hysterical dispositions, this might be taken as depreciating the value of her spiritual teaching, especially as the ' shewings '—on which Julian's doctrine is mainly based—began immediately after the crisis of her sickness, when she was suddenly released from it. Hence we must ask whether the sights form part of and result from a neurotic sickness or whether their origin and nature has to be explained by a special intervention of God.

The second aspect of this question, that is to say, *the possible relationship between sickness and sights*, has frequently been considered;[1] but the first, viz. the *possible neurotic*

---

[1] P. Renaudin (op. cit. p. 60) having cited the relevant passage, says: ' Before we proceed any further a question occurs to our mind. We have here the case of a vision, which had been prepared by a long period of desire and expectancy. Could we not say: excited by this expectancy? Could it not be that the vision was created by the desire itself? The ecstasy takes place during an illness, in a body which had been weakened by it, in a person who had lost, at least in part, normal consciousness and touch with reality. Have we not sufficient matter to recognize in this ecstasy a pathological character; that is to say do not the circumstances of the ecstasy strengthen the hypothesis of auto-suggestion (—leaving Julian's good faith intact—), this hypothesis being already suggested by the perfect correspondence between the anchoress' desires and their realization?' The attitudes taken by the commentators with regard to this problem have been various and they range from a more sound attitude of prudence (cf. Renaudin, op. cit., ibid.; Tyrrell, *The Faith*, pp. 12 ff.; Knowles, *The English Mystics*, pp. 130 ff.; Coleman, *English Mystics*, pp. 138 ff.) to hasty statements not sufficiently substantiated, or at least to a less cautious employment of technical terms such as ' state of hypnotism ' (cf. Inge, *Studies of English Mystics*, p. 58); Grace Warrack shows sympathy for the theory of ' physical illusion ', ' trance state ' visions, etc. (Cf. Introduction, pp. xxxvii-xxxviii); R. H. Thouless says: ' Then [in the sickness] her normal mental life was weakened, and the scenes of the Passion with which meditation had stored her mind welled up to the surface of consciousness and presented themselves with *hallucinatory* vividness ' (Thouless, *The Lady Julian*, p. 25); C. Pepler, O.P., speaks of ' extreme pathological state ', of ' acute neurosis induced perhaps by an over-enthusiastic life of penance and solitude. But she appears to have retained consciousness throughout, except in the final dream ' (C. Pepler, ' Visions and Shewings ', in *Life of the Spirit*, 3 (1949), p. 486).

C

origin of the sickness itself seems so far to have escaped the attention of the authors.

Both these aspects need to be considered simultaneously. In fact if it could be proved that the sickness had its origin only in neurosis, pathological hysteria, etc., suspicion as to the origin and nature of the sights which followed the sickness would be justified. If, on the other hand, it can be proved that neurosis must be ruled out, and that a preter-natural divine intervention has to be admitted as the cause of the sickness, neurosis as the sole cause of the subsequent sights is also extremely improbable.

The consideration of the sickness and sights in close rela-tionship with Julian's previous desire for both will also throw light on the continuity in Julian's spirituality before, during, and after both sickness and sights.

Analysis of the sickness

1. *Was Julian's ' sickness' the manifestation and crisis of an organic disease already affecting her body, or a temporary abnormal condition?*

We read of a paralysis of the lower parts of the body, of speechlessness and difficulty in raising the eyes. At a certain moment everything goes dark except for the image of the Crucifix, and this darkness is absolute. Meanwhile the paralysis is spreading to the upper parts of the body and causes shortness of breath. At this critical moment, when Julian thinks that death is imminent, there is a sudden release from all pains and Julian feels well again ' as ever I was before '.

The phenomena here described are not at all rare or extraordinary: they could be, and in fact frequently are, manifestations of advanced or final stages of a number of purely organic diseases. But the *sudden* appearance of the sickness in such an advanced and serious stage is certainly strange, and though it does not exclude the possibility that these phenomena, as described by Julian, were caused by a previous organic disease, it makes this explanation less likely. This is as much as can be said, since more precise data concerning the bodily conditions of Julian during the time preceding the sickness are not available.

We must, however, note that up to the time of her illness she appears to have enjoyed reasonably good health—another reason for assuming the unlikelihood of a gradual progress to such a serious crisis.

Again, if the crisis were provoked by purely organic conditions, it would be extremely difficult to explain the sudden cure and the absence of a repetition of such a crisis for the rest of her life [1] without having recourse to a preter-natural cause.

Hence from the purely medical point of view it seems more probable that her sickness was due to a temporary abnormal condition of her psycho-physical system, and not to a purely organic and permanent deficiency already affecting Julian.

2. *If the sickness was a temporary abnormal condition of Julian's psycho-physical system, was it the effect of a neurotic or hysterical disposition or the result of a special activity of God?*

If we remember that the sickness had been desired by Julian, the further question arises whether her temporary abnormal conditions (the supposed nervous paralysis and the concomitant and subsequent phenomena) were due to preternatural divine activity, or whether they must be attributed to purely natural causes, viz. to a strong neurotic or

---

[1] As noted at p. 7, from the Introduction by the copyist of the MS. (A), we gather that Julian lived at least for another forty years. In the Longer Version (written at least twenty years after the experience of 1373) there is no mention of a repetition of the sickness.

hysterical disposition, stimulated and excited to excess by religious ideas and aspirations.[1]

An accurate and unprejudiced inquiry is therefore essential. In fact there is no theological principle from which it would follow that an extraordinary divine activity on the psychological and physiological apparatus of the recipient must produce phenomena intrinsically different from those associated with hypnotism, hysteria, neurosis, and the like. Nor can it be excluded on theological grounds that God may grant mystical experiences to sick persons or to those who are inclined to some form of neurosis; nor even that divine Providence may make use of such tendencies within certain limits.

Hence a right and prudent judgement on these cases will be found not by considering the extraordinary phenomena in themselves, but rather by contemplating them in the light of what is known about the character and personality of the subject, particularly with regard to both the immediate and the permanent effects of such phenomena on the moral and religious reactions and activities of the person concerned.

In short, modern psychology, far from abolishing the classic principles of St Ignatius of Loyola and St John of the Cross on the discernment of spirits, rather confirms their value and even postulates a greater care in their application.[2]

[1] It is, of course, entirely superfluous to discuss here the opinion of those who, on account of their materialistic principles, deny every possibility of a genuine mystical experience. For the same reason such people immediately attribute the various categories of mental diseases indiscriminately to all who claim to have been granted extraordinary religious experiences, particularly if those experiences are associated with the phenomenon of bodily sickness. On the other hand, I wish to observe that it is neither prudent nor in conformity with the teaching and the practice of the Church to pronounce hastily in favour of extraordinary divine interventions.

[2] This is also the conclusion, e.g., of Fr Carlos Maria Staehlin, S.J., *Mystische Täuschungen. Zur Beurteilung einiger mystischer Phänomene*, GL, 27 (1954), pp. 276-290. Cf. also the introductory remarks of the editor of GL, ibid. p. 276: ' The result of this study is finally that a definitive judgement on the " mystical

Applying these principles to Julian's case, it should be noted first of all that the account of her sickness certainly does not exclude a divine origin. Again, a state of hypnosis, trance, or catalepsis must be excluded, because during the sickness Julian was highly conscious [1] and certainly far from hysterical.[2] Nor is there any likelihood that Julian's desire for a sickness had become an obsession which could have produced a pathological condition. On the contrary, she desired the sickness only as means to the attainment of higher spiritual graces: compassion, purgation, longing towards God. 'These two desires aforesaid [for bodily sight and sickness] passed from my mind, and the third dwelt with me continually.' (Ch. I, p. 3.) And she had asked for them 'with a condition': 'Lord, Thou knowest what I would have. If it be Thy will that I have it, grant it me; and if it be not Thy will, good Lord be not displeased, for I will not but as Thou willest.' (Ch. I, p. 3.) It

---

phenomena" cannot be given as long as one limits oneself exclusively to the psychic data, since the psychic mechanism is the same in all cases. Before one may conclude to a preternatural cause it is therefore necessary to have recourse to criteria which do not belong to the psychic order. The classic rules of the distinguishing of the spirits are not called in doubt hereby, but their application to the concrete case has become considerably more difficult.'

[1] She was able to reason and pass judgement on what was happening about her: she was aware of the coming of the curate; she listened to his words; she obeyed him in setting her eyes on the crucifix that he placed before her.

[2] Fr Tyrrell, speaking of the absence of hysterism in Julian, says that 'the hysterical mind is one in which large tracts of consciousness seem to get detached from the main body, and to take control of the subject for the time being, giving rise to the phenomena rather foolishly called double or multiple 'personality'. This is a disease proper to the passive-minded, to those who give way to a 'drifting' tendency, and habitually suffer their whole interest to be absorbed by the strongest sensation or emotion that presents itself. Such minds are generally chaotic and unorganized, as is revealed in the rambling, involved, interminably parenthetical and digressive character of their conversation. But when, as with Mother Juliana, we find unity and coherence, we may infer that there has been a life-long habit of mental control, such as excludes the supposition of an hysterical temperament.' (G. Tyrrell, *The Faith*, p. 18.)

is difficult to conceive that a desire so expressed could cause the sickness.

It is also necessary to stress the fact that neither Julian's account of her sickness nor anything else in her Revelations provides us with the slightest indication that Julian was not in good faith when she related her experience and expressed her conviction that the sickness and the other extraordinary experiences derived from God.   Examination of the internal evidence, as well as the esteem of her contemporaries,[1] seems to exclude absolutely such an hypothesis which, indeed, as far as I am aware, has never been advanced by anyone. (This does not, of course, prove the divine origin of her sickness and sights, but it serves as negative evidence which is far from negligible.) Moreover, Julian's account of her sickness is free from all affectation and from any trace of neurotic exhibitionism.   She has no desire to impress the reader, rather she wishes to direct attention away from herself to God alone:

> But God forbid that ye should say or take it thus, that I am a teacher, for *I do not mean that, nor meant I ever so.*
>
> For I am a woman, unlettered, feeble and frail. . . .
>
> Because I am a woman should I therefore believe that I ought not to tell you about the goodness of God since I saw at the same time that it is His will that it be known?   And that shall ye see well in the same matter that follows after, if it be well and truly received.
>
> *Then shall ye soon forget me that am a wretch,* and act so that I hinder you not, *and behold Jesus* who is Teacher of all.   (Ch. VI, p. 17.)

Anyone who has had to do with reports in which really neurotic persons enlarge upon their experiences, will be

---

[1] As I said, we have a testimony of this esteem in the book of Margery Kempe where it is said that ' she [Margery] showed to the ankress to learn if there were any deceit in them [her visions], *for the ankress was an expert in such things and good counsel could give* '.   (Quoted by Hudleston, p. xxviii.)

struck by the sober and detached way of Julian's description.[1] In fact her simplicity, freshness and modesty stand in complete contrast with what is usually considered typical of neurotic cases.

Perhaps the strongest indication of the divine origin of her sickness is her behaviour—her spiritual attitude—during its course and particularly at the crisis. In the midst of severe pains, when she was convinced that the shadow of death was upon her, she remained in an attitude of spiritual peace, of self-detachment, of readiness to do God's will in suffering and dying:

> . . . and on the third night I thought often times to have passed away and so too thought they who were about me. But in this I was right sorry and loath to die (though not for anything that was on earth that me liked to live for, nor for anything that I was afeared for; for I trusted in God). But it was because I would have lived on to have loved God better and for a longer time—that I might, by the grace of that living, have the more knowing and loving of God in the bliss of heaven, for methought all the time that I had lived here so little and so short in the regard of endless bliss. (Ch. II, p. 4).

All this manifests abundantly that during the sickness Julian's spiritual energies, as well as the natural force of mind and will, far from being diminished, were 'proved' and strengthened.[2] Julian had asked for a sickness so that she might be 'purged, by the mercy of God, and after live

[1] See, e.g., the simple expressions used to indicate her belief in the divine origin of the sickness and her cure: ' God sent me a bodily sickness ' (ch. II, p. 4). . . . ' And in this ' suddenly all my pain was away from me : I was all whole as ever I was before or afterwards, and especially in the upper part of my body.   I marvelled at this change, for me thought it was a secret working of God and not of nature.' (Ch. II, p. 6.)

[2] And this is highly significant, because the effects of neurotic phenomena definitely take another course.   The validity and importance of the principle here applied is generally recognized.   With direct application to the cause of Julian it is formulated by P. Renaudin at p. 60 of his study (cf. infra).

more to the worship of God because of that sickness'
(Hudleston, ch. 2, p. 4). The last quotation shows that the
aim of this prayer had evidently been realized: one more
indication in favour of the divine origin both of the desire
and of its fulfilment.[1]

It may therefore be concluded that there is no basis for
argument in proof of the neurotic origin of these phenomena, whereas there are several indications which would
point to a preternatural, divine origin. This conclusion
concerning the nature and origin of Julian's sickness is
(as pointed out on pp. 23-25) of great importance for a
right judgement on the parallel question concerning the
nature and the origin of the sights, which began immediately
after the sudden release from the sickness.

In a note to page 23 I have already recorded the judgements
of a number of authors. Proceeding merely from the
description of the sickness, they attribute the sights to a
'state of hypnotism', 'physical illusion', 'trance-state',
'hallucination', etc. I trust that my own analysis of the
sickness will have established with sufficient clarity that such
secular attributions are inadmissible, since they are over-
hasty and superficial. Furthermore, it should have cast very
strong doubts on a merely neurotic interpretation of the
sickness, and be a warning, too, against interpreting the
sights themselves as neurotic phenomena.

[1] The following passage, which gives an account of the immediate effects
of the whole experience, is also indicative of the divine origin: ' Suddenly it
came to my mind that I should desire the second wound, of our Lord's gift
and of His grace: that He would fill my body with mind and feeling of this
blessed Passion, as I had before prayed. For I would that His pains were
my pains, with compassion and then with longing for God. Thus methought
that I might with His grace have His wounds that I had before desired. But
in this I desired never of God either bodily sight or any manner of shewing,
but compassion such as methought a kind soul might have towards our Lord
Jesus, that for love willed to become a mortal man. With Him I desired to
suffer whilst I lived in this mortal body, as God would give me grace.'
(Ch. III, p. 7.)

While a study of the phenomena (the sights) entirely as such is essential, it is nevertheless utterly insufficient in itself. Due attention should also, or principally, be given to Julian's reactions, to her attitude before the shewings, to her appreciation of them, and particularly to the effects that the sights produced on her spiritual life and on her doctrine.[1]

In short, the criteria invoked to aid judgement concerning the nature and origin of the sickness, must now be applied to the phenomena of her sights.

[1] I am therefore in agreement with P. Renaudin, who says: ' It would be useless to try to find an immediate answer to this problem. On the contrary we must leave the question open. This is the procedure that one should follow when judging extraordinary facts in the lives of the mystics, because it is impossible to determine the supernatural character of these facts basing oneself merely on phenomenological grounds. For there exist, too, many analogies between these extraordinary facts and others which are merely natural; moreover, these extraordinary happenings are deeply connected with the whole psychical and even physiological substratum of the subject. In order to pronounce a judgement, one should wait and examine the effects they produce. The increase of spiritual energies that they bring to the soul —in contrast to the diminution of the same powers which is brought about by phenomena which are pathological—is, after all, the only safe criterion of their origin and their supernatural character.' (Op. cit. p. 60.)

2

JULIAN'S 'SHEWINGS'

JULIAN had formulated two desires concerning the concrete means by which she wished to arrive at a deeper union with God.

Having analysed and studied the first—viz. the desire for the sickness—in its actual fulfilment, and having seen also its impact on her spirituality—that is to say, how Julian by means of her sickness had attained to true detachment and an ardent desire for God alone—we may conclude that her wish 'to be purged by God' had been accomplished.

Because of this purification, during the sickness Julian had already abandoned her desire for a 'bodily sight' and only longed for compassion, more knowing and more love for Christ. It was in this state of mind that she first experienced a 'shewing', the first of a series of sixteen Revelations.

There is no doubt that the spiritual doctrine contained in the book of the Revelations finds its origin and immediate cause in these sights, because it was mainly in them and by them that Julian received a clearer light on various essential points of doctrine, so that the whole subsequent doctrinal development is woven round these experiences.

It was Julian's conviction that these sights conveyed to her intellect a special light, by which she saw and grasped the inner and real value of those vital truths which are at the basis of our life. However, she is concerned not with the perception of these truths in the abstract, but with their impact on our relationship towards God, with the understanding of the way in which this relationship should be lived. She saw that we should progressively unite ourselves to him, not by way of speculative knowledge but by an intimate clinging to him which is effected through the will, though the mind also plays its part through a luminous deepening of faith.

Since Julian's sights were both the occasion and the immediate cause of this clearer understanding of and closer union with God, and also because extraordinary communications often accompany such intense union and have an effect on it, we must examine Julian's own attitude to these sights and recognize the importance she attached to them in the ascent to God; and this not only for herself, but for all her even-Christians.

Although initially Julian herself speaks of sickness and sight equally as means for the attainment of higher spiritual good without stressing the importance of the sight over the sickness, the sights occupy in Julian's further exposition a much greater importance. For her initial desire contemplated only a ' bodily sight ', but the fulfilment went far beyond the limits of this inferior type of sight and extended also to *intellectual* sights.

We shall therefore analyse first the various types of sight in Julian's account, and examine them in the light of the classical treatment of mystical phenomena.

Secondly, the consideration of Julian's own appreciation of them will enable us to estimate their value relatively to what Julian considers to be the substance of the spiritual life, and will help us greatly in forming our judgement on the problem concerning their divine origin.

JULIAN'S DESCRIPTION AND CLASSIFICATION OF HER ' SIGHTS '

Julian summarizes and concludes the account of the first Revelation by saying:

All this was shewed by three [ways]: that is to say, by bodily sight,
and by word formed in mine understanding,
and by ghostly sight.

But the ghostly sight I cannot nor may not shew it as openly nor as fully as I would. But I trust in our Lord God Almighty that he shall of his goodness, and for your love, make you to take it more ghostly and more sweetly than I can or may tell it. (Ch. 9, p. 18.)

Since Julian introduces here a technical terminology to classify the different types of her experience, before analysing its content we need to consider the exact meaning of these terms as she understands them.

'Bodily sight'

The Revelations begin with a vision of the suffering Christ:

In this suddenly I saw the red blood trickling down from under the Garland hot and freshly and right plenteously, as it were in the time of his Passion when the Garland of thorns was pressed on his blessed head [that was] both God and Man, the same that suffered thus for me. (Ch. 4, p. 7.)

Even though in the immediate context Julian does not refer explicitly to this vision as a 'bodily sight', she nevertheless makes use of this term when shortly afterwards she tells us that the vision of the bleeding Christ continued throughout the time of the Revelation.

In all the time that he shewed this that I have said now in ghostly sight,

I saw the bodily sight lasting *of the plenteous bleeding* of the Head. The great drops of blood fell down from under the Garland like pellets, seeming as it had come out of the veins; and in the coming out they were brown-red, for the blood was full thick; and in the spreading-abroad they were bright-red; and when they came to the brows, then they vanished; notwithstanding, the bleeding continued till many things were seen and understood.

The fairness and the liveliness is like nothing but the same;

the plenteousness is like to the drops of water that fall off the
eaves after a great shower of rain, that fall so thick that no man
may number them with bodily wit; and for the roundness,
they were like to the scale of herring, in the spreading on the
forehead. These three came to my mind in the time: pellets,
for roundness, in the coming out of the blood; the scale of
herring, in the spreading in the forehead, for roundness;
the drops off eaves, for the plenteousness innumerable. (Ch. 7,
pp. 13-14.)

To enable us to determine more accurately what Julian
means by 'bodily sight', it will be helpful to cite some
other texts which offer descriptions of a strictly similar type:

And after this *I saw*, beholding, *the body plenteously bleeding* in
seeming of the Scourging, as thus: the fair skin was broken
full deep into the tender flesh with sharp smiting all about the
sweet body.

So plenteously the hot blood ran out that there was neither seen
skin nor wound, but as it were all blood.

And when it came where it should have fallen down, then it
vanished.

Notwithstanding, the bleeding continued awhile: till it might
be seen with avisement.

And this was so plenteous, to my sight, that methought if it
had been so in kind and in substance at that time, it should
have made the bed all one blood, and have passed over about.
(Ch. 12, p. 24.)

Again, in ch. 16:

After this Christ shewed part of his Passion near his dying.

I saw his sweet face as it were dry and bloodless with pale dying.
And later, more pale, dead, languoring; and then turned more
dead unto blue; and then more brown-blue, as the flesh turned
more deeply dead. For his Passion shewed to me most specially
in his blessed face, and chiefly in his lips: there I saw these four
colours, though it were afore fresh, ruddy, and liking, to my
sight. This was a sorrowful change to see, this deep dying.

And also the nose clogged and dried, to my sight, and the sweet body was brown and black, all turned out of fair, lively colour of itself, unto dry dying.

For that same time that our Lord and blessed Saviour died upon the Rood, it was a dry, hard wind, and wondrous cold, as to my sight, and what time the precious blood was bled out of the sweet body that might pass therefrom, yet there dwelled a moisture in the sweet flesh of Christ, as it was shewed.

Bloodlessness and pain dried within; and blowing of wind and cold coming from without met together in the sweet body of Christ. And these four,—twain without, and twain within— dried the flesh of Christ by process of time. And though this pain was bitter and sharp, it was full long lasting, as to my sight, and painfully dried up all the lively spirits of Christ's flesh. Thus *I saw the sweet flesh* dry in seeming by part after part: drying with marvellous pains.

And as long as any spirit had life in Christ's flesh, so long suffered he pain.

This long pining seemed to me as if he had been seven nights dead, dying, at the point of outpassing away, suffering the last pain. And when I said it seemed to me as if he had been seven nights dead, it meaneth that the sweet body was so discoloured, so dry, so clogged, so deathly, and so piteous, as [if] he had been seven nights dead, continually dying.

And methought the drying of Christ's flesh was the most pain, and the last, of his Passion. (Ch. 16, pp. 30-31.)

From these descriptions we may conclude that the salient feature of the ' bodily sights ' is that they have reference to a corporeal object—mainly the Humanity of Christ—which is by its nature perceptible to the senses, and thus may be described in a detailed and realistic way.[1] Precisely because

---

[1] When we speak here of senses and sense-perception we do not refer exclusively to the external senses, but include similarly the so-called *sensus interni* (imagination, sense-memory, etc.). The importance of this will be understood later in connection with the question whether the ' bodily sight ' of Julian's terminology has to be classified under ' corporeal vision ' or ' imaginative vision ' as understood in the classical terminology.

the object of this type of 'sight' falls within the boundaries of sense-perception Julian is able to describe her experience with such vividness that the reader may almost *see* with her the suffering Christ.

But, as we have already remarked, the 'bodily sight' which had originally been the only object of Julian's petition, was not the only type of 'sight' she had: it was rather the beginning of higher experiences, an appreciation of which will also help to determine more precisely the nature of the 'bodily sight'.

'Ghostly sight'

From Julian's classification, as well as from her terminology, a comparison is called for between the 'bodily sight' and what she calls 'ghostly sight'. The terms themselves, 'bodily' and 'ghostly', already point to the existence of some essential differences; and analysis of the sights which Julian qualifies as 'ghostly' will show the distinctive properties of each.

Chapter 22

Then said our good Lord Jesus Christ: 'Art thou well paid that I suffered for thee?' I said: 'Yea, good Lord, gramercy, Yea, good Lord, blessed mayst thou be.'

Then said Jesus, our kind Lord: 'If thou art paid, I am paid: it is a joy, a bliss, and endless liking to me that ever suffered I passion for thee; and if I might suffer more, I would suffer more.'

In this feeling my understanding was *lifted up* into heaven and there *I saw* three heavens: of which sight I *greatly marvelled*.

And though I see three heavens—and *all in the blessed manhood* of Christ—none is more, none is less, none is higher, none is lower, but [all] even-like in bliss.

For the first heaven, *Christ shewed* me *his Father; in no bodily* likeness, but *in his property* and *in his working*.

That is to say, I saw in Christ that the Father is. (Ch. 22, p. 40.)

Julian speaks here of a ' sight ' (' I saw '—' which sight '
—' shewed ') which is effected in the ' understanding ', not
perceived by the senses.   The understanding is ' lifted up ',
viz. elevated by a special intervention of God.   The expression ' lifted up ' presents the sight as taking place suddenly
without any indication of a connection with what has been
said previously.   The sight causes a feeling of ' great
marvel ';   the object of the sight is ' three heavens ' which
are seen in the ' blessed manhood of Christ '.[1]

Christ shewed ' *his Father* ', in ' *no bodily likeness* ' (hence
without dependence on or association with any phantasm,
or imaginative picture), but ' *in his property* and *in his working* '.
That is to say, ' *I saw in Christ that the Father is* '.   Therefore
the object seen in this type of sight is of a strictly spiritual
character: God himself, his attributes and activity, but
most of all the relationship between the First and the Second
Person of the Blessed Trinity—Julian's sight of the Father
' in the Son '.

Chapter 5

In this same time *our Lord shewed* me a *ghostly sight of his homely
loving*.

I saw that he is to us everything that is good and comfortable
for us.

He is our clothing that for love wrappeth us, claspeth us, and
all becloseth us for tender love, that he may never leave us;
being to us all thing that is good, as to mine understanding.
(Ch. 5, p. 8.)

As in the previous instance, this ' sight ' also is introduced
suddenly;   the object of the vision up to this point is our
Blessed Lady.   This ' ghostly sight ' is concerned with so
spiritual an object as the Creator's active and loving presence.

[1] Cf. the strict parallelism of ideas with the explanation that Julian gives in
ch. 4: ' for where Jesus appeareth, the blessed Trinity is understood '.   This
text will be considered later.

Chapter 25

. . . our good Lord looked down on the right side and brought to my mind where our Lady stood in the time of his Passion; and said: 'Wilt thou see her?'

And in this sweet word [it was] as if he had said: 'I wot well thou wouldst see my blessed Mother: for, after myself, she is the highest joy that I might shew thee, . . .'

as if he said: 'Wilt thou see how I love her, . . .?'

as if he said: 'Wilt thou see in her how thou art loved? For thy love I made her so high, so noble and so worthy; and this liketh me, and so will I that it doth thee.'

For after himself she is the most blissful sight.

But hereof *am I not* learned so long *to see her bodily* presence while I am here, *but the virtues of her blessed soul:* her truth, her wisdom, her charity; whereby I may learn to know myself and reverently dread my God.

And when our good Lord had shewed this and said this word: '*Wilt thou see her?*' I answered and said: 'Yea, good Lord, gramercy: yea, good Lord, *if it be thy will.*' Oftentimes I prayed this, and I *weened to have seen her in bodily presence, but I saw her not so.*

And Jesus in that word *shewed* me *ghostly sight of her:* right as I had seen her *afore,* little and simple, so *he shewed* her *then, high* and *noble* and *glorious,* and *pleasing* to him above all creatures. (Ch. 25, pp. 45-46.)

Here again we find that the sight is presented as being granted immediately by Christ himself and hence not connected with or deriving from Julian's own reflection: '*Wilt thou* see her?'—'Yea, good Lord, *gramercy:* yea, . . . *if it be thy will*'—'And Jesus . . . shewed me ghostly sight of her.' Notwithstanding that Julian 'weened to have seen her *in bodily presence*', she states explicitly 'I saw her not *so.*' 'Jesus . . . shewed me ghostly sight' of her. In fact what she sees is our Lady '*high* and *noble* and *glorious,*

and *pleasing* to him above all creatures ', viz. our Lady in her
spiritual glory and excellence.   And most significantly, Julian
adds: ' hereof am I not learned so long to see her bodily
presence while I am here, but the virtues of her blessed
soul. . . .'

Chapter 67

And then our Lord *opened* my *ghostly eye* and *shewed* me *my soul*
in midst of my heart.

I saw the soul so large as it were an endless world, and as it
were a blissful kingdom.   And by the conditions that I saw
therein I understood that it is a worshipful City.

In the midst of that City sitteth *our Lord Jesus, God and Man*,
a fair Person of large stature, highest Bishop, solemnest King,
most worshipful Lord; and I saw him clad solemnly.

And worshipfully he sitteth in the Soul, even-right in peace
and rest.

And *the God-head* ruleth and sustaineth heaven and earth and
all that is—sovereign Might, sovereign Wisdom, and sovereign
Goodness—[and] the place that Jesus taketh in our Soul he
shall never remove it, without end, as to my sight: for in us is
his homeliest home and his endless dwelling.

And in this [sight] *he shewed the satisfying that he hath* of the
making of Man's soul.   (Ch. 67, pp. 138-139.)

Again Julian takes care to note explicitly that her ' *ghostly
eye* ' was *opened* by our Lord; and this appears to have been
done all of a sudden.   She saw her ' *Soul* ' (spiritual object)
and ' *our Lord Jesus, God and Man* [1] dwelling in it.   One

---

[1] We draw particular attention to this expression: ' our Lord Jesus, *God
and Man* ' when Julian is speaking of God's presence in the soul.   A similar
assertion is made by St Teresa: ' It is not like another kind of consciousness
of the presence of God which is often experienced, especially by those who
have reached the Prayer of Union and the Prayer of Quiet. . . . The soul
distinctly sees that *Jesus Christ, the Son of the Virgin, is present*.   In that other
kind of prayer there come to it influences from the Godhead; but in this
experience, besides receiving these, we find that *the most sacred Humanity*
becomes our Companion and is also pleased to grant us favours.'—*Life*,
ch. xxvii, n. 4 (ed. cit. p. 171.)

aspect of this vision is directly concerned with the 'God-head '[1] that ' ruleth and sustaineth heaven and earth ', in other words we find here again the highest possible type of the purely spiritual, viz. the Divinity seen in its own proper life and activity.

From these examples [2] it is not difficult to discover what Julian means by ' ghostly sight ': it is a vision granted freely by God himself without direct and intrinsic connection with any sense-experiences. It is exclusively concerned with purely spiritual objects (mainly God himself) which are not described in detail. For Julian, then, there exists an essential difference between ' ghostly ' and ' bodily ' sights and in fact they are described as such.

Julian, who gives so many proofs of her extraordinary powers of description [3]—not least in her vivid narrative of the bodily sights—confesses ' But the ghostly sight I cannot nor may not shew it as openly nor as fully as I would.' (Ch. 9, p. 18.) And in another passage, where she explicitly compares the two types of sight, she points out this contrast:

For the bodily sight, I have said as I saw, as truly as I can;

and for the words, I have said them right as our Lord shewed them to me;

and for the ghostly sight, I have said some deal, but I may never fully tell it: . . . (Ch. 73, p. 148.)

[1] I draw attention again to the admirable theological precision of Julian's statement.

[2] Other examples can be found, though the technical term ' ghostly sight ' is not used by Julian in each separate instance to specify this type of sight. Because of elements found in the relation, I would consider as ' ghostly sights ', e.g.: ' With this sight of the blessed Passion, with the Godhead that I saw in mine understanding . . . ' (Ch. 4, p. 8.) And in the same Shewing suddenly the Trinity fulfilled my heart most of joy. . . . (Ibid. p. 7.) And with this sweet enjoying he shewed unto mine understanding the blessed Godhead. . . .' (Ch. 24, pp. 44-45.)

[3] For the beauty of Julian's prose and the literary worth of Revelations of Divine Love, cf. R. W. Chambers's classic treatise On the Continuity of English Prose from Alfred to More and his School, especially p. cxvii. Cf. also Reynolds, Introd., pp. x-xvii.

Here is her own criterion for classifying the sights, that the 'ghostly sight' is, because of its spiritual nature, ineffable; whereas the 'bodily sight' because of its connection with the visible and the tangible, can easily be described in real and pictorial terms. For Julian, then, 'bodily sight' and 'ghostly sight' are different in kind, not only because each has its own proper object, but also because of the way in which the object is known and the striking difference in the expression of this knowledge.[1]

All this throws light on a third more complex type of sight which we now come to consider; it is called by Julian 'Ghostly in bodily likeness and more ghostly, without bodily likeness.' (Ch. 51, p. 91.) The terminology itself creates the expectation that elements proper both to the 'bodily sight' and to the 'ghostly sight' will be found.

Sight 'ghostly in bodily likeness' and 'more ghostly without bodily likeness'

The terms 'ghostly in bodily likeness' and 'more ghostly without bodily likeness' occur only twice in the book of the Revelations: at ch. 4 and ch. 51.[2]

In these two sights the object seen, though representing a thing which is in itself perceptible to the senses, is *seen* not simply 'bodily', but 'spiritually': '*ghostly* sight *in bodily likeness*'. In fact, the descriptions Julian gives of these objects are shorter and less detailed, less vivid and pictorial, less realistic; they are descriptions not of objects *seen* ' *bodily* ', but ' *in bodily likeness* '. In the examples adduced for ' bodily

---

[1] I am aware that in the field both of the ' bodily ' and the ' ghostly ' sight many questions could still be considered. But my only concern here is to draw attention to the existence of various irreducible types of sight and to outline the most typical characteristics of each of them, and thus to arrive at an understanding of Julian's classification.

[2] But it cannot be concluded that she had only two ' sights ' of this type. Frequently Julian is not concerned with technical terminology and does not take care to specify the type of each one of her experiences.

sights' it is as though the reader were invited to *see* with Julian; not so with the ' ghostly sight in bodily likeness '.

This vision is accompanied by a '*more* ghostly' sight, from which even the ' bodily *likeness* ' is absent; this ' more ghostly sight ' does not introduce itself ' suddenly ', but is presented as a progressive illumination of the mind. But we shall also see that for Julian this progressive ' understanding ' must not be identified with her own reflections and reasonings—though these have a part to play—but rather to shewings and sights directly communicated by God (the intellect is *led* to perceive and understand the spiritual meaning contained in or hidden behind the object seen in ' bodily likeness ').

Chapter 51

And then our courteous Lord answered in *shewing* full mistily a wonderful example of a Lord that hath a servant:

1st element

and he gave me *sight to my understanding of* both.

2nd element

} of this more complex type of sight.

Which sight was shewed *doubly* in the Lord and *doubly* in the Servant:

the one part was *shewed ghostly in bodily likeness*, and

1st element

the other part was *shewed more ghostly, without bodily likeness.*

2nd element

}

For the first [sight], thus, *I saw two persons in bodily likeness:* that is to say, a Lord and a Servant;

1st element

and *therewith* God *gave* me a ghostly understanding.

2nd element

} of *this particular instance* of the more complex type of sight.

The Lord sitteth solemnly in rest and in peace; the Servant standeth by, afore his Lord reverently, ready to do his Lord's will. The Lord looketh upon his Servant full lovingly and sweetly, . . .

The Servant not only he goeth, but suddenly he starteth, and runneth in great haste, for love to do his Lord's will. And anon he falleth into a slade, and taketh full great hurt. And then he groaneth and moaneth and waileth and writheth, . . .

And of all this the most mischief that I saw him in, was failing of comfort: . . .

And right thus continually his loving Lord full tenderly beholdeth him. . . .

. . . full meekly and mildly, with great ruth and pity,
—and *this was of the first* [*sight*]:

another inward, *more ghostly*,— and this was *shewed with a leading of mine understanding* into the Lord, [in the] which *I saw* him highly rejoicing for the worshipful resting and nobleness that he will and shall bring his Servant to by his plenteous grace:

and *this was of that other shewing.*

description of the object seen ' ghostly in bodily likeness ': less realistic, more spiritual.

2nd element: ' more ghostly ',

not sudden

' without bodily likeness '

And now [was] my understanding *led again into the first* [sight]; both keeping in mind . . .

Repetition of the same process: 1st element.

And in this an *inward ghostly Shewing of the* Lord's *meaning* descended into my soul: in which I saw that it behoveth . . . (Ch. 51, pp. 91-93.)

2nd element: not sudden, but progressive illumination and understanding of the first element.

Chapter 4

In this *he brought* our blessed Lady to my understanding. *I saw her ghostly, in bodily likeness:*

1st element.

a simple maid and a meek, young of age and little waxen above a child, in the stature that she was when she conceived with child.

description of the 'ghostly sight in bodily likeness'.

Also God *shewed in part the wisdom* and the truth of her soul:

2nd element: more ghostly (the virtues of her soul being the object of this sight).

wherein I understood the reverent beholding that she beheld her God and Maker [with], marvelling with great reverence that he would be born of her that was a simple creature of his making. And this wisdom and truth—knowing the greatness of her Maker and the littleness of herself that was made—, caused her to say full meekly to Gabriel: 'Lo me, God's handmaid.'

the object of this sight can be described in some ways.

In this sight I *understood* soothly that she is more than all that God made beneath her in worthiness and grace; for above her is nothing that is made but the blessed [Manhood] of Christ, as to my sight. (Ch. 4, p. 8.)

The same scheme and elements can be easily traced in other sights or shewings, where we do not find the technical terminology: e.g.

Also in this he shewed [me] a little thing, the quantity of an hazel-nut, in the palm of my hand; . . .

I looked thereupon with eye of my understanding, . . .

And *I was answered in my understanding:* . . .

In this Little Thing *I saw three properties*, etc.   (Ch. 5, p. 9.)

Through comparison of the elements found in this type of sight with the previous considerations on the ' bodily sight ' and the ' ghostly sight ', it is possible to distinguish the existence of an intermediate type of sight; to determine more accurately its proper characteristics; and thus to arrive at a clearer understanding of each type of sight in Julian's classification.

In the analysis of the ' bodily ' and ' ghostly sight ' the simultaneous presence of the two types of sight has been observed: ' In this suddenly I saw the red blood . . . And *in the same Shewing* suddenly the Trinity fulfilled my heart most of joy.' (Ch. 4, p. 7.)

In such a case this coexistence, and the reason for it, are clearly indicated by Julian: ' And this was shewed in the First [Shewing] and in all: *for where Jesus appeareth, the blessed Trinity is understood*, as to my sight ' (ibid.).

Moreover, the 'ghostly sight' was said explicitly to have come 'suddenly'[1] as a new vision not directly connected with the previous 'bodily sight'.

On the other hand, with regard to this third type of sight, we are first of all struck by the fact that it is not a question of mere coexistence of the sight 'in bodily likeness', and the 'more ghostly, without bodily likeness'. We are to understand that the two sights are in close harmony and possess an intrinsic relationship one to the other, so that the 'more ghostly, without bodily likeness' is considered as explaining and developing what has been seen in 'bodily likeness'. Julian never introduces the 'more ghostly' element by saying that it came 'suddenly'; rather there seems to be a more gradual transition: 'with a leading of mine understanding'—'an inward ghostly Shewing of the . . . meaning descended into my soul'.[2] Further, Julian never separates out the 'more ghostly, without bodily likeness' from the 'ghostly in bodily likeness'. Hence my assertion that we have here a third type of sight—complex indeed but a unity—is fully justified. And if we remember that the two elements of this unity are allied, the one ('ghostly in bodily likeness') to the 'bodily sight', the other ('more ghostly without bodily likeness') to the simple ghostly sight, there can be no doubt that this third type is intermediate between 'bodily sight' and 'ghostly sight'.

[1] '*Suddenly* the Trinity fulfilled. . . .' (Ch. 4, p. 7.)
[2] 'To lead forth the understanding' (and Julian's synonymous expressions) explains most precisely the characteristics of this type of 'sight' in so far as it differs from the 'ghostly sight' which is sudden intuition. There is no danger of confusing Julian's use of 'understanding' in this context with the 'natural understanding' or reasoning of the mind, because she specifies that this 'understanding' is due to the 'leading of God' (this way of speaking openly points to the passivity), and uses simultaneously such expressions as 'shewed' and 'sight'. Cf. e.g. ch. 51, p. 91: 'He [God] *gave sight* to my *understanding*', '*therewith* God *gave* me a ghostly understanding'.

Schematically then, according to Julian, we have:

1. First type: ' bodily sight '

2. Second type: ' intermediate type' $\left\{\begin{array}{l}\text{' ghostly sight in bodily} \\ \text{likeness '} \\ \text{' more ghostly sight with-} \\ \text{out bodily likeness'.}^1\end{array}\right.$

3. Third type: ' ghostly sight '

[1] The question arises whether any one of these types predominates in Julian's mystical experience. From her account of the Revelations it would appear not. Not only does each type occur frequently, but often two or even all three, in one and the same Shewing: e.g. the first Revelation:

' In this suddenly I saw the red blood trickling down from under the Garland hot and freshly and right plenteously. . . .

' And in the same Shewing suddenly the Trinity fulfilled my heart most of joy. . . .

' In this he brought our blessed Lady to my understanding.

' I saw her ghostly, in bodily likeness: a simple maid and a meek, young of age. . . .

' Also God shewed in part the wisdom and the truth of her soul: wherein I understood the reverent beholding that she beheld her God and Maker, . . .' (Ch. 4, pp. 7-8.)

For other examples cf. the 9th Revelation (chs. 22-23), and the 10th Revelation (ch. 24).

3

JULIAN'S PERSONAL EVALUATION OF HER 'SHEWINGS'

As I have said, Julian's shewings are of vital importance for a true understanding and appreciation of her doctrine on prayer and contemplation. And this not only because her teaching found its immediate cause and origin in the shewings, but also because visions, revelations, etc., often go together with a life of intense union with God and play an important part in it. Hence, Julian's own evaluation of visions, revelations, etc., and of their function and importance in the life of prayer and union with God, will provide us with a valuable criterion with which to judge the soundness of her doctrine on prayer and contemplation.

It will be helpful for us to consider first how Julian esteemed these extraordinary phenomena *before the shewings began*.

She had asked for a 'bodily sight' (and a sickness), but she knew that this petition 'passed the common course of prayers' (Reynolds, ch. I, pp. 1, 3). Because of this reason she had asked for it only with a condition. '. . . If it be Thy will that I have it, grant it me; and if it be not Thy will, good Lord be not displeased, for I will not but as Thou willest.' (Ib., p. 3.) But, more important, she had asked for it only as a means to obtain a greater spiritual union with God: 'And this was my meaning: that I should afterwards, because of that showing, have the more true mind in the Passion of Christ.' (Ib., p. 2.) Later she changed her attitude and no longer wished for a bodily sight: 'But in this I desired never of God either bodily sight or any manner of

49

shewing.' (ibid. ch. III, p. 7), but only for ' compassion such as methought a kind soul might have towards our Lord Jesus' (ibid.), that is to say, a very high degree of unitive love: ' With Him I desired to suffer whilst I lived in this mortal body, as God would give me grace ' (ibid.).

From what we know of her life before the shewing we may therefore conclude that nothing betrays an unsound attitude towards the ' bodily sight '. On the contrary, Julian reveals the necessary prudence and moderation, and most of all an appreciation of the bodily sight as a means.

When we come to consider Julian's attitude during and after the experience of the shewings, we notice that she considered them to be of divine origin; but nevertheless she did not consider them to be of essential importance for the life of mystical union with God.

Julian considered her shewings to be of divine origin

Julian frequently manifests her conviction that her shewings came from God: at the opening of the book we read: ' This is a Revelation of Love that Jesus Christ, our endless bliss, made in Sixteen Shewings ' (ch. 1, p. 1). And still more explicitly in ch. 4 she says: ' I conceived truly and mightily that it was himself shewed it me, without any mean.' (Ch. 4, p. 7.)

In the last chapter Julian concludes her account of the Revelations by saying:

And from that time that it was shewed I desired oftentimes to witten what was our Lord's meaning. And fifteen years after, and more, I was answered in ghostly understanding, saying thus:

' Wouldst thou witten thy Lord's meaning in this thing? Wit it well: Love was his meaning.'

Who shewed it thee? Love.

What *shewed he* thee ? Love.

Wherefore *shewed* it *he?* For Love. (Ch. 86, p. 169.)

Julian also reveals herself as by no means inclined to give credence to extraordinary phenomena. In fact, at least at times, she asked herself objectively and explicitly whether the shewings were an illusion or a real visitation from God.

This Second Shewing was so low and so little and so simple, that my spirits were in great travail in the beholding,—mourning, dread-full, and longing—for I was some time in doubt whether it was a Shewing.

And then diverse times our good Lord gave me more sight, whereby I understood truly that it was a Shewing. (Ch. 10, p. 19.)

We also know that she expressed her doubts to a ' Religious person ', who reassured her by giving his approval: [1]

Then came a Religious person to me and asked me how I fared.

I said I had raved to-day.

And he laughed loud and inwardly.

And I said: ' The Cross that stood afore my face, methought it bled fast.'

And with this word *the person that I spake to waxed all sad and marvelled.*

And anon I was sore ashamed and astonished for my recklessness, and I thought: ' This man taketh sadly the least word that I might say.'

Then said I no more thereof. And when I saw that *he took it sadly* [2] *and with so great reverence*, I wept, full greatly ashamed, and would have been shriven; but at that time I could tell it no priest, for I thought: ' How should a priest believe me? I believe not our Lord God.' (Ch. 66, p. 137.)

It was only then that Julian began to realize that to persist in an attitude of doubt would have been an offence against God, due to lack of faith: ' Ah! lo, wretch that I

[1] Clearly he was one who had no difficulty in taking Julian's words at their face-value in spite of their extraordinary nature.

[2] ' sadly ' = ' seriously ' (see also the preceding sentence: ' waxed all sad ' = ' all serious ').

am: this was a great sin, great unkindness, that I for folly of feeling of a little bodily pain, so unwisely lost for the time the comfort of all this blessed Shewing of our Lord God.' (Ch. 66, p. 137.)

There is a passage, however, in which Julian seems to have collected the various elements that sustained her conviction of the divine origin of her shewings:

> But God forbid that ye should say or take it thus, that I am a teacher, for I do not mean that, nor meant I ever so. For I am a woman, unlettered, feeble and frail. But I know well this that I say—I have it on the shewing of Him who is Sovereign Teacher—and truly charity urgeth me to tell you of it, for I would that God were known and my fellow-Christians helped (as I would be myself), to the more hating of sin and loving of God. Because I am a woman should I therefore believe that I ought not to tell you about the goodness of God since I saw at the same time that it is His will that it be known? And that shall ye see well in the same matter that follows after, if it be well and truly received. Then shall ye soon forget me that am a wretch, and act so that I hinder you not, and behold Jesus who is Teacher of all. I speak of those who shall be saved, since at this time God showed me none other. But in all things I believe as Holy Church teaches, for all things in this blessed shewing of our Lord I beheld as one with the teaching of Holy Church in God's sight; and never did I understand a thing therein (i.e. in the shewing) which harms me or withdraws me from the true teaching of Holy Church.' (Reynolds, ch. VI, pp. 17-18.)

The importance of this passage can scarcely be over-emphasized. It clearly contains Julian's *subjective* conviction that her source is 'the shewing of Him who is Sovereign Teacher'; and further it contains statements which offer precious *objective* data for the solution of the problem concerning the divine origin of the shewings. In fact, Julian here shows her belief that the visions are from God, yet she emphasizes that they do not convey new revelations, or communications of hidden truths not already contained in the Revelation entrusted to the Church.   This is an explicit though negative criterion which is of importance for us (as for Julian herself) with regard to the divine origin of her shewings.   We also see that Julian's attitude, in spite of her unshakable conviction that the shew- ings are directly from God, is fundamentally that of a truly humble child of Holy Church; always ready to reject what she conceived to be a light from God, if this was not in full accord with the Church's teaching.[1]

I mentioned above Julian's negative criterion for the divine origin of her shewings.   But in the fact that she considers them as lights giving her a deeper understanding of the truths of faith we have also a positive criterion:

> Our Lord God shewed two manner of privities.   *One* is *this great privity* with all the privy points that belong thereto: and these privities he willeth we should know [as] hid until the time that he will clearly shew them to us.   *The other* are the *privities that he willeth to make open and known to us;* for he willeth that we wit that it is his will that we should know them.
>
> They are privities to us not only for that he willeth that they be privities to us, but *they are privities to us for our blindness and our unknowing;*
>
> and thereof he hath great ruth, and therefore he will himself make them

---

[1] Cf. also: ' But in all things I believe as Holy Church believeth, preacheth, and teacheth.   For the Faith of Holy Church, the which I had aforehand understood and, as I hope, by the grace of God willingly kept in use and custom, stood continually in my sight: [I] willing and meaning never to receive anything that might be contrary thereunto, and with this intent I beheld the Shewing with all my diligence: for in all this blessed Shewing I beheld it as one in God's meaning.'   (Ch. 9, p. 18.)   See also chs. 30, 32, 33, 34, 46, 61, 62, 66.   The fact that she returns on the same point so often reveals the depth of her humble faith.   One may find similar expressions in the writings, e.g. of St Teresa (ch. *Interior Castle*, VII, ch. vi, ed. cit. vol. II, p. 351)—*Way of Perfection*, Protestation, ed. cit. vol. II, p. xxvi.   The theo- logians stress that the humility of the ' favoured soul ' is an essential factor in the prudent evaluation of the origin of private revelations.

more open to us, whereby we may know him and love him and cleave to him.

For all that is speedful for us to wit and to know, full courte-
ously will our Lord shew us: *and* [of] *that is this* [*Shewing*], with
all the preaching and teaching of Holy Church. (Ch. 34,
pp. 59-60.)

It is common teaching that the divine purpose in private
revelations which touch on points of doctrine is precisely
to give a clearer understanding of the truths of faith. It is
the argument of this present study that Julian's account of
her shewings gives this clearer understanding ' whereby we
may know him and love him and cleave to him ', and hence
in the last analysis any reasoned judgement as to the divine
origin of Julian's Revelations must follow the judgement on
the soundness of her whole teaching.

*Though considered as divine favours, the shewings were not esteemed
by Julian as of essential importance for the life of union with
God*

Julian states this explicitly in ch. 6 (Shorter Version),
where she clearly asserts that the shewings were gratuitous
gifts, which did not make her better by the mere fact that
they were given to her:

Because of the shewing I am not good, but only if I love God
the better, and so may, and so should, each one do who sees it
and hears it with good will and true intent. And so is my
desire—that it should be for every such man the same profit as
I desired for myself. Thereto was I moved by God the first
time when I saw it, for since we are all one, the shewing is
common to all. I am certain I saw it for the profit of many
another, for in truth it was not shewed me that God loves me
better than the least soul that is in grace; *I am certain there are
full many who never had shewing nor sight but of the common teaching
of Holy Church and who love God better than I.*

For if I look at myself in particular I am right naught, . . .
(Reynolds, ch. VI, pp. 15-16.) [1]

From the whole quotation it is clear that according to
Julian the shewings are far from essential for a life of love
and union.   In the light of this principle we may understand
the other passage where Julian states that the condition of
those who seek for God in pure faith, without the help of
these extraordinary favours, is as good as the condition of
those who are granted the grace of beholding God in special
shewing:

> And thus was I learned, to mine understanding, that seeking
> is as good as beholding, for the time that he will suffer the soul
> to be in travail. . . .

> For a soul that only fasteneth it[self] on to God with very trust,
> either by seeking or in beholding, it is the most worship that
> it may do to him, as to my sight.   (Ch. 10, p. 21.)

However the shewings are ' profitable ': ' and that is most
worship to him and profit to thyself, and [the soul then]
most receiveth of meekness and virtues with the grace and
leading of the Holy Ghost ' (ch. 10, p. 21), and they have
to be used as means to increase in ' more knowing ' and
' loving ' of God: ' and therefore I desired a bodily sight
wherein I might have more knowledge of the bodily pains of
our Saviour and of the compassion of our Lady. . . .'
(ch. 2, p. 3).   But they must not be asked for in order to
satisfy curiosity and the natural desire for knowledge.

---

[1] Julian's humility appears ever more clearly from the sentences which
precede the above quoted passage: ' And therefore I pray you all for God's
sake, and counsel you for your own profit, that ye leave the beholding of the
wretched, worldly, sinful creature that it was shewed unto; and that ye mightily,
wisely, lovingly and meekly behold God, that of His courteous love and of
His endless goodness willed to shew generally this vision, in comfort of us
all.   And ye that hear and see this vision and this teaching, which is of Jesus
Christ, to the edification of your souls, it is God's will and my desire that ye
take it with as great joy and delight as if Jesus had shewn it to you as He
did to me.'   (Ibid. p. 15.)

E

An illustration of this theoretical and practical appreciation, e.g. of 'bodily and imaginary sights', is contained in
ch. 25, where it appears that the aim is to arrive at a perception of spiritual truths, not the sight in itself:

> And with this same cheer of mirth and joy our good Lord
> looked down on the right side and brought to my mind where
> our Lady stood in the time of his Passion; and said: 'Wilt
> thou see her?' . . . *But hereof am I not learned so long to see her
> bodily* presence while I am here, *but the virtues of her blessed
> soul*: her truth, her wisdom, her charity; *whereby I may learn to
> know myself and reverently dread my God.*
>
> And when our good Lord had shewed this and said this word:
> 'Wilt thou see her?'
>
> I answered and said:
>
> 'Yea, good Lord, gramercy: yea, good Lord, if it be thy will.'
> Oftentimes I prayed this, *and I weened to have seen her in bodily
> presence, but I saw her not so.* And Jesus in that word shewed
> me ghostly sight of her: right as I had seen her afore, little
> and simple, so he shewed her then, high and noble and
> glorious, and pleasing to him above all creatures. (Ch. 25,
> pp. 45-46.)

Thus, though Julian received all her shewings with great
gratitude and love, throughout she was convinced that they
were no more than alternative and not essential means to
advancement in the love of God: means, moreover, which
are to be used with great prudence and always in full accord
with the will of God in granting them.

Julian's evaluation of her shewings is therefore in perfect
agreement with the classical teaching on this matter. In
fact, contrary to popular belief, the theologians insist that
extraordinary phenomena [1] may be associated with the
mystical life, either as a preparation for it or simply as the

---

[1] The term 'extraordinary phenomena' is taken here in the sense in which
it is commonly used by the modern authors, and refers to physical phenomena
(stigmatization, etc.), to corporeal or imaginary visions, apparitions, etc.

manifestation of a deeper union already acquired; but they do not belong to the essence of mystical experience.[1]

According to most authorities, the mystical life consists in a really intimate union with God, which affects the soul much more deeply than do the 'extraordinary phenomena'. In fact, we may speak of mystical life when the soul, under the influence of a special actual grace—at times experienced and felt—acquires a particular awareness of its habitual union with God and his divine presence.[2]

In this state of union, precisely because it is participating more consciously in God's life, in God's knowing and loving of himself, the soul is also flooded by his light: a light which penetrates its substance ever more intensely. The soul is thus constantly enlightened by 'many privy touchings of sweetly ghostly sight and feeling', and it is by these that the soul, in this state, knows, is aware of God.

These lights and touchings are the mystical knowledge of God and hence are inseparable from infused contemplation

---

[1] Cf. e.g. Gabriele di S. Maria Maddalena, *Visions and Revelations in the Spiritual Life*, pp. 10-11: 'Notwithstanding, we have no wish to assert that visions and revelations, if authentic, are not mystical graces. They have their place in the mystical life, and, as we shall see later, even an estimable place; but we wish to demonstrate clearly, making use of Teresian teaching, that this place is entirely *secondary and accidental*. Hence, such graces cannot be considered as the characteristic of the mystical life. We must get rid, once for all, of this wholly mistaken idea which, in practice, gives rise to serious errors.' (See also the whole section.) On the same subject see among others: C. M. Staehlin, *Apariciones*, Madrid, 1954; *Mystische Täuschungen. Zur Beurteilung einiger mystischer Phänomene*, in GL, 27 (1954), pp. 276-290. J. Lhermitte, *Mystiques et faux mystiques;* H. Thurston, *The Physical Phenomena of Mysticism*, edited by J. H. Crehan.

[2] I do not attempt a solution of the problem of a satisfactory definition of mystical life, but merely point to the main elements which would seem to constitute it. On this subject, see e.g. J. De Guibert, *Une définition des grâces mystiques*, in RSR, 18 (1928), pp. 269-280; M. De la Taille, *Théories mystiques*, in RSR, 18 (1928), pp. 297-325; J.-V. Bainvel, Introduction to the 11th edn. of Fr Poulain's *Des grâces d'Oraison* (Paris, 1931), pp. xxiv-xciv; Butler, *Western Mysticism, Afterthoughts*, pp. ix-lviii.

and are of the essence of mystical experience.[1] In the
context of infused contemplation then, they cannot be
considered as 'extraordinary'. To the soul living in this
state God can obviously grant intellectual visions far in
excess of these 'lights and touchings'; and such visions,
even in the higher states of mystical union, would rightly
be considered special graces.

*   *   *   *   *

Having seen that, according to Julian's mind, the part
played by extraordinary phenomena in the spiritual life is
only accidental, we are enabled to see the general intention
of her writings, namely, to lead the soul to perceive and
understand that the essence of union with God consists in
an ever purer faith and trustful love; and that only thus will
the soul gradually acquire understanding and habitual
consciousness of its relations towards God, that is to say,
will be ever more flooded by his light and enflamed by his
love.

The following study, in Part II, of Julian's doctrine
on the essential elements of the spiritual life will also provide
the final criterion for judgement concerning the divine origin
of her extraordinary experience.

---

[1] 'It is evident from experience that corporeal and imaginative visions and
locutions may be received apart from infused contemplation, and that infused
contemplation may be possessed even in a high degree without these visions
or locutions. However, one may ask whether this is true of *intellectual visions
also, at least of those visions* which St John of the Cross calls ' (to speak more
properly) . . . knowledge of naked truths ' (*Ascent of Mount Carmel*, II,
ch. 26, n. 2, Allison Peers' edn., vol. I, p. 194), *which are visions of God Himself*.
The Saint himself asserts that ' these lofty manifestations of knowledge can
only come to the soul that attains to union with God, for they are themselves
that union '. (Ibid. ed. cit. p. 196.) Cf. J. De Guibert, *The Theology of the
Spiritual Life*, n. 442, p. 356. Cf. also M. Ledrus, *Introductio in doctrinam
theologicam Sancti Joannis a Cruce de Contemplatione*, XVIII, *Coruscationes Extaticae*,
XIX, *Tactus Dei*, pp. 42-45.

Note: St John of the Cross and St Teresa on how to conduct one-self when visited by extraordinary phenomena.

Whereas St John of the Cross teaches in general that the soul should always bear an attitude of prudence with regard to all types of visions, but that it can and must enjoy the intellectual apprehensions (*noticias de verdades desnudas:* that is, generic illustrations resulting from the mystical union itself), when he speaks of corporeal and imaginary visions he insists that they should be constantly refused. They have to be rejected for they cause ' distinct' and ' special' notions which, if accepted, would satisfy the curiosity of the human intellect rather than sustain and engender love; they may thus constitute a hindrance to the purity of faith on which the essence of mystical union is based. (For this cf. Philippus a SS. Trinitate, *Summa Theologiae Mysticae* (Friburgi, 1874), Pt. II, pp. 425 ff., where he summarizes beautifu.ly the teaching of St John of the Cross; see also P. Gabriele di S. M. Maddalena, op. cit. pp. 96 ff.).

To say this does not mean that St John denies that corporeal and imaginative visions may come from God and hence play a part in the spiritual progress. But he maintains that when these favours are granted by God, they produce directly the effect intended by him if the soul does not fix its attention on them, deriving thus some satisfaction for its natural faculties.

This rigid attitude of refusal with regard to the lower forms of supernatural apprehensions, however, is not shared entirely by all spiritual writers. As M. Lépée has shown quite conclusively, St Teresa, at least in practice, would appear to have accepted and positively used these visions as means towards a higher mystical union (cf. M. Lépée, *Sainte Thérèse Mystique*, Pt. III, ch. vi, especially pp. 190-191, 203-204. M. Lépée's thesis goes counter to the interpretation of other authors, e.g. P. Gabriele di S. M. Maddalena, op. cit. Pt. III, pp. 87 ff.). But, even so, I wish to stress the fact that for St Teresa, also, corporeal and imaginative visions do not constitute the essence of mystical union, but they are only means, which have to be accepted with great prudence and should never become the end of the soul's attention and desire.

This attitude seems to be identical with that of Julian.

APPENDIX

Julian's Classification of her 'Shewings' compared with the Traditional Scheme of Mystical Theology

CONSIDERATION of the classification of the sights discovered in Julian's writings cannot be completed without comparing it with the one which in mystical theology is recognized as classic.[1]

[1] Fr J. de Tonquédec gives the following historical note on the origin of the division of supernatural apprehensions which, he says, is 'devenue classique': 'Saint Augustin (*Contra Adimantum*, cap. ult., PL, 42, 171; *De Genesi ad litteram*, lib. 12, cap. 6 sq., PL, 34, 458 sq.) suivi par saint Isidore de Seville (*Etymologiarum*, lib. 7, cap. 8, n. 37 sq., PL, 82, 286-287), par saint Thomas (I, q. 93, 6, 4m; II-II q. 174, 1, 3m; q. 175, 3, 4m, etc.), et par la plupart de ceux qui ont écrit sur cette matière, divise les visions en trois espèces: les corporelles, perçues par les sens extérieurs; les imaginatives (qu'il appelle 'spirituelles') perçues par les sens intérieurs; les intellectuelles, qui s'adressent à l'esprit seul. (Cf. J. de Tonquédec, S.J., *Apparitions*, DSp., I, c. 803.) It is a well known fact that this scheme of supernatural visions, apparitions, locutions, etc. has become classic mainly because of its application to prophecy and inspiration. 'Haec Sancti Augustini doctrina de visionibus, etsi non immediate prophetiam et inspirationem considerat, summi momenti facta est in nostra quaestione [de inspiratione] quia magna ex parte in tractatum S. Thomae 'de prophetia' transiit et ab eo ad systema philosophicum aristotelicum accomodata ad modum cognitionis propheticae explicandum adhibetur.' (Cf. A. Bea, S.J., *De Inspiratione et Inerrantia S. Scripturae*, p. 16.) Its present application to the field of mystical theology is largely due to the influence of St John of the Cross (cf. *Ascent*, bk. II, ch. 11, 16), followed by the manuals of Mystical Theology: cf. Philippus a SS. Trinitate, *Summa Theologiae Mysticae*, Pt. II, D. IV, pp. 396 ff. D. Schram, *Institutiones Theologiae Mysticae*, Pt. II, c. IV, pp. 185 ff. Josephus a Spiritu Sancto, *Enucleatio Mysticae Theologiae S. Dionysii Areopagitae*, Pt. I, q. 23, pp. 105 ff. In substance the classification has remained unchanged since then. From amongst the many modern authors, cf.: Antonius a Spiritu Sancto, *Directorium Mysticum*, T. III, D.V., nn. 311 ff., pp. 354 ff.; T. a Valgornera, *Mystica Theologia Divi Thomae*, T. I, Q. III, D.V., pp. 495 ff.; A. Poulain, *Des Grâces d'Oraison*, ch. xx, pp. 311 ff.; J. De Guibert, *Theologia Spiritualis Ascetica et Mystica* (English trans.), *Theology of the Spiritual Life*, n. 441 ff., p. 355 ff.; E. Underhill, *Mysticism*, Pt. II, ch. V, pp. 319 ff. I follow the excellent summary of this classification as presented by Fr J. De Guibert.

A distinction is made between *corporeal*, *imaginative*, and *intellectual* visions. This distinction can also be applied to preternatural locutions.

In corporeal visions and locutions there is real perception by the *external senses;* the person who is seen or heard may be really present, or (in corporeal visions) the body which appears may be formed in the air, or a change may be effected at the moment the light-rays impinge on the eye, or (in corporeal locutions) a real acoustical vibration may be produced in the ear.

In imaginative visions and locutions there is no perception by the external senses but, rather, a Divine action on *the imagination or the internal senses*, stirring up and uniting perceptions already received through sight or hearing.

In intellectual visions and locutions the Divine action directly affects *the intellect*. God may use *intelligible species* already possessed and then the intellectual vision or intellectual locution is always *accompanied by a phantasm*. It is precisely according as this phantasm is visual or verbal that an intellectual vision differs from an intellectual locution. Or, on the contrary, God may grant *new and purely intellectual species*, which result in a wholly preternatural and angelic mode of knowledge. In this case an intellectual vision can be distinguished from an intellectual locution only by some kind of analogy.[1]

If De Guibert's exposition is reduced to an outline and compared with Julian's classification, one is at first glance tempted to conclude that the two classifications correspond to one another because of the identity of some of the terms, e.g. bodily-corporeal; ghostly-intellectual.[2]

[1] Cf. De Guibert, op. cit. n. 441, pp. 355-356.

[2] Basing a comparison on terminology alone we have this classification:

Julian	Traditional
bodily sight	corporeal vision
intermediate { in bodily likeness	imaginative vision
without bodily likeness	
ghostly sight	intellectual vision

However, since Julian's 'more ghostly sight without bodily likeness', as contained in the 'intermediate type', can hardly be said to correspond to the term 'imaginative vision', but seems rather to belong to what in the classic terminology is called 'intellectual vision' (on account of the absence of every bodily element—cf. Pt. I, ch. 2), mere correspondence of terms is clearly no criterion of identity.

But it is important to notice that the two classifications are arrived at by very distinct methods. Julian is concerned to give a simple and straightforward account of her experience, and this remains true even when she classifies; but in the classic scheme the various types of vision are distinguished by means of the principles and data of rational psychology, particularly in the technical language used in estimating the origin of these phenomena.

Hence we must look not to the terms themselves but to their meaning.

'Bodily sight'—corporeal vision?

'Corporeal vision' by its very definition implies that the *external* senses are stimulated by an external agent: '*In corporeal visions* . . . there is a real perception by the *external senses*. In *imaginative visions* . . . there is *no perception by the external senses*. . . .' But Julian's descriptions of her 'bodily sights', though depicting an object perceptible to the external senses, do not tell us whether or not, in fact, such a stimulation took place.

Julian certainly does not indicate that external sense perception is an *essential* element of her 'bodily sight'; and as analysis of all the cases of 'bodily sight' reveals that, though the stimulation of the external senses is not to be excluded, there is no definite proof that Julian's external senses were ever affected.

In her sight of the bleeding crucifix, Julian says, 'And this was so plenteous, to my sight, that methought *if it had been so in kind and in substance at that time*, it should have made the bed all one blood, and have passed over about.' (Ch. 12, p. 24.) It follows from this that there is here certainly no question of a 'perception by the external senses' in which 'the person who is seen' is 'really present'; nor probably of one in which 'the body which appears' is 'formed in the air'. Moreover, the fact that Julian is conscious of these circumstances, though it does not apodictically exclude the third possibility of 'corporeal vision' as contemplated by De Guibert, may perhaps be considered as an indication that this 'bodily sight' belongs rather to the 'imaginative vision'.

De Guibert's third explanation, 'perception by the external

senses ' in which ' a change may be effected at the moment the light-rays impinge on the eye, or (in corporeal locutions) a real acoustical vibration may be produced in the ear) always remains possible, and in fairness to those who tend to identify ' corporeal vision ' and ' bodily sight ',[1] Julian's own descriptions of so many of her sights are so vivid and ' lively ' as to persuade us even against our better judgement that this third explanation may in many cases be the correct interpretation.

However, as Fr K. Rahner, S.J., remarks, in any concrete case it is extremely difficult to prove apodictically that a vision is really a ' corporeal vision '.[2]

And what one tends to forget is that the ' imaginative vision ' remains completely within the sphere of the senses. Hence all the characteristics of Julian's ' bodily sight ', including the vividness and liveliness of the descriptions, apply equally well to the ' imaginative vision '; precisely because the divine intervention can infuse into the interior senses phantasms (or imaginative pictures) which are indistinguishable from those acquired through the stimulation of the exterior senses.

My conclusion, then, is that Julian's ' bodily sight ' can reasonably be explained as ' a Divine action on the imagination or the internal senses, stirring up and uniting perceptions already received through sight or hearing' ; namely, as ' imaginative vision '.[3]

---

[1] Several commentators seem to have drawn this conclusion, e.g. E. I. Watkin, in his valuable study on Julian: see *Poets and Mystics*, p. 78; cf. also C. Kröger, op. cit. p. 172 ff.

[2] ' To sum up: . . . I cannot very well see how one could raise *fundamental* objections to the possibility of there being corporeal visions; but on the other hand I think that it will be possible only rarely to provide a cogent proof in any given case that we have to do with such type of vision.' (GL, 21, 1948, p. 190.)

[3] It is relevant to note, in this context, that St Teresa explicitly states that all her ' visions ' which could be considered as ' corporeal ' were, in fact, ' imaginative ' (cf. *Life*, ch. 28, ed. cit. vol. I, p. 179; *Interior Castle*, 6th Mansion, ch. 9, ed. cit. vol. II, p. 315). Commenting on this, K. Rahner remarks acutely that it is probably due to the fact that ' . . . she [St Teresa] has observed more accurately than those who conceive their visions to be corporeal and who are hence inclined to consider corporeal visions to be the normal type '. (Ibid. p. 187, n. 16.)

'Ghostly sight'—intellectual vision?

There is also a *prima facie* identity between ' ghostly sight ' and ' intellectual vision '.

At the conclusion of my analysis of the ' ghostly sight ' I said that it is a vision exclusively concerned with a spiritual object not perceivable by the senses and which consequently transcends adequate description. Thus there can be no correspondence between ' ghostly sight ' and ' imaginative vision ' (and *a fortiori* ' corporeal vision '). Therefore the only term of comparison can be the ' intellectual vision '.

But the ' intellectual vision ' is divided into two species:

In intellectual visions . . . the Divine action directly affects the intellect.

God may use intelligible species already possessed, and then the intellectual vision . . . is always accompanied by a phantasm.

Or, on the contrary, God may grant new and purely intellectual species, which result in a wholly preternatural and angelic mode of knowledge.

Does Julian's description of the ' ghostly sight ' correspond to either of these kinds of vision or to both?

The previous analysis has shown that the ' more ghostly sight without bodily likeness ' is, according to Julian, a new progressive understanding originated by God's direct action. This action gives the soul not only new sight, but one closely related to the ' ghostly sight in bodily likeness ' and the ideas and phantasms (or imaginative pictures) involved in this. The purely ' ghostly sight ' is, on the contrary, characterized by sudden introduction into the mind of an entirely new intellectual apprehension, which Julian presents as not being connected with or even related to phantasms and ideas already existing in the mind. Therefore Julian's purely ' ghostly sight ' as distinct from the ' more ghostly without bodily likeness ' would appear to exclude an identification with the intellectual vision ' which is not ' wholly preternatural '. Rather it would seem to possess all the elements proper to the ' intellectual vision ' which is ' wholly preternatural ', and in particular the characteristic which commentators maintain to be typical and distinctive of this type of intellectual vision, viz. that it can only be explained by the direct infusion of new intellectual species.

Indeed the *sudden* sight of a *highly spiritual object*, which by its very nature *cannot* be *seen* by our faculties without a very particular intervention of God,[1] and the extreme difficulty of describing what transcends human powers of description,[2] provide a proof that this type of sight cannot be explained as partly deriving from phantasms and ideas already existing in the mind ('intelligible species already possessed').

Intermediate type of sight ('ghostly sight in bodily likeness' and 'more ghostly without bodily likeness')

It might be thought that the intermediate type of sight, composed as it is of two elements, would fit into the framework of the traditional classification, 'ghostly sight in bodily likeness' being equated with 'imaginative vision',[3] and the 'more ghostly without bodily likeness' with the 'intellectual vision'. But this is too facile a conclusion, precisely because there is an intrinsic and dynamic unity between the two elements of Julian's intermediate type of sight, whilst the 'imaginative vision' and the 'intellectual vision' of the classical scheme are not conceived as having a mutual connection but as independent phenomena. Of course it must be conceded that the 'ghostly sight in bodily likeness' is an 'imaginative vision', because of the infused phantasm, but clearly, from Julian's own description, it is different from and of a higher type than 'imaginative vision' as usually explained in the manuals. In this the infused phantasm is normally conceived to be a faithful representation of a real object wholly perceivable by the senses; whilst the understanding grasps all that is conveyed to it through the imagination.

[1] Cf. Julian: 'He [God] strengtheneth the creature above the self.' (Ch. 43, p. 78.)

[2] Cf. Julian: 'But the ghostly sight I cannot nor may not shew it as openly nor as fully as I would.' (Ch. 9, p. 18.) '. . . and for the ghostly sight, I have said some deal, but I may never fully tell it' (ch. 73, p. 148).

[3] The qualification 'in bodily *likeness*' clearly rules out any identity with the 'corporeal vision'.

On the contrary, in the ' ghostly sight in bodily likeness ' the phantasm is not of a ' real ' object, but of a parabolic or allegorical object.[1] The mind, far from grasping what is conveyed in the imaginative representation (the infused phantasm), is in a state of wonder, and realizes that of itself it is incapable of penetrating to the true meaning of the ' sight in bodily likeness ' which has been granted to it.[2]

Hence the ' more ghostly sight ' is postulated—a second moment in which the ' species ' already present to the mind (but ' shewed full mistily ') are re-presented by God in a new and superior light (' and *therewith* God *gave* me a *ghostly* understanding ', ch. 51, p. 91) (' a beginning of teaching which I *saw in the same time* ', ch. 51, p. 95). But this new sight is no longer an ' imaginative vision ' (even in Julian's ' extended ' sense of the term), for it is ' without bodily likeness '. Julian specifically states that ' at this point [when the more ghostly shewing was granted] the shewing of the example vanished ' (ch. 51, p. 93); and it is ' more ghostly ': namely, in the re-presentation the divine light is focused on the meaning, the inner reality of the previous sight (' . . . this was shewed with a leading of mine understanding *into* the Lord ', ch. 51, p. 92; ' . . . in this an inward ghostly Shewing *of the Lord's* meaning descended into my soul ', ch. 51, p. 93).

Thus we are left in no doubt that the ' more ghostly sight without bodily likeness ' is an ' intellectual vision '. However, as already indicated, the theologians distinguish two kinds of intellectual vision: ' higher ' and ' lower '. The ' more ghostly sight without bodily likeness ' exactly corresponds to the ' lower type of intellectual vision ' in which ' the Divine action directly

---

[1] Julian calls it, at ch. 51, p. 91, ' a wonderful *example* of a Lord and a Servant '. The imaginative side of the experience seems to be equivalent to an elaborate mime or ' acted allegory ' where each detail has its symbolic significance, but does not define or particularize the object.

[2] See the whole of ch. 51. I quote but one passage: ' It belongeth to thee to take heed to all the properties and conditions that were shewed in the example, though thou think that they be misty and indifferent to thy sight. I assented willingly, with great desire, and inwardly [beheld] with avisement all the points and properties that were shewed in the same time, as far forth as my wit and understanding would serve: . . . And this was a beginning of teaching which I saw in the same time, . . .' (Ch. 51, pp. 94-95.)

affects the intellect. God may use intelligible species already possessed, and then the intellectual vision . . . is always accompanied by a phantasm.'

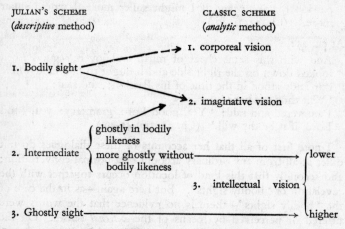

JULIAN'S SCHEME
(*descriptive* method)

CLASSIC SCHEME
(*analytic* method)

1. Bodily sight

1. corporeal vision

2. imaginative vision

2. Intermediate
{ ghostly in bodily likeness
more ghostly without bodily likeness }

lower

3. intellectual vision

3. Ghostly sight

higher

Locutions (' Words formed in mine understanding ')

It will have been noticed that in the classifications of supernatural apprehensions reference is made to ' locutions ' as well as to visions. This is true also for Julian: ' All this was shewed by three [ways]: that is to say, by bodily sight, and *by word formed in mine understanding*, and by ghostly sight.' (Ch. 9, p. 18.) [1] The locutions, however, do not appear to be all of the same type and nature. But whereas Julian is fairly accurate in classifying the various species of her sights, she does not appear to do the same with regard to the locutions. Yet it is legitimate to suggest that there exists a certain parallelism between the various types of sight and locution.

1. We may group together several instances in which Julian seems to be listening to and speaking with our Lord. Such dialogues occur, for example, at ch. 22:

Then said our good Lord Jesus Christ: ' Art thou well paid that I suffered for thee ? '

[1] Cf. also ch. 73, p. 148.

> I said: ' Yea, good Lord, gramercy.   Yea, good Lord, blessed
> mayst thou be.'
> Then said Jesus, our kind Lord: ' if thou art paid, I am paid:
> it is a joy, a bliss, and endless liking to me that ever suffered I
> passion for thee; and if I might suffer more, I would suffer
> more.'   (Ch. 22, p. 40.)

At ch. 25:

> And with this same cheer of mirth and joy our good Lord
> looked down on the right side and brought to my mind where
> our Lady stood in the time of his Passion; and said:
> ' Wilt thou see her?' . . .
> I answered and said: ' Yea, good Lord, gramercy: yea, good
> Lord, if it be thy will.'   (Ch. 25, pp. 45-46.)

I note first of all that her accounts of these dialogues do not
differ at all from any ordinary account of a normal conversation;
and secondly that this kind of locution occurs together with the
revelation of ' bodily sights '.   But here again—as in the case of
the ' bodily sights '—there is no evidence that the words were
uttered or perceived by means of the *external* senses.   On the
contrary, Julian's explicit statement—' Then he, *without voice and
opening of lips*, formed in my soul these words: " Herewith is the
Fiend overcome ".   These words said our Lord, meaning his
blessed Passion as he shewed it afore.'   (Ch. 13, p. 26)—proves
that at least in this case there is no question of *external* locution.
Confirmation of this can be found in the terminology used by
Julian: ' word formed *in mine understanding* '.

It may also be noted that the ' bystanders ' do not seem to
have overheard anything of these conversations.   Hence there is
nothing to prove that these locutions correspond to the so-called
' exterior locutions '.   On the other hand, there are definite
indications that these ' words ' should rather be identified with
' imaginary or imaginative locutions '.[1]

2. There is another group of locutions in Julian's narrative
which remind us of the ' intellectual locutions ' spoken of by
St Teresa, e.g. in ch. 27 of her *Life* (ed. cit. pp. 172-173).[2]

This group must obviously be considered as on a par with

[1] Cf. P. Gabriele di S.M. Maddalena, *Visions and Revelations in the Spiritual Life*,
pp. 41 ff.   [2] See Allison Peers (*Complete Works of St Teresa*), vol. II, p. 279, n. 1.

Julian's highest form of vision, viz. the ghostly sight. The clearest example can be found in ch. 26:

> And after this our Lord shewed him[self] more glorified, as to my sight, than I saw him before [in the Shewing] wherein I was learned that our soul shall never have rest till it cometh to him, knowing that he is fulness of joy, homely and courteous, blissful and very life.
>
> Our Lord Jesus oftentimes said: 'I it am, I it am: I it am that is highest, I it am that thou lovest, I it am that thou likest, I it am that thou servest, I it am that thou longest for, I it am that thou desirest, I it am that thou meanest, I it am that is all. I it am that Holy Church preacheth and teacheth thee, I it am that shewed me here to thee.'
>
> The number of words passeth my wit and all my understanding and all my might. And they are the highest, as to my sight: for therein is comprehended—I cannot tell,—but the joy that I saw in the Shewing of them passeth all that heart may wish for and soul may desire.
>
> Therefore the words be not declared here; but [let] every man, after the grace that God giveth him in understanding and loving, receive them in our Lord's meaning. (Ch. 26, p. 47.)

The fact that these words were perceived during a ghostly sight ('shewed him more glorified'), that their number 'passeth my wit and all my understanding and all my might', and that they 'are the highest' and 'therefore . . . be not declared' is a sufficient justification of our assertion that this type of locution is parallel to the 'ghostly sight' ('intellectual vision').

3. Though I would hesitate to say that there is a third type of locutions corresponding exactly to the intermediate type of sight which we have examined at length in the previous chapter, there are, nevertheless, some indications of such correspondence; e.g.

> Also in this he shewed [me] a little thing, the quantity of an hazel-nut, in the palm of my hand; and it was as round as a ball. I looked thereupon with eye of my understanding, and thought: 'What may this be?' And *it was generally answered* thus: 'It is all that is made.' I marvelled how it might last,

for methought it might suddenly have fallen to naught for little[ness].   And I was *answered in my understanding:* ' It lasteth, and ever shall [last] for that God loveth it.'   And so all thing hath the Being by the love of God.   (Ch. 5, p. 9.)

2

THE ESSENTIAL ELEMENTS
OF THE SPIRITUAL LIFE

From Julian's own testimony we know that for the rest of her life she 'dwelled' in prayerful recollection of the spiritual meaning of her 'shewings', often renewed by new interior lights (cf. ch. 65). These were not extraordinary communications of the nature of the Shewings of the year 1373, but rather 'lightings and touchings', that is to say actual graces given by the Holy Ghost to 'enlighten her mind and enflame her will' in the knowledge and the love of God; they were the participation in God's light and love proper to the souls who have reached a high stage of union with God.

The results of the insight acquired during those years of prayer and contemplation are set down in the Longer Version. It is from this that I shall try to reconstruct systematically Julian's doctrine on the soul's ascent to God.

I

PRELIMINARY METHODOLOGICAL REMARKS

Nature and purpose of the book ' Revelations of Divine Love '

THE 'Revelations of Divine Love' *is not a technical treatise* on prayer and contemplation, viz. it does not proceed from a number of technical definitions of terms and rigorously proved theses, with the intention of arriving at a methodological coherent system. Julian in fact does not pretend to be a teacher,[1] and she openly declares herself ' a creature that could no letter ' (ch. 2, p. 3). She merely intends to give an account of her personal experience, and wishes to communicate to her ' even-Christians ' the deep knowledge of the love of God, as revealed to her. Hence her aim is to help good souls to make progress and to unite themselves entirely to God.[2]

---

[1] See Shorter Version: ' But God forbid that ye should say or take it thus, that I am a teacher, for I do not mean that, nor meant I ever so. For I am a woman, unlettered, feeble and frail. But I know well this that I say—I have it on the shewing of Him who is Sovereign Teacher—and truly charity urgeth me to tell you of it, . . .' (Reynolds, ch. VI, p. 17.)

[2] That this is the purpose of Julian's account of the Revelations appears from various texts: cf. e.g. Shorter Version, Reynolds, ch. VI, p. 17: ' and truly charity urgeth me to tell you of it, for I would that God were known and my fellow-Christians helped (as I would be myself), to the more hating of sin and loving of God '. (See also Renaudin, *Quatre Mystiques Anglais*, pp. 90-93.) It is clear also from the fact that she addresses herself to souls who are really turned to God and are eager to live for him, cf. chs. 65, 73. For this purpose see also the addition of the scribe of the MS. Sloane 2499: ' I pray almighty God that this book come not but to the hands of them that will be his faithful lovers, and to those that will submit them to the faith of holy Church, and obey the wholesome understanding and teaching of the men that be of virtuous life, sad age, and profound learning: for this Revelation is high Divinity and high wisdom, wherefore it may not dwell with him that is thrall to sin and to the Devil.' (Hudleston, p. 170.)

This however brings her necessarily to speak of prayer, which tends to unite man to God, and of contemplation [1] in which man more deeply realizes and lives his union with God. Therefore, though we say that Julian did not mean specifically to compose a treatise on contemplation, it is obvious that the book contains some very definite teaching on this subject.[2]

My purpose is to collect the various elements of Julian's teaching on prayer and contemplation, and to present them in a coherent and somehow systematic way.[3] In making this objective investigation we are greatly helped by the acknowledged fact that we find in the course of the exposition of the Revelations a major section in which Julian herself discusses at length and directly, though not systematically, the process of ascent to God and speaks of some stages of prayer and contemplation (chs. 41-43).

[1] The word ' contemplation' occurs only 3 times in the Longer Version, cf. Hudleston, ch. 64, p. 134; ch. 71, p. 145; ch. 78, p. 159; only once in the Shorter Version, cf. Reynolds, ch. XIII, p. 38.   The word ' contemplative' occurs only once in the Shorter Version, cf. Reynolds, ch. XIII, p. 38.   The word ' contemplatively ' occurs only once in the Shorter Version, cf. Reynolds, ch. IV, p. 11.

[2] Hence it is rather disconcerting to read such a statement as this: ' unlike St Teresa, she [Julian] was not writing for those who were aspiring to be contemplatives, so she is little occupied with analysing her soul states'. (Thouless, *The Lady Julian*, p. 89.)   If such a statement merely means that St Teresa was primarily writing for her own nuns devoted *ex professo* to the ' life of contemplation ', whereas Julian is writing for all her even-Christians, we could scarcely quarrel with it.   But in the light of the words ' so she is little occupied with analysing her soul states ' we are driven to the conclusion that Mr Thouless is in danger of misconceiving the whole purpose of Julian's writing, viz. to enable all readers of good will to strive after the same loving union with God which she herself, by his grace, has attained; this striving is nothing more nor less than to aspire to be contemplatives—' *to live contemplatively* ' (Shorter Version, Reynolds, ch. IV, p. 11), and this by a very careful analysis of her own experience in the life of the spirit.

[3] In trying to systematize Julian's doctrine I shall take great care in discovering from the text itself which are the guiding principles in the development of her thought.   The study, therefore, will not be a selection of passages gathered without a principle, or without any strict objective link, but a selection based on internal examination of the book.

Having those chapters as the main basis for analysis I shall extend the examination to other parts of the book, which will clarify and complete what is contained in the main section (41-43).   In order to find these other parts or sections concerning my subject, I shall pay attention not only to the recurrence of the same words, but also, and more particularly, to the descriptions of the different stages in the life of prayer and the connections between the different elements described.[1]

The main theme of chs. 41-43 is ' prayer ': but, as will be seen later, this term in Julian's writing is not to be understood in the ordinary sense of ' petition ' (i.e. to ask for things or graces in particular) but as ' unitive prayer ', the aim and perfection of which is ' a true, gracious, lasting will of the soul oned and fastened into the will of our Lord by the sweet inward work of the Holy Ghost '.   (Ch. 41, p. 72.)

It is a prayer which precedes the gratuitous gift of God which is infused passive contemplation.   And because it is a very high form of prayer, it is understandable that some critics [2] should have said that the author of the Revelations simply presupposes the ordinary teaching on the lower stages of prayer, and is little occupied with the ascetical work.

But a more careful reading of the Revelations shows that Julian's teaching on prayer in this section embraces also chs. 39-40, in which she gives a very clear—though brief—teaching on the preparatory stages.   In fact these chapters (39-40) describe the so called ' second conversion '[3] and the progress

[1] As will appear from the following pages, these sections are contained mainly in chs. 5, 6, 7, 10, 46, 54, 68, 73.   [2] E.g. Warrack, Introd., p. xxxiii.

[3] In the terminology of Spiritual Theology the ' second conversion ' (in contradistinction to the ' first conversion ', that is to say from heathenism to faith) is a fuller donation of self to God on the part of one who already possesses faith.   Hence it corresponds to the beginning of a life in which man deliberately and explicitly orientates his existence towards God.   In that life God becomes the centre of man's thought and desires, and man tries to model his conduct according to God's will and pleasure.   Cf. H. Pinard de la Boullaye, *Conversion*, DSp, II, c. 2261.   R. Garrigou-Lagrange, *Les trois âges de la vie intérieure*, vol. 2, chs. 1 and 2.

of the soul to God up to the time when prayer develops into ' unitive prayer '.

Therefore I maintain—and shall prove later—that chs. 39-40 should be added to the following three as constituting together with them an integral teaching.

It is true that Julian does not dwell too long on these lower stages (and this confirms my assertion that she addresses her teaching to souls who really intend to unite themselves to God, viz. to be contemplatives) because if the work of the ' purgative way ' were prolonged too much, these souls could become spiritually self-centred; and this would hinder their progress. According to Julian, when the main work of purgation is accomplished, the purified souls should be led to fix their eyes more on God than on themselves: by so doing, they will more easily forget self and ' cleave ' to him, behold him and be brought to the grace of contemplation.

Here is precisely where Julian is so original in her teaching: as we shall see at length later, she leads the soul to a complete detachment from self by taking and directing it more positively to God.

On the other hand, I think that unless we extend attention to chs. 39-40, and view the doctrine contained in chs. 41-43 in the light of the preceding two, we might be led erroneously to think that Julian is rash, unsound, and blind to the necessity of an active work of purification, mortification, etc.

In order to facilitate for the reader the task of following the particular examination of each stage, it will be useful for him to have the general outlines of Julian's thought and teaching before his eyes.

Ch. 2. The 'second conversion': contrition, compassion, longing for God (chs. 39-40).

Supplementary teaching on the 'longing' as found in ch. 5:

longing for God alone: 'God, of thy goodness, give me thyself';

how the longing arises: from the realization of God's homely loving;

the necessity of detachment from creatures in order to fulfill the desire of having God (the longing);

this detachment from creatures more easily obtained by fixing our attention on God;

the longing as corresponding to the will of God.

Ch. 3. Unitive 'prayer'—union of the wills (chs. 41-43).

In what manner and how we should use our 'prayer'.

The end and fruit of 'prayer'.

The source of our 'prayer'.

Ch. 4. From the union of the wills to contemplation ('beholding') = ch. 43 and ch. 10.

'Beholding which is special shewing': when the union of the wills is established, God shows himself, of his special grace if and when he wills.

Characteristic elements of the 'Beholding' which is 'Shewing'.

The 'Beholding' which is 'Shewing' compared to the Beatific Vision.

Ch. 5. A second type of 'Beholding' (ch. 7). 'Beholding' (infused contemplation) which is not 'Special Shewing'.

Complementary teaching on the second form of 'Beholding' as found in ch. 10 and ch. 43.

Characteristic elements of this type of 'Beholding'.

Difference between the two types of 'Beholding'.

THE 'SECOND CONVERSION':
CONTRITION; COMPASSION; LONGING
FOR GOD

Analysis of chs. 39-40

JULIAN's teaching in chs. 39-40 is a clear and simple summary of the traditional doctrine on the 'second conversion'. Here she describes with great precision the elements and the soul-states proper to this stage, in which man, moved by the grace of God, sees the disorder of his life, deliberately turns to God and begins to desire him ardently, perceiving that he alone can satisfy the soul's longing.

I shall simply reproduce here, side by side, the main corresponding passages of the two chapters in question, so that by this parallelism and the clarification given by the diversity of expressions, we shall see the essence of the 'second conversion', as described by Julian, with greater accuracy. The same process is described in each chapter; but whereas ch. 39 is more concerned with the part of man, ch. 40 envisages more directly God's activity in this process.[1]

---

[1] I intend merely to analyse and not to study this stage of the soul in her progress to God, because my purpose is to study more carefully and directly the subsequent phases of the spiritual life. These pages, though a simplified analysis and description, could not be omitted for the right appreciation of Julian's subsequent doctrine on the higher forms of prayer and union with God.

Ch. 39, pp. 67-68

Ch. 40, pp. 69-70

'*Sin* is the sharpest scourge that any chosen soul may be smitten with:

[and yet] 'This is a sovereign friendship of our courteous Lord that he keepeth us so tenderly while we be in *sin*';

[not only this, but] 'and furthermore he toucheth us full privily and sheweth us our *sin* by the sweet light of mercy and grace'.

[the consequence is] 'we see our self *so foul*',

'which scourge all forbeateth man and woman, and maketh him so *noisome* in his own sight'.

'so far forth that *after*-while he *thinketh* himself he is not *worthy* but as to *sink in hell*,—

then ween we that God were *wroth with us* for our sin,

till [that time] when *contrition forceth* him *by touching of the Holy Ghost*,

and then are we *stirred of the Holy Ghost* by *contrition*

and turneth the bitterness in hopes of God's mercy.

unto prayer

And then he beginneth his wounds to heal, and the soul to quicken [as it is] *turned unto* the *life of Holy Church*.

The Holy Ghost leadeth him to *confession*,

and desire for the *amending* of our life

wilfully to shew his sins nakedly and truly,
with great sorrow and *great shame* that he hath defouled the fair image of God.

Then undergoeth he *penance* for every sin [as] enjoined by his doomsman that is grounded in Holy Church by the teaching of the Holy Ghost.

And this is one meekness that greatly pleaseth God ; '

with *all our mights,*

to slake the wrath of God,

unto the time we find a rest in soul and a softness in conscience.

Then hope we that God hath forgiven us our sins: and it is sooth.' [1]

[1] Similar descriptions of the ' second conversion ' are frequent in classic spiritual literature. (See e.g. the texts collected by Fr R. Garrigou-Lagrange, from the writings of St Benedict, St Catherine of Siena, Blessed Henry Suso and Tauler; op. cit. vol. 2, ch. 3, *La seconde conversion selon plusieurs spirituels*, pp. 38-50.) I draw particular attention, however, to the strikingly similar passage written by one of Julian's contemporary English mystics: ' At the beginning of his conversion a man who has been much stained with worldliness and sins of the flesh generally dwells most on his sins. He feels great compunction and sorrow; he weeps abundantly, humbly and earnestly asking mercy and pardon of God. And if he is strongly touched with compunction, because God wishes to cleanse him quickly, his sins will seem to be always in his sight, and to be so foul and horrible that he hardly knows what to do with himself. And however exactly he confesses, his conscience will prick him, so that he thinks he has not made a good confession. He can feel no rest, and the strain would become intolerable, if God in His mercy did not sometimes comfort him with feelings of great devotion—it may be to the passion, or whatever seems best to Him. God works in some men's hearts in this way —to a greater or less degree, according as He wills. And this is the great mercy of God, that He will not only forgive the sin but will remit also the pain of purgatory for a little pain of conscience here. Also, if God wishes to prepare a man to receive a special gift of His love, He must first cleanse him by making him feel the fire of compunction for the great sins he has committed. David speaks of this work in many places of the Psalter and especially in the psalm *Miserere mei Deus*—Ps. L.' (Walter Hilton, *The Scale of Perfection*, edited by G. Sitwell, p. 49.)

Having spoken of penance, freely and willingly accepted by the soul, Julian introduces other elements of the same process: trials sent by God: 'And this [penance] is *one* meekness that greatly pleaseth God; and also bodily sickness of God's sending, and also sorrow and shame from without, and reproof, and despite of this world, with all manner of grievance and temptations that he will be cast in, bodily and ghostly.' (Ch. 39, p. 68.) [1] By these words are clearly indicated various forms of purification, and the function of these trials (sickness and bodily afflictions, the contempt and obloquy of others, temptations and spiritual trials, obscurity and darkness, aridity and feelings of abandonment by and the remoteness of God) is explicitly explained by Julian:

On each person that he loveth, *to his bliss for to bring* [them], he layeth something *that is no lack* in his sight, whereby they are blamed and despised in this world, scorned, mocked, and outcasten. And *this he doeth* for *to let the harm* that they should take from the pomp and the vain-glory of this wretched life, and *make their way ready to come to Heaven, and up-raise them* in his bliss everlasting. For he saith: '*I shall wholly break you of* your vain affections and your vicious pride; and after that *I shall together gather you*, and make you *mild and meek*, clean and holy, by *oneing* to me.' (Ch. 28, p. 50.) [2]

These trials are therefore 'laid by God' himself on 'each person' that he 'loveth', with the intention of 'oneing' them to him.

But as the soul which undergoes this trial is usually exposed to the danger of feeling its dereliction so much as to be unaware of the cause of it, Julian therefore shows more clearly the main feature of this process: she speaks

[1] Cf. a similar description in the 'Epistle of Privy Counsel', ch. 12 (*The Cloud of Unknowing and other treatises by a 14th century English Mystic*, edited by J. McCann, pp. 131-133).

[2] Cf. also ch. 27, p. 48: '. . .; (for we be all partly naughted, and we shall be naughted following our Master, Jesus, till we be full purged, that is to say, till we be fully naughted of our deadly flesh and of all our inward affections which be not very good)'.

clearly of the hidden and inward work that God carries on in the soul in order to establish a ' well high ' degree of union: [1]

> *Full preciously* our Lord *keepeth us* when *it seemeth to us* that we are *near forsaken* and *cast away* for our sin and because we have deserved it.
>
> And because of meekness that we get hereby, *we are raised well-high* in God's sight *by his grace*, with so great contrition, also with compassion and *true longing* to God.
>
> *Then they be suddenly delivered* from sin and from pain, and *taken up to bliss*, and made even high saints.   (Ch. 39, p. 68.) [2]

[1] Obviously this teaching of Julian corresponds to the classic doctrine on the nature of the contemplative ' night '. To give but one quotation I reproduce the following passage from A. Poulain, S.J., *The Graces of Interior Prayer*, pp. 200-201: ' As St John of the Cross has given us a careful description of this state, and has called it the first of the *two nights of the soul*, we had better explain what it is that he understands by these two nights. He gives this name to two *successive states of prayer*, or, as he expresses himself, two degrees of the *contemplation* of God. These states are the cause of sufferings; but the sufferings are a secondary element only, a *consequence*. People make mistakes about this sometimes, because of the difficulty of defining the exact nature of the principal element, the *contemplation* of God. They prefer only to consider the sufferings, which have nothing mysterious about them (aridity, the sight of sins, etc.). In a word, instead of endeavouring to penetrate into the saint's real meaning, they are satisfied with adapting his language to ordinary things which are already familiar to them.' Fr Poulain then proceeds to explain the nature of the ' nights ' by showing how these sufferings, aridities, etc., are consequences and signs of a deeper communication effected by God. On this point see the excellent article *Lumière de la contemplation dans la nuit mystique* by K. Truhlar, S. J., *Nouvelle Revue Théologique*, 71 (1949), pp. 1063-1071.

[2] Cf. a similar passage in Walter Hilton, *The Scale of Perfection:* ' For the consolation of those who are tempted in this way, so that *they seem forsaken of God*, our Lord said by his prophet: " In modico dereliqui te, et in momento indignationis meae percussi te, et in miserationibus meis multis congregabo te." (Isa. liv. 7.) For a little time I forsook you, that is to say, I allowed you to be tormented a little, and in a moment of indignation I struck you; that is to say all the penance and the pain that you undergo here is but a moment of my indignation compared to the pain of hell or purgatory; and yet in my manifold mercies *I shall enfold you*, and *when you think you are forsaken*, I shall in my great mercy *gather you again* to me. For *when you think* you are lost, our Lord will help you, as Job says: " Cum te consumptum putaveris, orieris ut lucifer et habebis fiduciam ". (Job, xi. 17.) That is to say, when you are brought so low by the affliction of temptation that you think you have no

This work of purification in which God 'preciously keepeth us' aims therefore at introducing into the soul the disposition of 'meekness'[1] 'because of [which] we are raised well high in God's sight by his grace' and we begin to have 'true longing to God'.

The adjective 'true' clarifies Julian's mind for us: the longing is not a mere aspiration, but an effective love that brings man to be truly turned to God, anxious to find him and to be united to him. This loving disposition will establish an ever increasing union with God, and will enable man to receive a special grace of God, if and when he will give it. Hence Julian summarizes her teaching thus: 'By contrition we are made clean, by compassion we are made ready, and by true longing to God we are made worthy.' (Ch. 39, p. 68.) 'Worthy', that is, of the special grace which she briefly describes in ch. 40, that is to say, after the 'second conversion' and the following stages of trial and wilful longing:

> And then sheweth our courteous Lord himself to the soul—well merrily and with glad cheer—with friendful welcoming as if it had been in pain and in prison, saying sweetly thus: 'My darling, I am glad thou art come to me: in all thy woe I have ever been with thee; and now seest thou my loving and we be oned in bliss.' (Ch. 40, p. 70.)

---

help and no consolation but are as it were forsaken, yet stand firmly in hope and pray to God, and in truth *you shall suddenly spring up* as the day star in gladness of heart and have true confidence in God according to the word of Job.' (Ed. cit. bk. I, ch. 38, p. 55; italics mine.)

[1] This attitude, described by Julian in terms of 'meekness' and the corresponding adjectives 'mild and meek' is considered as a necessary disposition to a higher union with God, and re-echoes, of course, the Evangelical teaching contained, e.g. in the following text of St Matthew: 'At that time Jesus spoke and said, "I praise thee, Father, Lord of heaven and earth, that thou didst hide these things from the wise and prudent, and didst reveal them to little ones. . . . Come to me, all you who labour and are burdened, and I will give you rest. Take my yoke upon you, and learn from me, for I am meek and humble of heart; and you will find rest for your souls. For my yoke is easy, and my burden light."' (Ch. 11, 25-30.)

We may conclude, then, that Julian conceives of the 'second conversion' as blossoming out into the 'longing for God', which is explicitly mentioned as the fruit and conclusion of the preparatory stages described in chs. 39-40.

Since, however, the 'longing' is the immediate preparation for the higher stages of 'prayer and contemplation'—of which Julian speaks at length in chs. 41-43—and even more because the 'longing' which becomes 'true' is practically the essence of 'prayer', it is of vital importance to examine more carefully the meaning of this term. 'Longing', though mentioned in chs. 39-40, is not explained and worked out there; but a much fuller explanation is given in ch. 5.

The supplementary teaching on the 'longing' as found in ch. 5.

The fruit of the process described by Julian in chs. 39-40 is, as we have seen, the 'longing towards God', namely, the supernatural desire of possessing God, a desire that will be fully satisfied only in the beatific vision:

> By contrition we are made clean, by compassion we are made ready, and by true longing to God we are made worthy.
>
> These are three means, as I understand, whereby that all souls come to heaven:
>
> that is to say, that have been sinners in earth and shall be saved: . . . (Ch. 39, p. 68.)
>
> For our kindly will [1] is to have God, and the Good Will of God is to have us; and we may never cease from willing nor from longing, till we have him in fulness of joy: and then may we no more will. (Ch. 6, p. 12.) [2]

[1] On the meaning of the term 'kindly will', cf. note 4 at p. 85 below.

[2] Hence Mr Watkin may rightly say: 'This wilful longing is for Julian the substance of religion and of prayer. It is "the affectuous stirring of love to God for Himself", the "sharp dart of longing love" on which the anonymous mystic, contemporary and fellow countryman, who wrote "The Cloud of Unknowing" insists and of which he says "this is only by itself that work that destroyeth the ground and the root of sin" and that "all virtues shall be subtly, and perfectly conceived, felt and comprehended in it, without any mingling of thine intent".' (E. I. Watkin, *Poets and Mystics*, p. 77.)

The soul which is brought to the 'longing' is therefore in that wilful desire for God, which re-echoes the words of the Psalmist:

O God, my whole soul longs for thee, as a deer for running water; my whole soul thirsts for God, the strong, the living God; shall I never again make my pilgrimage into God's presence? (Psalm 41, 1-2.) [1]

It is in ch. 5 that Julian explains more in detail what she means by this 'longing'.[2]

Longing for God alone. In ch. 5 Julian speaks at length of the process whereby the soul that begins to see the 'homeliness of God',[3] feels the supreme desire of adhering to him *as the only object* that can satisfy its desire. This truth is so deeply felt by the soul that it expresses its aspiration in an ardent prayer, in which it asks for God alone:

For this is the kind yearnings of the soul,[4] by the touching of the Holy Ghost (as by the understanding that I have in this Shewing). God, of thy Goodness, give me thyself: for thou art enough to me, and I may nothing ask that is less, that may be full worship to thee; and if I ask anything that is less, ever me wanteth,—but only in thee I have all. (Ch. 5, pp. 9-10.) [5]

[1] St. Augustine has developed this idea beautifully in his *Enarratio in Ps. 41*; cf. PL, 36, 464 ff.

[2] In ch. 5 Julian does not use the term 'longing' but the corresponding one 'yearning'.

[3] On the concept of the 'homeliness of God', cf. Pt. III, chs. 1-2 of this study.

[4] The terminology in 'kind [= natural] yearnings of the soul' must here of course not be taken as implying an opposition to or contradistinction from a supernatural desire. The whole context shows that Julian is thinking of a desire caused by grace (' by the touching of the Holy Ghost', ' of thy Goodness '). What she wants to say is, simply, that once the soul is under the influence of this grace she *spontaneously* conceives the desire. . . .

[5] This prayer, like the whole chapter, is very reminiscent of St Augustine's ' Fecisti nos [Domine] ad te et inquietum est cor nostrum donec requiescat in te '. (*Confessiones*, I, i, 1; PL, 32, 661.) ' Thou madest us for thyself, and our heart is restless, until it repose in thee.' For other passages that ' call to mind at once the writings of St Augustine ', cf. Sister Reynolds, LSE, pp. 22-23.

How the ' longing ' arises: from the realization of God's home-liness.   At the basis of this ' longing towards God ' is the realization of the love and homeliness of God; a realization which is the effect of the work of the Holy Ghost in the soul (the ' touching of the Holy Ghost '), and which enables the soul to see God in an entirely new light.   God is no longer conceived as a remote entity, but the God who ' cometh down to the lowest part of our need.'   (Ch. 6, p. 11.)

The contrast between the idea of God ' who is so reverend and dreadful ' (ch. 4, p. 7), and the perception of his home-liness leads the soul to see that he is a loving God.   Hence the soul sees him as the One who ' is to us everything that is good and comfortable for us.   He is our clothing that for love wrappeth us, claspeth us, and all becloseth us for tender love, that he may never leave us; being to us all thing that is good, as to mine understanding.'   (Ch. 5, p. 8.)

Of this truth Julian had a vision (' ghostly sight in bodily likeness ') in which she saw a hazel-nut in the palm of the hand:

Also in this he shewed [me] a little thing, the quantity of an hazel-nut, in the palm of my hand; and it was as round as a ball.

I looked thereupon with eye of my understanding, and thought: ' What may this be?'   And it was generally answered thus: ' It is all that is made.'

I marvelled how it might last, for methought it might suddenly have fallen to naught for little[ness].

And I was answered in my understanding:

' It lasteth, and ever shall [last] *for that God loveth it*.'   And so all thing hath the Being by the love of God.

In this Little Thing I saw three properties.

The first is that God made it:

the second is that God loveth it:

the third, that God keepeth it.

But what is to me soothly the Maker, the Keeper, and the Lover,—I cannot tell; for till I am substantially oned to him,

I may never have full rest nor very bliss: that is to say, till I be so fastened to him, that there is right naught that is made betwixt my God and me. (Ch. 5, p. 9.)

I have quoted this text at length because it contains one of the fundamental ideas of Julian's doctrine: the idea of the homeliness of God, which comprehends the elements expressed also in the characteristic description of God as 'the Maker, the Keeper, the Lover'; it is a love tender and intimate, an active and constant love.

This realization of the homeliness of God, causes the creature to bend before God in reverent adoration and admiration: ' And therefore we may with grace and his help stand in ghostly beholding, with everlasting marvelling in this high, overpassing, one, inestimable Love that Almighty God hath to us of his Goodness.' (Ch. 6, p. 12); [1] to move towards Him: cf. all that has been said above concerning the 'longing' and the 'continual seeking'; to be filled with an ardent desire of loving and possessing Him who is the lover:

and we may never cease from willing nor from longing till we have him in fulness of joy: and then may we no more will. (Ch. 6, p. 12.)

For this is the kind yearnings of the soul, by the touching of the Holy Ghost. . . .

God, of thy Goodness, give me thyself: for thou art enough to me, and I may nothing ask that is less, that may be full

---

[1] This quotation can be easily substantiated by several others; e.g. Julian's own attitude when God revealed himself to her: ' And I said: " Benedicite, Domine." This I said for reverence in my meaning, with a mighty voice; and full greatly was astonied *for wonder and marvel* that I had, that he, that is *so reverend and dreadful*, will be *so homely* with a sinful creature living in wretched flesh.' (Ch. 4, p. 7.) Our Lady's attitude is seen and described by Julian in the very same context: ' Also God shewed in part the wisdom and the truth of her soul: wherein I understood the reverent beholding that she beheld her God and Maker [with], *marvelling with great* reverence that he would be born of her that was a simple creature of his making.' (Ch. 4, p. 8; cf. also ch. 7, p. 13.)

worship to thee; and if I ask anything that is less, ever me wanteth,—but only in thee I have all.   (Ch. 5, pp. 9-10.) [1]

The necessity of detachment from creatures in order to fulfil the desire of possessing God.   Having related her ' ghostly sight ' of God's homely loving, Julian proceeds to explain that:

It needeth us to have knowing of the littleness of creatures and to naughten all thing that is made, for to love and have God that is unmade.

For this is the cause why we be not all in ease of heart and soul: that we seek here rest in those things that be so little, wherein is no rest, and know not our God that is Almighty, All-wise, All-good.   For he is the Very Rest.

God will[eth to] be known, and it liketh him that we rest in him; for all that is beneath him sufficeth not us.

And this is the cause why that no soul is rested till it is naughted of all things that are made.

When it is wilfully naughted, for love to have him that is all, then is it able to receive ghostly rest.   (Ch. 5, p. 9.)

From this citation and the preceding one, two distinct elements are discernible: union with God as our end, and detachment from creatures.

Union with God is described in the following terms: ' Substantially *oned* to him [God] '; ' *fastened* to him '; ' to love and *have* God '; ' to *have* him that is all '; and in this way ' to *rest* in him '.

Detachment from creatures: in order to be fastened to him, ' to have ' God, Julian explicitly insists that: ' it needeth us to have knowing of the littleness of creatures ', ' to hold as nought all thing that is made ' (naughten), because ' all thing that is beneath him sufficeth not us ', and ' the cause

---

[1] Here the teaching of Julian seems to walk hand in hand with what is called the Benedictine spirituality.   Cf. note at the end of this chapter (p. 92.)

why we be not all in ease of heart and soul: that we seek here rest in those things that be so little, wherein is no rest '.

The intrinsic relationship between these two elements is clearly indicated by Julian's saying: ' when it is wilfully *naughted*,[1] for love *to have him* that is all, then is it able to receive ghostly *rest* '. (Ch. 5, p. 9.)

To regard as ' naught ' ' all thing that is made ', and to act accordingly, namely, to deprive oneself of all creatures to the end that the soul may at some future date come into the possession of God, is of course the common teaching of all ascetical treatises. In fact this effort is the very essence of all asceticism (*askesis* meaning precisely the effort). But what is characteristic of Julian's teaching is the stress laid on the words: ' when it is *wilfully* naughted, for *love* to have him that is all '.[2]

Detachment from creatures more easily attained by fixing our attention on God. It is characteristic of Julian's teaching that the stress is laid on the words ' when it is *wilfully* naughted, *for love to have* him '. She does not dwell so long on what may be called the turning away from creatures; but quickly draws attention towards the positive element of this reality, which is the possession of God. She is obviously aware of the necessity of detachment from creatures and that we have ' to hold as nought all thing that is made ', but she is more concerned with a constant insistence on the

---

[1] ' to naughten ' means ' to make naught of '; hence ' naughted ' = ' made naught of, emptied of, detached from '; cf. the modernized words used by Miss Warrack in her edition of the *Revelations:* ' to hold as nought ', ' made nought ', p. 11; and the notes in Hudleston's edition, p. 9.

[2] This is the punctuation according to Fr Hudleston. Other editors have punctuated this sentence differently: e.g. Warrack, ' When it is willingly made nought, for love, to have Him that is all.' Tyrrell, ' When she is wilfullie naughted for love to have him that is all.' Harford, ' When he is noughted for love to have him that is all.' Reynolds, ' When he is fully emptied, for love, to have Him who is all that is good.'

attachment to God ('cleave to the Goodness of God', ch. 6, p. 10).

This teaching is surely very sound: it corresponds to the psychological necessity of foreknowing and even, to a certain extent, foretasting a higher good, the desire of which alone can reasonably induce the renunciation of limited and lesser goods. Thus she obtains a much greater detachment from those things which are not worthy of our attention; when the heart is full of the One who is worthy of all attention, all else is eclipsed and seems as nothing compared to it. This is her teaching when, in summarizing the meaning of the first Revelation, as described in ch. 5 and ff., she says:

> In which Shewing I understood six things: . . .
> The third is the blissful Godhead that ever was, is and ever shall be: Almighty, All-Wisdom, All-Love.
> The fourth is, all thing that he hath made.—
> For well I wot that heaven and earth and all that is made is great and large, fair and good;
> *but the cause why it shewed so little to my sight was for that I saw it in the presence of him that is the Maker of all things:*
> for to a soul that seeth the Maker of all, all that is made seemeth full little. (Ch. 8, pp. 15-16.) [1]

This is the true Christian detachment from creatures: detachment from and not contempt of the 'things which are made': in fact they are 'great and large, fair and good' (ch. 8, p. 15), because God makes them and keeps them for love. In other words Julian leads the soul to estimate created things at their true value and to love them in so far as they ought to be loved, that is to say, because 'He that

---

[1] The last words of this sentence are said to be the only direct extra-biblical quotation known to us. It is from St Gregory's *Life of St Benedict* (cf. PL, 66, 200); see Sister Reynolds, LSE, p. 23. Here again attention may be drawn to the already indicated parallelism between Julian's doctrine and the Benedictine spirituality. Cf. note at the end of this chapter (p. 92).

made all thing for love, by the same love keepeth [it], and
it is kept and shall be without end.' (Ch. 8, p. 16.)[1]

The soul which is full of God and knows God with that
deep spiritual sight which is given 'by the Holy Ghost'
will not be seduced by created things: in fact 'to a soul
that seeth the Maker of all, all that is made seemeth full
little' (ch. 8, p. 16). Hence the soul, which has contemplated God, will experience with regard to created things
that feeling of dissatisfaction to which Julian refers in ch. 5,
where she says: 'For this is the cause why we be not all in
ease of heart and soul: that we seek here rest in those things
that be so little, wherein is no rest, and know not our God
that is Almighty, All-wise, All-good. For he is the Very
Rest.' (Ch. 5, p. 9.)

In order to reach this perfection the eyes of the soul must
be fixed on God himself: Julian concentrates the attention
on God, on his goodness, on his love, so that the soul may

[1] Hence Gerald Bullett rightly says: ' Julian does not mean that created
things are to be despised, or regarded as valueless, but only that their value
is derived from the one life, or love, that *sustains* them. In the vision and
contemplation of that, not in attachment to things as such, is our " rest ".
This is the ancient doctrine of non-attachment, purged of the insufferable
disdain of natural things that too often infects it. For God, says Julian,
" hath no disdain of that which he hath made, nor any disdain to serve us at
the simplest offices that belong in nature to our body. For as the body is
clad in cloth, and the flesh in skin and the bones in flesh, and the heart in the
whole, so are we, soul and body, clad in the goodness of God and beclosed.
Yea, and more homely; for all these may waste and wear away, but the
goodness of God is ever whole, and more near to us." She is quite explicit
on this point: that the allegory of the hazel-nut does not imply a disdain of
creatures and things. " Well I wot that heaven and earth and all that is made
is great and large, fair and good. The cause why it shewed so little to my
sight was that I saw it in the presence of him that is the Maker of all things.
For to a soul that seeth the Maker of all, all that is made seemeth full little."
But the goodness can be in little things as easily as in great; for " God is all
that is good, as to my sight, and the goodness that each thing hath, it is he." '
(*The English Mystics*, London, 1950, pp. 58-59.) I call attention to the similarity of Julian's ideas as expressed in these passages with various points of
the so called *Contemplatio ad amorem* by St Ignatius of Loyola, cf. *Exercitia
Spiritualia*, nn. 35-37.

be ravished by him and consequently forget self and all other things: 'for truly our Lover desireth that our soul cleave to him with all its might, and that we be evermore cleaving to his Goodness. For of all things that heart may think, this pleaseth most God, and *soonest speedeth* [the soul].' (Ch. 6, p. 12.) Again at the end of ch. 6 Julian explicitly says:

For *he willeth that we be occupied in knowing and loving* till the time that we shall be fulfilled in Heaven; and *therefore was this lesson of love shewed*, with all that followeth, as ye shall see.

For *the strength and the Ground of all was shewed in the* First Sight. *For of all things the beholding and the loving of the Maker maketh the soul to seem least in his own sight, and most filleth it with reverent dread and true meekness;* with plenty of charity to his even-Christians. (Ch. 6, p. 12.)

There can be little doubt that for Julian, all progress in the ascent to God depends largely on our fixing the attention on God rather than on ourselves.

These ideas, explained in detail in the preceding pages are beautifully expressed in the prayer:

God, of thy Goodness, give me thyself : for thou art enough to me, and I may nothing ask that is less, that may be full worship to thee ; and if I ask anything that is less, ever me wanteth —but only in thee I have all. (Ch. 5, p. 10.)

in which Julian, having seen the homeliness of God, and hence having realized that nothing 'that is made' can satisfy her longing, *asks* for God alone.

Asking for God alone is therefore the manner in which the 'longing' finds its concrete realization.

Note: JULIAN AND BENEDICTINE SPIRITUALITY

The following citations from Dom De Puniet (*Benoît et Bénédictins* in DSp, I, c. 1388 ff.) will illustrate more clearly than any words of mine the remarkable similarity between Julian's thought and what is called the Benedictine spirituality (cf. my remarks on pp. 88 and 90).

' The deep consciousness of God's nearness gives to prayer a quality that is highly recommended by St Benedict, as the most important of all, that is to say simplicity.

" He who wishes to pray on his own—St Benedict says—let him enter

quite simply into the oratory and let him give himself simply to prayer—
'Simpliciter intret et oret' (*Rule*, ch. LII)."

What is required when one desires to speak to our Lord is not a multitude
of words nor loud exclamations, but rather purity of the heart which
enables man to love God in spite of the petty attractions of worldly things,
and devotion, by which man gives himself totally to God. A short and
sincere prayer is preferable to a long discourse. Only fervent love can cause
a man to prolong his prayer, while preserving its simplicity. St Benedict
wishes that such should be the prayer of his disciples. It is the love of God
which has brought them to their monastery; it is charity that inspires all
their religious activity; it is love at the root of their obedience which makes
them obey with joy and readiness, even in difficult things (*Rule*, ch. V, and
ch. LXVIII); it is the *desire of finding God* in order to know him and love him
better that drives them to seek God.

This is what they must do from the very beginning: and this is what St
Benedict himself did for the whole of his life.

The testimony left to us by his Rule and by the life written by St Gregory,
both give evidence that this was his spiritual attitude:

" St Benedict was dominated by a strong and all-embracing aspiration
towards God alone; he sought God's face" (Dom I. Ryelandt, *Essay sur la
physionomie morale de saint Benoît*, 1924, Coll. Pax., p. 23). St Benedict wants
to see his neighbour act and live as he did, " if they really seek God" (*Rule*,
ch. LVIII; cf. Dom Marmion, *Le Christ, idéal du moine*. I, Chercher Dieu;
XV, L'Oraison monastique.-Dom C. Butler, *Benedictine Monachism*, ch. VI,
St Benedict's teaching on prayer). " To seek God with the noble desire of
possessing him, means to tend towards him, and towards him alone, with all
the faculties and powers of the soul; it is in truth the *élan* of the whole being
towards God, it is the perfect prayer, that is to say prayer full of boundless
wonder, deep respect and humble adoration of the creature bent before its
Creator (*Rule*, ch. XVI); prayer of praise and thanksgiving to the Lord and
Master of all things " (ibid. ch. XX) c. 1403.

' The constant attention to the presence of God led St Benedict to an
intimate union with our Lord, and procured for him—according to St Gregory
—exceptional graces of contemplation which are granted only to few. However, it must be noted that St Gregory's opinion is that this is the normal
outcome of an intense spirit of faith and prayer, in a soul which is totally
dominated by the thought of God, present in the soul.

" Videnti Creatorem angusta est omnis creatura "

St Gregory, *Dialogues*, II, ch. XXXV.

God's presence reveals to the contemplative soul the littleness of created
things in comparison to the Creator, and the nothingness of all which is not
God. This is the best lesson that can be derived from a constant intercourse
with the Truth; when the soul attains to this degree of deep appreciation of
the things of God, it approaches perfect charity. And according to St
Benedict, it is this perfect charity that leads the soul to fulfil its daily duties
out of pure love and desire of doing good. (*Rule*, ch. VII) '. c. 1404.

3

UNITIVE 'PRAYER'—UNION OF THE WILLS

(Chs. 41-43)

The ' longing ' of the soul as corresponding to the ' good will of God '

IMMEDIATELY after the prayer ' God, of thy Goodness, give me thyself ', in which the soul asks for God alone, Julian proceeds to explain that this petition is ' full lovesome to the soul ' (ch. 5, p. 10), because she realizes that, by this prayer, her longing is in process of being fulfilled. But a new element, of extreme importance for the right appreciation of Julian's doctrine on prayer, is introduced here: these words of her prayer do not only correspond to the ' kind yearnings of the soul ', but at the same time ' full near touch they the will of God ' (ch. 5, p. 10).

The new element is the will of God who wants to possess us. Hence these two movements, the one of the soul aspiring and tending towards God, and the other of God desiring to have us, are shown by Julian as intrinsically joined, as two aspects of one reality, when she says: ' our kindly Will is to have God, and the Good Will of God is to have us ' (ch. 6, p. 12).

The first part of this passage ' our kindly will is to have God ' summarizes the first teaching on prayer—the one found in chs. 39-40, 5 and ff., viz. the ' longing '. The second part, ' the Good Will of God is to have us ', is the key to the union between that teaching and chs. 41-43, where the teaching on prayer concerns the union of the wills.[1]

---

[1] For a right understanding of chs. 41-43 it is necessary, as I have pointed out, to consider chs. 39-40 as part of the main section concerning prayer.

In fact, the 'natural will' ('kind yearnings') 'to have God' is given to the soul by God himself: 'for this is the kind yearnings of the soul, by the touching of the Holy Ghost' (ch. 5, 9). But the reason why God infuses this 'natural will' is that the soul must go to him as to its last end: 'He hath made us only to himself' (ch. 5, p. 10). God wants to have us: it cannot be otherwise, because God cannot renounce his glory. Hence: 'the good will of God is to have us' (ch. 6, p. 12).

When Julian says that 'it is God's will to have us', she is clearly considering the actual relation which exists between the soul and God who has not only created it but has lifted it up to be a partaker of the divine nature. It is thus that he inspires the soul with the desire of possessing him, so that by following its deepest desire ('for this is the kind yearnings of the soul'), under the prompting of the Holy Spirit ('by the touching of the Holy Ghost'), the soul unites itself to God's will, and fulfils it by attaining the end for which it has been created. Thus by going to God (which is the primary end of creation), the creature finds its full satisfaction (which is the secondary end of creation).

The reader may now see the full import of the sentence so far considered only by sections:

> And these words are *full lovesome to the soul*, and *full near touch they the will of God* and his Goodness.
> For his Goodness comprehendeth all his creatures and his blessed works, and overpasseth without end. *For he is the endlessness, and he hath made us only to* himself, and restored us by his blessed Passion, and keepeth us in his blessed Love; and all this is of his Goodness. (Ch. 5, p. 10.)

The two aspects, viz. the 'longing' and the 'good will of God', are here openly indicated. But their intrinsic connection is also stated, with like clearness.

The union of the wills and prayer

Merely by longing for God, man corresponds to God's will: hence a certain degree of union of the wills is already established. But this is only an initial union: in fact it is —on man's part—only the level of aspiration, which if it is to develop into full union must become more concrete and exercise its influence on man's life. Therefore from the union of aspiration or of desire, Julian proceeds to the union of the wills by means of prayer.

Her teaching on this matter is mainly contained in chs. 41-43.

'. . . our Lord . . . said:

' I am Ground of thy beseeching:
First it is my will that thou have it;
and after, I make thee to will it;
and since, I make thee to beseech it and thou beseechest it,
how should it then be that thou shouldst not have thy beseech-
    ing?' (Ch. 41, p. 72.)

Our Lord God willeth [that] we have true understanding, and especially in three things that belong to our prayer.
The first is by whom and how that our prayer springeth.
By whom, he sheweth when he saith:
' I am [the] Ground ';
and how, by his Goodness: for he saith first:
' It is my will.'
The second is: in what manner and how we should use our
    prayer and that is; that our will be turned unto the will of
    our Lord, enjoying: and so meaneth he when he saith:
    ' I make thee to will it.'
The third is that we should know the fruit and the end of our
    prayers: that is, that we be oned and like to our Lord in all
    things. (Ch. 42, p. 74.)

Prayer oneth the soul to God.

For though the soul be ever like to God in kind and substance, restored by grace, it is often unlike in condition, by sin on man's part.

Then is prayer a witness that the soul willeth as God willeth; and it comforteth the conscience and [en]ableth man to grace.

And thus he teacheth us to pray, and mightily to trust that we shall have it.

For he beholdeth us in love and would make us partners of his good deed, and therefore he stirreth us to prayer for that which it liketh him to do.

For which prayer and good-will, that we have of his gift, he will reward us and give us endless meed. . . .

And thus the soul by prayer accordeth to God.   (Ch. 43, p. 76.)

In these texts may be found the following elements of Julian's doctrine on prayer.

I. ' *In what manner and how we should use our prayer; and that is that our will be turned unto the will of our Lord, enjoying.*'

' Prayer ' is the means that brings the soul from the state of mere aspiration (' longing ') to the union of wills in the practical life: ' Prayer oneth the soul to God. *For though the soul be ever like to God in kind and substance*, restored by grace, *it is often unlike in condition*, by sin on man's part.' (Ch. 43, p. 76.) We are dealing here with the concrete situation of fallen man and the difficulties which he encounters on his way to union with God.   In fact, though the ' kind yearning[s] of the soul ' is ' to have God ', man is ' unlike in condition ' because of sin.   Thus God ' teacheth us to pray ' (ch. 43, p. 77), viz. ' He stirreth us to prayer for that which it liketh him to do.'   (Ch. 43, p. 77.)

To do what ' liketh him ' (= what pleases God) implies in our present situation that at least from time to time our will must be ' turned ' so as to be in accord with God. ' Our Lord God willeth [that] we have true understanding, and specially in three things that belong to our prayer. . . . in what manner and how we should use our prayer; and that is *that our will be turned unto* the will of our Lord, enjoying.' (Ch. 42, p. 74.)

That this 'turning' of the will into the will of God may assume at times the proportion of a serious effort is known to Julian. She is fully aware that the state of ardent longing and sweet consolations may alternate with times of hardness and tempest: and this is the time to 'pray':

> But when we see him not so, then feel we need and cause to pray, for failing and for unabling of our self, to Jesus.
>
> For when the soul is tempested, troubled, and left to itself by unrest then it is time to pray, for to make itself supple and buxom [1] to God. (Ch. 43, p. 77.)

This teaching is no mere theorizing, but reflects Julian's own experience.

It is in these practical difficulties of our life that the soul —through 'prayer'—is 'made pliable and obedient to God': thus union with God is no longer confined to union of 'aspiration', but is obedience, by which man lives, works and does what God wants him to do: and this is a deeper union than the one obtained through mere 'longing' and hence more acceptable to Him:

> God accepteth the good-will and the travail of his servant, howsoever we feel: wherefore *it pleaseth him that we work both in our prayers and in good living*, by his help and his grace. (Ch. 41, p. 73.)
>
> . . . and therefore he stirreth us to prayer for that which it liketh him *to do*.
>
> For which *prayer and good-will*, that we have of his gift, he will reward us and give us endless meed. (Ch. 43, p. 77.)

This teaching is all briefly summed up in Julian's own words: 'And thus the soul by prayer *accordeth* to God' (ch. 43, p. 77); 'Prayer *oneth* the soul to God.' (Ch. 43,

---

[1] In modern English: 'for to make itself pliable and obedient to God' (Warrack, p. 91).

p. 76.) Therefore when Julian gives explicit teaching on 'prayer', this term has to be understood, not as petition of things, but in the precise and technical sense of 'unitive prayer' leading to the union of wills.

II. '*The fruit and the end of our prayer: that is that we be oned and like to our Lord in all things.*'

It is obvious that prayer thus understood constitutes and establishes a much deeper union between God and man than does mere longing. Whereas longing does not require special effort and sacrifice on man's part—longing being rather 'full lovesome to the soul' (ch. 5, p. 10)—the effect of being 'turned' to God through prayer submits the longing to the test of 'good-will' and 'living'; viz.: engages the sincerity of man's will for union with God in a much deeper and more demanding sense.

This is a high degree of union, expressed by Julian in her definition of prayer: 'Beseeching is a new, gracious, *lasting* will of the soul, oned and *fastened* into the will of our Lord by the sweet inward work of the Holy Ghost' (ch. 41, p. 72), that is to say the substantial union with God by which man is 'oned and like to God in all things'. But it is not the highest union. In fact if, on the one hand, this degree of union established by prayer 'comforteth the conscience' (ch. 43, p. 76), on the other hand it '[en]ableth man *to grace*' (ibid).[1] The grace that Julian has here in mind is the entirely gratuitous grace of 'special Shewing' which will be analysed in the following chapter.

By stating that 'prayer' constitutes a high degree of union with God and by adding that it 'enableth man' to still higher graces, Julian gives us to understand that prayer has always to be seen in the light of our progressive

[1] Cf. ch. 43, p. 77: 'And thus the soul by prayer accordeth to God. But when our courteous Lord of his grace sheweth himself to our soul, we have that [which] we desire.'

unification with God, and that it is the necessary stage preceding the highest forms of union.[1]

From this point of view we can appreciate why Julian, from the very beginning, does not conceive of prayer as petition of things from God, or as an effort to bend God's will to our needs, but as ' unitive prayer '.[2]

And this conception is typical of contemplative souls. Indeed prayer so understood is an act of full glorification of God: it is ' petition ', but petition of the highest of all goods: God himself. And this petition is ' most worshipful to God ' because it postulates the conscious acknowledgment of the absolute reality of God as the creature's last end. For he is cause and end of all ' things which are made ', and source and explanation of every created value.

III. ' *By whom and how that our prayer springeth. By whom, he sheweth when he saith: I am* [*the*] *Ground of thy beseeching.*'

Prayer being thus conceived as the means of fulfilling, in the practical order, our longing for union with God, it is not surprising to find Julian insisting again upon God being the cause of our prayer.

---

[1] This teaching of Julian is of course in perfect harmony with the doctrine of the great mystical writers. Cf. e.g. on the teaching of St Francis of Sales, A. Saudreau, *L'Oraison d'après Saint François de Sales* (extrait de ' La Vie Spirituelle '), particularly chs. 2, 4 and 6. On the teaching of St Jeanne de Chantal, A. Saudreau, *L'Oraison d'après Sainte Jeanne de Chantal*, Saint-Maximin (extrait de ' La Vie Spirituelle '), particularly pp. 25-31. It would be labouring the obvious to say that this is also the teaching of St John of the Cross.

[2] Cf. ch. 6, p. 10: ' And in that time the custom of our praying was brought to mind: how we use for lack of understanding and knowing of Love, to make many means. Then saw I soothly that it is more worship to God, and more very delight, that we faithfully pray to himself of his Goodness.' And ch. 43, p. 77: (' But the soul *by no manner* of prayer maketh God supple to it; for he is ever alike in love.') See also R. H. Thouless, ' The keynote of all Julian's teaching on prayer is struck in this chapter—that it is asking of boons from a lover, not an attempt to bend a stern alien will to our needs.' (*The Lady Julian*, p. 91)—though I would like to make some qualification of this judgement; and E. I. Watkin, *Poets and Mystics*, pp. 98-99: ' like other contemplatives . . . [Julian] insists upon the unitive nature of genuine prayer '.

Julian mentions emphatically the priority of the divine element, in the text from ch. 42, where she refers directly to the words of ch. 41: 'I am [the] Ground':

> Our Lord God willeth [that] we have true understanding, and specially in three things that belong to our prayer.

> The first is by whom and how that our prayer springeth. By whom, he sheweth when he saith: 'I am [the] Ground'; and how, by his Goodness: for he saith first: 'It is my will.' (Ch. 42, p. 74.)

The Idea of God as the 'Ground of our beseeching' is specified even more clearly when she says that 'our beseeching is not cause of God's goodness' (ch. 41, p. 72),[1] but rather 'beseeching' is due to 'the sweet inward work of the Holy Ghost' (ch. 41, p. 72); in fact 'he stirreth us to prayer' (ch. 43, p. 77).

Consequently when we 'beseech' we follow the movement of God's will and hence, by this uniting of our will to his, we give him pleasure: 'And in the first reason,—where he saith: "and thou beseechest it", there he sheweth [his] full great pleasance, and endless meed that he will give us for our beseeching.' (Ch. 41, p. 72.) And this is at the same time the basis of Julian's insistence on *trust*:

> I am Ground of thy beseeching:
> first it is my will that thou have it;
> and after, I make thee to will it;
> and since, I make thee to beseech it and thou beseechest it,
> *how should it then be that thou shouldst not have thy* beseeching?
> (Ch. 41, p. 72.)

And in the second reason, where he saith:

> 'How should it then be?' etc.,

this was said for an impossible [thing].

> *For it is most impossible that we should beseech* mercy and grace, *and not have it.* (Ibid.)

---

[1] The immediate context of this passage is concerned with Julian's optimism. As I shall show later, Julian finds the reason for this optimism precisely in the consideration of God being, in this sense, 'the Ground'.

This conception is so logically united with the fundamental idea of prayer as an act of glorification of God, that Julian teaches explicitly that we do not comply with God's will for glorification, unless we abandon ourselves wholeheartedly to this trust in God:

> For this is our Lord's *will*, that our prayer and our trust be both alike large.
>
> *For if we trust not as much as we pray, we do not full worship to our Lord in our prayer*, and also we tarry and pain our self.
>
> The cause is, as I believe, that we know not truly that our Lord is [the] Ground on whom our prayer springeth; and also that we know not that it is given us by the grace of his love.
>
> For if we knew this, it would make us to trust to have, of our Lord's gift, all that we desire.[1] (Ch. 42, pp. 74-75.)

A more detailed analysis of this ' trust ' brings Julian to determine more accurately how the divine and human elements collaborate in the progressive realization of the union:

> Then meaneth he thus: that we [should] see *that he* doeth it, *and that we* [should] pray therefor. For the one is not enough. *For if we pray and see not that he doeth it*, it maketh us heavy and doubtful; and that is not his worship.
>
> *And if we see that he doeth, and we pray not*, we do not our debt, and so may it not be: that is to say, so is it not [the thing that is] in his beholding.

[1] As is obvious from this text, according to Julian the greater part of our ' pain ' and worries comes from the fact that we do not realize that as God is the inspirer of our desires—he is also the one who will bring us to the fulfilment of our desires. Cf. ch. 42, p. 75—viz. the passage which follows immediately: ' But sometimes it cometh to our mind that we have prayed long time, and yet we think to ourselves that we have not our asking. But herefor should we not be heavy. For I am sure, by our Lord's meaning, that either we abide a better time, or more grace, or a better gift. He willeth that we have true knowing in himself that He is Being; and in this knowing he willeth that our understanding be grounded, with all our mights and all our intent and all our meaning; and in this ground he willeth that we take our *stand and our oneing*. . . .' (MS. (S1): ' stede and our wonynge ' = our stand (= place) and our dwelling.)

But to see that he doeth it, and to pray forthwithal,—so is he worshipped and we sped.

All thing that our Lord hath ordained to do, it is his will that we pray therefor, either in special or in general.   And the joy and the bliss that it is to him, and the thanks and the worship that we shall have therefor, it passeth the understanding of creatures, as to my sight. . . .

Thus it belongeth to us to do our diligence; and when we have done it, then shall us yet think that [it] is naught—and sooth it is.   But if we do as we may, and soothly ask [for] mercy and grace, all that faileth us we shall find in him.   And thus meaneth he where he saith: ' I am Ground of thy beseeching.'

And thus in this blissful word, with the Shewing, I saw a full over-coming against all our weakness and all our doubtful dreads.   (Ch. 42, pp. 75-76.)

As may be seen from this text, *the idea of God being the cause* of our prayers (which is the source of real trust), as well as *the idea of God expecting this trust* as his proper glorification, are *at the root* of what we believe to be the most typical and important teaching of Julian in the spiritual life: viz. the full detachment from self by fixing the eyes on God.

In fact, by realizing that God is not only the inspirer of man's desire for union, but also the principal agent in the process of its realization, man becomes aware of his own insufficiency and gives up trust in himself.   But at the same time, instead of being discouraged, he is comforted and filled with joy by the knowledge that God, in his love, will do all. ' And thus he teacheth us to pray, and *mightily to trust that we shall have it.'*   (Ch. 43, p. 77.)

H

FROM THE 'UNION OF THE WILLS' TO 'BEHOLDING' (CONTEMPLATION): 'BEHOLDING' WHICH IS 'SPECIAL SHEWING'

(Ch. 43 and Ch. 10)

WHEN the union of the wills has been effected, the soul has reached the accord with God: 'And thus the soul by prayer accordeth to God' (ch. 43, p. 77); 'Beseeching is a new, gracious, lasting will of the soul, oned and fastened into the will of our Lord by the sweet inward work of the Holy Ghost' (ch. 41, p. 72), the soul is in the attitude of expecting God. Not distracted by any created good, she is fixed in God, 'oned and fastened' to him.

While the soul is in this condition a special communication of God may take place:

And thus the soul by prayer accordeth to God.

But when our courteous Lord of his grace sheweth himself to our soul, we have that [which] we desire. And then we see not, for the time, what we should more pray, but all our intent with all our might is set wholly to the beholding of him.[1]

And this is an high unperceivable prayer, as to my sight. (Ch. 43, p. 77.)

---

[1] Cf. Hugh of St Victor, *De modo orandi*, PL, 176, 980: 'Pura oratio est, quando ex abundantia devotionis mens ita accenditur, ut cum se ad Deum postulatura converterit, *prae amoris eius magnitudine etiam petitionis suae obliviscatur;* et cum amore eius, quem videt, perfrui vehementer concupiscit totaque jam illi vacare desiderat, ejus etiam, pro quo venit, curam libenter postponat.'

Julian introduces thus a higher type of prayer or union which is originated by a special 'shewing' of God and takes the form of simple 'beholding' of him.

The term 'beholding' does not occur only in this context, but is frequently used by Julian even when there is no mention of a 'shewing'. From all the instances in which this term is employed, we may gather that for Julian it does not signify the mere act of 'seeing', but the act by which a person fixes his whole attention on something. The simplicity and depth of this attention reveals that a particular attraction has been exercised by the object, and consequently that the person who beholds is showing an especial affection and love for the object, as well as a desire to penetrate more deeply into that property of it which has drawn the attention.

'Beholding' understood in this general sense would correspond to the word 'contemplation' when the latter is taken in its common acceptation.

We would consequently apply to the term 'beholding' the considerations of Fr J. Maréchal, S.J., with regard to the term 'contemplation':

Contemplation, as commonly understood, is not intuition, since the name 'contemplation' is also applied to an intellectual and imaginative activity.

Might it be defined at least as an inchoative intuition? Perhaps, in a way; yet it must be noted that sensible intuition, the only kind of which we normally have any experience, is not necessarily contemplation.

This latter seems to require in addition a certain fixity, a more prolonged or intimate communion. We recollect a visit we once made to a famous place in company with a band of tourists, some not very given to recollection, and others, more meditative, who kept to themselves; the former, content merely to 'see', were always impatient to go on, to the indignant despair of the latter, who would have preferred to 'contemplate' at least for a few moments; now attention acts on the psychological elements after the fashion of the poles of a magnet, which gather up iron filings into magnetic shapes.

Perhaps the characteristic of contemplation is rather a deep ' orientation' of the human being ' in ' an intuition or ' towards ' an intuition?

However this may be, there exist various kinds of contemplation.[1]

Even a casual reader of the Book of Revelations will advert to the fact that the term ' beholding' is used by Julian in different contexts. From them it is clear that the manner in which the contemplative attention is effected is not the same in all cases. Julian appears then to be aware that—at least in her experience—there are various forms of ' beholding '. She distinguishes between the simple act in which the attention is mainly the result of an activity of the will disposing the intellect to gaze and contemplate, and a higher form in which something imposes itself so vividly and luminously upon the intellect that it ' can do no more but behold '. (Ch. 43, p. 78.)

Following Julian's own terminology, I shall use the word ' beholding ' as a generic term, but I shall also analyse carefully the nature of the beholding, and study the various types contained in it, in so far as they constitute various forms of contemplation, that is, various stages in the life of union with God.

I begin with the most conspicuous form of beholding: viz. the one which Julian describes as being the consequence of a special grace in which God ' shews ' himself to the soul. This ' special shewing ' is so high and luminous that the soul is entirely absorbed: ' . . . when our courteous Lord *of his grace sheweth himself* to our soul, we have that [which] we desire. And then we see not, for the time, what we should more pray, but *all our intent with all our might* is set wholly to the beholding of him.' (Ch. 43, p. 77.)

[1] J. Maréchal, *Studies on the Psychology of the Mystics*, p. 168

I call this form of contemplation 'beholding which is special shewing', to distinguish it from another form of infused contemplation in which there is no 'shewing'. On this latter type I shall dwell later, and see how Julian conceives of a form of contemplation which is deprived of any extraordinary element and is very precious for our life of union with God. Her teaching on this matter is, to my mind, one of the most valuable and beautiful points of doctrine.

Beholding which is ' special shewing'

But when our courteous Lord of his grace sheweth himself to our soul, we have that [which] we desire. And then we see not, for the time, what we should more pray, but all our intent with all our might is set wholly to the beholding of him.

And this is an high unperceivable prayer, as to my sight: for all the cause wherefor we pray, it is oned into the sight and beholding of him to whom we pray;

marvellously enjoying with reverent dread, and with so great sweetness and delight in him that we can pray right naught but as he stirreth us, for the time.

And well I wot, the more the soul seeth of God, the more it desireth him by his grace. . . .

And this I saw: that what time we see needs wherefor we pray, then our good Lord followeth us, helping our desire;

and when we of his special grace plainly behold him, seeing none other needs, then we follow him and he draweth us into him by love.

For I saw and felt that his marvellous and fulsome Goodness fulfilleth all our might; and therewith I saw that his continual working in all manner of things is done so goodly,[1] so wisely, and so mightily, that it overpasseth all our imagining, and all that we can ween and think; and then we can do no more but behold him, enjoying, with an high, mighty desire to be all oned into him,—centred to his dwelling,—and enjoy in his loving and delight in his goodness. (Ch. 43, pp. 77-78.)

[1] MSS. (P) and (W) read ' godly ' instead of ' goodly '; (S1) ' godely '.

I have quoted this passage at length because of its importance, and while analysing it, I shall associate it with certain complementary expressions from a parallel passage in ch. 10.[1]

With the contrast between the two sentences: ' And thus the soul by prayer accordeth to God.' '*But when . . .*' Julian introduces the superior form of union, thus clearly stating the relationship and divergences existing between the two: the higher union (beholding) comes after the union of the wills, but it is not caused by this union. Union through ' prayer ' merely disposes the soul to the ' beholding ' which is entirely gratuitous and is granted ' when our courteous Lord of *his grace* sheweth himself to our soul '. This point is emphasized and twice repeated in the parallel passage of ch. 10, p. 21: ' he shall shew us himself of *his special grace when he will.*'

The meaning and the end of ' prayer ' is—as we have seen—that ' our *will* be turned unto the *will* of our Lord ' (ch. 42, p. 74), and hence we may arrive at the stage in which the will is united to God: ' new, gracious, lasting *will* of the soul *oned* and *fastened into the will* of our Lord ' (ch. 41, p. 72), whereas in the new type of union the soul is ' oned into the *sight* and *beholding* of him ', and ' all our intent with all our might is set to the beholding of him '. Nay even to a ' plain ' beholding: ' and when we of his special grace *plainly* behold him '. In the same category of ' sight ' and ' beholding ' rather than of union of the ' *wills* ', Julian typifies this new union by the term ' *clearness* of finding.' (Ch. 10, p. 21.)

The object of this beholding is God himself: ' behold *him* ', ' sheweth *himself* ', etc. We shall discover later what is here meant by the expression ' beholding *him* ', and find that the object of this beholding is the ' Godhead ', God ' the Maker, the Keeper, the Lover ', viz. God loving and thus operating in his creatures, and in man's soul in particular:

1 The content of ch. 10 is considered and studied in detail in the next chapter.

I saw that his continual working in all manner of things is done so goodly, so wisely, and so mightily . . . we can do no more but behold him, enjoying, with an high, mighty desire to be all oned into him,—centred to his dwelling,[1]—and enjoy in his loving and delight in his goodness.

The effects of this beholding on the soul are described by Julian in terms of ineffable joy: 'marvellously enjoying with reverent dread, and with so great *sweetness* and delight'; '*enjoy* in his loving and *delight* in his goodness'. In fact, in this contemplation 'we have that [which] we desire', so that Julian may say that the beholding 'pleaseth the soul and fulfilleth it with joy'. (Ch. 10, p. 21.)

In Julian's own words 'beholding which is special shewing' is a 'high unperceivable prayer'. Yet, of the soul who has been granted the shewing, she says: 'the more the soul seeth of God, the more it desireth Him'; which means that even the 'beholding which is special shewing' does not fully satisfy the soul: this will be done only in the open Vision of Heaven. Julian herself points out *the difference between the 'shewing' and the Beatific Vision*, and by so doing she clarifies her mind on the essence of the former.

And then shall we all come into our Lord, our Self clearly knowing, and God *fully having;*
and we shall *endlessly* be all had in God:
him *verily seeing* and *fulsomely feeling*, him *ghostly hearing*, and him delectably smelling, and [of] him sweetly swallowing.[2]

---

[1] MS. (S1) reads 'and entred to his wonying' ('entred' = entered, instead of 'centred'; 'wonying' = dwelling); MS. (W) has 'and entende to his wonying'; and MS. (P) 'and entend to his motion'. I shall consider this text at length in Pt. III, ch. 2.

[2] I draw attention to the explicit mention of the so-called *spiritual senses*. On this point, cf. e.g. A. Poulain, *The Graces of Interior Prayer*, ed. cit. ch. VI, pp. 88 ff.; K. Rahner, *Le début d'une doctrine des cinq sens spirituels*, RAM, 13 (1932), pp. 113-145; C. Truhlar, *De Experientia Mystica*, pp. 21-24. A famous passage of St Augustine is found in *Confessions*, X, 6, 8 (PL, 32, 782-783). A few other texts, drawn from the writings of St Augustine, St Gregory, and St Bernard, which bear on this point, can be found, e.g. in: Butler, *Western Mysticism*, pp. 46, 73-74, 104, etc.

And then shall we see God *face to face*, homely and fulsomely.

The creature, that is made, shall see and *endlessly behold* God, which is the Maker. (Ch. 43, p. 78.)

It is clear then that according to Julian's mind the beholding which is special shewing is not comparable with the Beatific Vision; the one differs from the other as the picture from the reality, as the part from the whole. If in the Beatific Vision—as opposed to the beholding—will be verified the 'full having', 'verily seeing', 'face to face', 'endlessly' beholding, this means that in the Shewing one does not possess or see God fully, verily, face to face, endlessly.

However, the beholding which is special shewing is nevertheless conceived as an infusion of light, as a beam coming through a chink, which enables the soul to see and penetrate momentarily what it is not permitted to see ' while we are here ':

I had, in part, touching, sight, and feeling in three properties of God, in which the strength and effect of all the Revelation standeth: and they were seen in every Shewing, and most properly in the Twelfth, where it saith oftentimes: [' I it am ']. The properties are these: Life, Love, and Light. (Ch. 83, p. 166.)

Therefore in the beholding which is special shewing there is only a part of the full sight that we shall enjoy in Heaven: '. . . he shewed unto mine understanding, in part, the blessed Godhead, stirring then the poor soul for to understand, as it may be said, that is, to think on the endless Love that was without beginning, and is, and shall be ever.' (Ch. 24, pp. 44-45.)

This partial understanding or light is of such a nature that it exceeds the natural capacities of man. For this reason the creature needs special help in order to *be fortified and lifted up above its natural capacities* and its usual way of acting: '. . . when he [God] of his special grace will shew himself here, he strengtheneth the creature above the self. . . .' (Ch. 43, p. 78.)

And this explains also why the creature who has been granted a shewing, is then *incapable of expressing in human* language what it has experienced and known during the extraordinary communication.[1]

> But the ghostly sight I cannot nor may not shew it as openly nor as fully as I would.

> But I trust in our Lord God Almighty that he shall of his goodness, and for your love, make you to take it more ghostly and more sweetly than I can or may tell it. (Ch. 9, p. 18.)

> And how a soul shall have him in its beholding, he shall teach himself. . . . (Ch. 10, p. 21.)

But for our purpose of analysing Julian's doctrine on prayer and contemplation the most relevant factor that characterizes the 'beholding which is shewing' is *the special operation of God in the soul*. This gratuitous and extraordinary action is the cause and the explanation of the exceeding height of this type of contemplation. In fact if, as Julian says, 'all our intent with all our might *is set wholly* to the beholding of him' and 'we can do no more but behold him', this is due to the fact that 'his marvellous and plentiful

---

[1] Similar remarks on this and other points concerning the special shewing can be found in the following passage by the contemporary author of *The Cloud of Unknowing*: 'Then will he sometimes peradventure send out a beam of light, piercing this "cloud of unknowing" that is betwixt thee and him, and show thee some of his secrets, the which man may not and cannot speak. Then shalt thou feel thine affection inflamed with the fire of his love, far more than I can tell thee, or may or will at this time. For of that work that pertaineth only to God dare I not take upon me to speak with my blabbering fleshly tongue: and, shortly to say, although I durst I would not. But of that work that pertaineth to man, when he feeleth himself stirred and helped by grace, I like well to tell thee: for therein is the less peril of the two.' (*The Cloud of Unknowing and other treatises by a 14th Century English Mystic*, edited by McCann, ch. 26, p. 43.) As I have pointed out, the ineffability is one of the most salient features of the 'ghostly sight', cf. Pt. I, ch. 2, of this study.

goodness *fulfilleth all our powers* ' and because God ' *stirreth us* for the time '.

Therefore the special grace of shewing is a passive form of contemplation, in which the soul no longer acts according to its normal way: ' we can pray right nought ', but in a new and higher manner ' but as he stirreth us ', so that ' when we of this special grace plainly behold him, . . . then *we follow him*, and *he draweth us* unto him by love '.

Precisely because this beholding totally exceeds our ordinary way of acting, it is presupposed that ' He [God] *strengtheneth* the creature *above* the self '. But this special action of God on the soul which is lifted up above itself and acts because ' stirred ' and ' drawn ', can only last ' *for the time* '—as Julian implies repeatedly. In fact this grace is given by God ' after his own will, and it is profitable for the time '.

Resuming all the various elements of this new and higher type of union, we may say that the beholding is a special grace which consists in some kind of ' sight ' of God. It is a form of temporary passive contemplation in which the soul feels and follows the movement by which God, taking her captive and fulfilling all her faculties, draws her ' into him by love '. This special beholding fills the soul with indescribable joy and sweetness.

A simple comparison between the ' beholding which is special shewing ' and the description of mystical experience given, e.g. by St Bernard in his *Sermo in Cantica*, xli, 3, will show how Julian's teaching is in perfect harmony with the classical doctrine on contemplation.

> This means, I think, nothing else than to weave certain spiritual likenesses, and in these to bring the meanings of Divine Wisdom into the sight of the mind which is contemplating, in order that *it may perceive, at least by a mirror and in a riddle, what it cannot as yet look upon face to face.*
> What I speak of are things divine, and wholly *unknown but to*

those who have experienced them, how, that is, *in this mortal body* while yet *the state of faith endures* and the substance of the clear Light is *not yet made manifest*, the contemplation of pure truth can yet anticipate *its action in us*, at least *in part* so that *some*, even among us, to whom this has been *granted from above*, can employ the Apostle's words ' Now I know in part ', and again ' We know in part, and we prophesy in part '.

For when something from God has *momentarily* and, as it were, *with the swiftness of a flash of light*, shed its *ray* upon the mind in ecstasy of spirit, immediately, whether *for the tempering of this* too great radiance, *or for the sake of imparting it to others*, there present themselves certain *imaginary likenesses* of lower things, *suited to the meanings which have been infused* from above, by means of which that most pure and brilliant ray is in a manner shaded, and both becomes *more bearable* to the soul itself, and more capable of being communicated to whomsoever the latter wishes.[1]

It may therefore be asserted that in Julian's description of the form of ' beholding ' as so far considered, may be found the typical signs of strictly supernatural infused contemplation as understood by the mystics,[2] who, as is known, on

[1] I cite the English translation of St Bernard's text as found in C. Butler, *Western Mysticism*, p. 105, which gives an amply documented exposition of the classic doctrine on contemplation according to St Augustine, St Gregory, and St Bernard.

[2] There is a difference in St Teresa and St John's terminology which needs to be indicated to the reader, since it will assist the understanding of certain expressions in the next chapter. While St Teresa reserves the term ' contemplation ' for those types of prayer which she calls ' supernatural prayer ', viz. when the action of God is not merely a silent working of grace, but an act of which the soul is sensibly and consciously aware, St John uses the same term ' contemplation ' and even ' infused contemplation ' of stages of prayer in which the action of God in the soul is present but still imperceptible. According to him ' the commencement of contemplation is in general secret, and unknown to him who is admitted to it '. Cf. *Dark Night*, Bk. I, ch. 9, ed. cit. pp. 396 ff.; *Ascent*, Bk. II, ch. 14, ed. cit. pp. 239-240. This difference in terminology has escaped the notice of many authors; hence many misunderstandings that could have been easily avoided if attention had been paid to this point, along the lines indicated by some early commentators of the two Saints (cf. e.g. Joseph a Jesu Maria).

the one hand do not identify their experiences with the Beatific Vision, whereas on the other hand they speak of them as the nearest possible approach to it.

Vision of God and mystical contemplation.

This exalted experience of the Christian mystery cannot be a direct vision of the divine essence—at least habitually, and very probably, never.

It always remains within the boundaries of the knowledge which is faith, though this is brought to such a high degree of perfection as cannot be imagined; even so it is always a kind of knowledge which is connatural to us.

It is true to say that some great mystics have described this foretaste of the joys of heaven given to them, from time to time when at prayer, in terms so strong and forthright as would seem to testify to a direct vision of the divine essence. Granted such an immediate intuition of the Holy Trinity, we would still have to distinguish it from the vision ' face to face ', on several very important counts: it would come upon the soul in a very extraordinary fashion—in rapture; it would be momentary and obscure; nor would it confer the plenitude of happiness. One is aware that the texts are a matter of controversy. Nor is there any need for us to take sides, nor even to consider the theological problem raised by an over-literal interpretation of the alleged testimonies—viz. whether or not a direct vision of the divine essence is possible here below. For even if this were the case, it would still remain that the highest mystical form of contemplation would be a direct vision of the divine essence granted only very rarely and by a very singular title.

Normally speaking, mystical contemplation is an experience of God, which is had in the light of faith. It is a development, so to say, a deepening of the knowledge one has through faith; it constitutes the organic development of this knowledge, though gratuitously given; normal development, but not very often found in its highest forms; it is a progress, but a remarkable one, for which there is no positive preparation on man's part.

The ascesis, which achieves a psychological and moral 'wholeness', is usually required as a necessary condition before contemplation may begin. But it is not its all-sufficing condition.

Everything depends on the initiative of the Holy Ghost, and on this alone. All the theologians seem to agree—following St Thomas and St John of the Cross—on the general statement that infused contemplation is the exercise of the theological virtues or of living faith to an extraordinary degree.

Similarly they all emphasize the predominant part played by the gifts of the Holy Ghost in the genesis of infused contemplation.[1]

As I indicated before, the same fundamental teaching on the 'special shewing' is contained in ch. 10, where Julian says that 'these are two workings that may be seen in this Vision: the one is seeking, the other is beholding. *The seeking* is common—that every soul may have with his grace, . . .' (Ch. 10, p. 21.) The sentence is here incomplete, but the obvious sequence is something like this: the beholding is not common; it is given by God as a special grace, to whom and when he wills.[2]

. . . the continual seeking of the soul pleaseth God full greatly: for it may do no more than seek, suffer and trust.

And this is wrought in the soul that hath it, by the Holy Ghost, and the clearness of finding, it is of his special grace, when it is his will.

The seeking, with faith, hope, and charity, pleaseth our Lord, and the finding pleaseth the soul and fulfilleth it with joy. . . .

It is God's will that we seek him, to the beholding of him, forby that he shall shew us himself of his special grace when he will.

And how a soul shall have him in its beholding, he shall teach himself: and that is most worship to him and profit to thyself, and [the soul then] most receiveth of meekness and virtues with the grace and leading of the Holy Ghost. . . .

[1] C. Baumgartner, *Contemplation: Conclusion générale*, in DSp. II, cc. 2188-2189.
[2] See also Tyrrell, XVI *Revelations*, p. 32, note.

and his appearing shall be sweet [1] and sudden. (Ch. 10, pp. 21-22.)

By this presentation of the two consecutive stages of 'prayer' and 'special grace' of contemplation, or in other words 'seeking' and 'beholding', we are spontaneously led to consider this conception as corresponding to the doctrine on prayer and contemplation still commonly proposed in the thirteenth century, when the mystics tell of their effort to ascend to God in contemplation and of their extraordinary experiences. [2]

According to this doctrine, the diffusion of which is greatly due to St Gregory, two principal movements may be distinguished: [3] that of the soul, which tends towards God

[1] MSS. (W) and (S1) read: 'swith sudden': (swith = very, exceedingly); MS. (S2) reads: 'very sudden'; MS. (P) reads: 'swete'.

[2] 'Throughout the thirteenth century a single view on contemplation held the field, one inspired by St Augustine, elaborated by St Gregory and rounded off by St Bernard. This spirituality, or "Western Mysticism" may be called classic in the sense that it gives a rightful place to all the essential elements of the spiritual life, love, knowledge of God and the practice of virtue, with no more than a normal interest in mystical phenomena such as ecstasy and visions. Whilst other spiritualities are centred round a single primitive idea, the mystical marriage of a Hadwig, for instance, or the dionysian unknowing of a Thomas Gallus, Western Mysticism is marked by the balance of its thought when faced with the complexity of spiritual realities. With the Masters of Western spirituality, one passes imperceptibly from " acquired " to " infused " (contemplation), for the " grace of contemplation " follows upon the efforts of " meditation ". As regards "feeling", it partakes quite naturally of the sweets of contemplation—admitting at the same time that the needs of the body will always put a limit, here below, to the time dedicated to intimate communion with God.' (P. Philippe, *Contemplation au XIIIe siècle in DSp, II,* c. 1967.) For more detailed information see C. Butler, *Western Mysticism,* and *Mediaeval Mystical Tradition and Saint John of the Cross* by A Benedictine of Stanbrook Abbey.

[3] St Gregory's conception of contemplation is formulated thus by C. Butler: ' It is a struggle wherein the mind disengages itself from thought of the things of this world and fixes its *attention wholly* on spiritual things, and thereby *raises itself above itself,* and by dint of a great effort mounts up to a *momentary* perception of the unencompassed *Light,* as through a chink; and then exhausted by the effort and blinded by the vision of the Light, it sinks back wearied to its normal state, to recuperate its spiritual strength by *exercising the works of the active life,* till in due time it can again brace itself for the effort of another act of contemplation.' (C. Butler, *Benedictine Monachism,* pp. 84-85—italics mine.)

and seeks him anxiously, ardently desiring to be united to him in contemplation; that of God, who 'for the time' visits the soul, thus granting her, through some 'sight' of him—a partial satisfaction of her desire, a foretaste of the union of the eternal bliss.

But when the beholding ceases, the soul sinks back into the less pleasing stage of 'seeking':

> Sometimes the soul is admitted to some unwonted sweetness of interior relish, and is suddenly in some way refreshed when breathed on by the glowing spirit; and is the more eager the more it gains a taste of something to love. And it desires that within itself which it feels to taste sweet within, because it has in truth, from the love of its sweetness, become vile in its own sight; and after having been able in whatever way to enjoy it, it discovers what it has hitherto been without it. It endeavours to cling closely to it, but is kept back from its strength by its own remaining weakness; and because it is unable to contemplate its purity, it counts it sweet to weep, and sinking back to itself, to strew the tears of its own weakness. For it cannot fix its mind's eye on that which it has with hasty glance seen within itself, because it is compelled by its own old habits to sink downwards. It meanwhile pants and struggles and endeavours to go above itself, but sinks back, overpowered with weariness, into its own familiar darkness.[1]

This corresponds to Julian's 'we can do no more than seek and suffer' (ch. 10). We may rightly suppose that this pain and suffering, caused by the cessation of the special beholding, induced Julian to analyse more deeply the process of ascent to God and contemplation.

[1] St Gregory the Great, *Morals*, XXIII, 43 (PL, 76, 277). English transl. by C. Butler, *Western Mysticism*, pp. 73-74.

5

A SECOND TYPE OF INFUSED CONTEMPLATION: 'BEHOLDING WHICH IS NOT SPECIAL SHEWING'

A MORE careful study of those passages in which Julian speaks of prayer and contemplation, will reveal a more complete doctrine. Comparing the different expressions used in the various passages, it may be asserted that she speaks at length of a type of infused contemplation succeeding the union of the wills and yet not attaining to the height of the form of infused, passive contemplation considered so far, viz. the special grace of shewing, in which the soul is conscious of being moved by God.[1]

The characteristic of this new form of contemplation is that while there is indeed an infused grace, this is not so intense as to give the 'clearness of finding' and the 'plain beholding' of God; and, at least in the initial stages, it is hidden from the eyes and experience of the soul. This infusion, without attaining to the 'shewing', nevertheless confers a new light, a deeper penetration into the truths of faith; but it does not give the soul that awareness of the infusion which is proper to the special beholding.

The importance for Julian of this form of contemplation is that it constitutes the essence of union with God and hence it should endure for one's whole life.

[1] I have shown in the preceding chapter that Julian refers to this strictly infused contemplation in various ways: God 'stirreth us'—'draweth us'—'fulfilleth all our powers'—'we follow him'—'with great sweetness and delight'.

As we have seen, there exists a parallelism between chs. 10 and 41-43, in which Julian speaks clearly of two main moments of the soul's ascent to God, calling them ' seeking ' and ' beholding '. But a new light is thrown on both chapters by the complementary teaching of ch. 7. Here is the chief passage:

But this marvellous homeliness may no man wot of in this time of life, *save he have it of special shewing* of our Lord, *or of great plenty of grace inwardly given of the Holy Ghost.*

But faith and belief with charity deserveth the meed: and so it is had, by grace;
for in faith, with hope and charity, our life is grounded.

The Shewing, made to whom that God will, plainly teacheth the same, opened and declared, with many privy points belonging to our Faith which be worshipful to know.

And when the Shewing which is given in a time is passed and hid, then the faith keepeth [it] by grace of the Holy Ghost unto our life's end.

And thus by the Shewing it is not other than the faith, nor less nor more; as it may be seen in our Lord's teaching in the same matter. (Ch. 7, p. 15.)

Here Julian clearly states that one can discover, penetrate, see—' fully see '—the ' homeliness of God ' [1] in two different ways: by ' special shewing ', that is, the form of contemplation ' beholding ', already considered in the last chapter; or by ' plenty of grace inwardly given of the Holy Ghost ', that is, by an abundant infusion of grace (we may note that this is attributed to the Holy Ghost). These terms point to *a form of infused contemplation, distinct from the ordinary grace, but also from the extraordinary grace* or ' shewing ', because deprived of some of its elements.

[1] On the ' homeliness of God ' as the main object of contemplation, cf. Pt. III, chs. 1 and 2 of this study.

I

It is worthwhile observing that:

(i) One or the other of these forms of *infused* contemplation is *necessary* in order to 'fully see', that is, to comprehend as far as is possible in this life the 'homeliness
of God', which is the object of contemplation.

(ii) The second form of contemplation, i.e. the intermediate stage, consists in a deepening of the life of
faith, hope and charity, a closer approximation to the
divine life. Though this is due to 'plenty of grace
inwardly given', it is far from being the clear 'sight' of
the 'special shewing'.

(iii) Further it is shown as being offered to all—'our
common working'—whilst the first form is given
gratuitously ('by grace') only to some: 'to whom
that God will'.

(iv) Neither form reveals new truths, but gives clearer
insight of the truths contained in the deposit of faith:
'by the Shewing it is not other than of faith, nor less
nor more'. (Ch. 7, p. 15.)

(v) Hence both forms of infused contemplation bear on
the same object, viz. the revealed truths entrusted to
the Church.

(vi) The excellence of the first form of contemplation (and
one not enjoyed by the second form) lies: (*a*) in the
different way in which it enlightens the soul '*plainly*
teacheth the same *opened* and *declared*' (these terms
correspond to that other expression Julian uses:
'clearness of finding'); (*b*) in the light which the
'shewing' confers on 'many privy points belonging
to our faith'; (*c*) in the resulting marvellous joy and
sweetness which are proper to the 'shewing' and do
not accompany the lower form.

(vii) The difference between the two forms thus seems to lie not in the quality of the grace infused, though in this there will be obviously varying degrees of intensity, but rather in the above-mentioned accessory and extra-ordinary elements which are present only in the case of the ' shewing '. The substantial element is common to both forms: viz. infused grace, the intimate work of God in the soul (which will make itself felt, in the case of the ' shewing ', when God wishes also to confer the accessory elements).

(viii) A final point of difference between the two forms lies in the fact that the shewing is transitory: the soul receives *passing* ' sights ', after which it returns to a state bereft of these extraordinary elements. And in this state it lives by faith sustained by the Holy Ghost: ' when the shewing, which is given in a time is passed and hid, then the faith keepeth [it] by grace of the Holy Ghost '. (Ch. 7, p. 15.)

The foregoing analysis of ch. 7 establishes that in Julian's doctrine there is a second form of contemplation or an inter-mediate stage between the union of the wills and the ' shew-ing '.

In the light of this discovery we must now reconsider chs. 10 and 41-43, and see the relationship which exists between this form of contemplation and both the ' seeking ' and the ' beholding '.

The second form of contemplation in chs. 10 and 41-43

Let us notice first of all that the ' seeking ' of which Julian speaks in ch. 10 is a form of prayer, whose distinctive note is the want of ' clearness of finding ' (this clearness of finding is a note peculiar to the beholding). ' The seeking ', then, extends from the ' longing ' to the lower limit of the state in which there is ' clearness of finding ' (that is, ' behold-ing which is special shewing '). Therefore it includes also the second form of contemplation.

If we analyse more carefully this ' seeking ' we shall find the same elements of the second form of contemplation as in ch. 7.

(a) *Three states within the ' seeking '*

The states which follow each other within this ' seeking ' seem to be outlined by Julian when she speaks of three conditions as being typical of it:

It is God's will that we have three things in our seeking:—

The first is that we seek wilfully and busily, without sloth, as it may be through his grace, gladly and merrily, without un-skilful heaviness and vain sorrow.

The second is that we abide him steadfastly for his love, without grudging and striving against him, to our life's end: for it shall last but a while.

The third is that we trust in him mightily of full sure faith, for it is his will. We know he shall appear suddenly and bliss-fully to all that be his lovers. (Ch. 10, pp. 21-22.)

1. The first refers chiefly to the human activity of search-ing, viz. the movement of the soul towards God. This anxious search, dictated by love, becomes more and more simple, is transformed into a loving union, in which the soul seeks to conform itself to the will of God, ' to one ' itself with him. (Cf. ch. 3 on ' unitive prayer '.)

2. After a while this state becomes even more simple, a mere expectancy, in which the soul is only desirous of God. But although God is already beginning to satisfy this desire by communicating himself in a more intimate way, the soul is not yet conscious of this; rather God seems more distant than before, and hence the soul is tempted to return to a previous form of prayer, more satisfying (more consoling).

This state is indicated by Julian when she lays down the second condition: ' The second is that we abide him stead-fastly for his love.'

3. By this ' steadfast abiding for love ' the soul comes to the third stage. Throughout this second stage, where effort was required in order to wait for God to show himself, faith has been purified and strengthened. This deeper and purer faith now enables the soul to live a life of loving trust, of full abandonment, of simple attention to God.

We think that these last two stages of the ' seeking ' constitute *the beginning* of infused contemplation, viz. the form of infused contemplation which is not ' special shewing '.

(b) *Analysis of the second state of ' seeking ': preparation for the third state—beginning of infused contemplation*

' The second is that we abide him steadfastly for his love, without grudging and striving against him, to our life's end: for it shall last but a while.' In these words Julian shows the essential attitude the soul should have in the state that comes after the union of the wills has been attained.

The soul may seem to be plunged into a state in which God appears to be far away from it. Then the soul must remain intent on God, out of pure love of him, even though it is in desolation. Hence she states that this ' abide stead-fastly ' consists in ' without grudging and striving against him '.

This brief description, though clear, can be usefully com-pleted by the more detailed notions given by Julian in chs. 41-43.[1] In fact in ch. 41, after introducing the subject of prayer and its initial stages, she observes that these are not limited merely to a petition that our will be united to God's; rather they already embrace and go as far as this substantial

[1] The strict parallelism not only of thought but of language between sections 10 and 41-43 should be noted. Such parallelism obviates the possibility of reading too much into Julian's words.

union of the will with God: 'Beseeching is a new, gracious, lasting will of the soul oned and fastened into the will of our Lord, by the sweet inward work of the Holy Ghost.' (Ch. 41, p. 72.)

In these expressions she clearly points to a permanent state of union of the will with God: 'new, gracious, *lasting* will of the soul, oned and fastened'.

It is at this very stage, as in ch. 10, that Julian brings in the need of faithful perseverance in this loving attention to God: because, though substantially united with God, the soul feels itself deprived of the accessory element of comfort and sweetness:

> Therefore he saith thus:
> Pray inwardly, though thee thinketh it savour thee not:
> for it is profitable, though thou feel not, though thou see naught; yea, though thou think thou mayst naught.
> For in dryness and in barrenness, in sickness and in feebleness, then is thy prayer well-pleasant to me, though thee thinketh it savour thee naught but little.
> And so is all thy believing prayer in my sight. (Ch. 41, p. 73.)

Every word of this sentence is weighty with profound doctrinal meaning:
'though *thee thinketh* it savour thee not':
even if the soul thinks that this form of prayer is useless, it should not be deceived; this impression is caused by the fact that God is depriving the soul of the consolations which formerly sustained it: for these are not essential and may even be a hindrance to that purity which he now desires for the soul.
'though *thou see* not':
it is a time of obscurity: the soul feels itself deprived of the knowledge that formerly was habitual to it and sustained it, and hence feels itself tempted to doubts about its spiritual state. But God reassures the soul; because this very

obscurity is due to a new superior light, infused by God, which is not perceptible to its natural powers. This infused knowledge is thus received without the soul's being aware of it: 'plenty of grace inwardly given of the Holy Ghost.'

'though *thou think thou canst not*':
we see here the incapacity in which the soul feels itself plunged.

But it is precisely in this want of savour, of security, of light, in this weakness felt by the soul, that the true beauty and secret of this state of prayer, of this walking in pure faith, is made manifest. The soul has no consolation, no satisfaction, and thus having nothing of itself it lives by faith, lives only for God, intent on God: 'for his love', and not for any consolation he may give.

And this is the prayer that pleases God: 'then is thy prayer well pleasant to me, though thee thinketh it savour thee naught but little.' (Ch. 41, p. 73.)

And now deprived of every comfort that it previously enjoyed, deprived also of that spiritual light which previously sustained it, the soul needs this simple advice: 'that we abide him steadfastly for his love, without grudging and striving against him. . . .'

Here we have a patient expectancy of God (without grudging). For God is working in the soul and wishes to see it in an attitude of simple adherence to and of utter dependence on himself.

In this state the soul feels its own incapacity and thus does not seek to go forward by its own powers, as it did formerly; for it is now in a state where it can only make progress by abandoning itself to God's action. At such a stage it would be a mistake to seek to go back to a form of prayer in which the soul *seemed* more active. This former state seemed more satisfactory because the soul was using its powers and was conscious of the progress it was making. We may perhaps compare this state to that of a child who instead of walking by its own efforts is taken up in its mother's arms and carried. While it is thus being carried it seems to be doing nothing because it is not using its legs, but in reality it is making more rapid progress than it was before. And it would be making a mistake to try to leave its mother in order to walk unaided. This is the point of Julian's warning: 'without striving against him', for a 'striving' in this sense would mean going against the action of God who is seeking to communicate himself in a superior way, one that exceeds the usual mode of knowledge and adherence to him.

How does one know in practice whether or not God is communicating himself to the soul in this special and secret way? This is an extremely important point and Julian is not one to overlook it. She offers as a criterion of judgement the behaviour of the soul in this state. If the soul lives a life of virtue then this will be a sign that such a form of prayer truly comes from God.

> God accepteth the good-will and the travail of his servant, howsoever we feel: wherefore it pleaseth him that we work *both in our prayers and in good living*, by his help and his grace, reasonably with discretion keeping our mights [turned] to him, till when that we have him that we seek, in fulness of joy: that is, Jesus. (Ch. 41, p. 73.)

To all who are acquainted, even slightly, with the teaching of St John of the Cross on the initial form of infused contemplation, these lines of Julian will recall not only his doctrine but even his words. His teaching is contained chiefly in Bk. II, chs. 12-14 of *The Ascent*, and in Bk. I, ch. 9 of *The Dark Night*.[1]

---

[1] In these passages St John is speaking of a form of contemplation in which the infused element plays the main part. See note 2 at p. 113.

(c) *The third state of 'seeking': loving attention in faith*

And so, after a time of trial, obscurity, dereliction, and faithful perseverance, the soul comes to the third state: a loving attention towards God; a full abandonment to him, sustained by faith alone: 'The third is that we trust in him mightily of full sure faith, for it is his will.'

This is an attention which is full of trustful love, a total abandonment in God. It is a simple union, rather than a knowledge: in fact there is no distinct knowledge of God, but a 'general' knowledge in faith, that enables the soul to exercise its love and remain intent on him. This is possible because faith is now sustained, increased, enlightened by the inward work of the Holy Ghost, which confers a deeper penetration into God and his love.

This type of contemplation is pleasing to God: '. . . then is thy prayer well-pleasant to me, though thee thinketh it savour thee naught but little. And so is all *thy believing prayer* in my sight.' (Ch. 41, p. 73)—words corresponding to those of ch. 10: ' the third is that we trust in him mightily of full sure faith '.

Within this type of contemplation there are various progressive stages: in fact in this state of union, precisely because it is more closely united to God, and by faith participates more consciously in God's life, the soul is flooded by his light: a light which penetrates its substance ever more deeply and confers an increase of the knowledge—and hence of the love in which union consists. The highest degree of this type of contemplation is therefore a state in which illuminations flood the soul that lives intent on God; and this is described more at length by Julian when she says:

And then shall we, with his *sweet grace*, in our own meek continuant prayer come into him now *in this life* by many *privy touchings* of *sweet ghostly sights* and feeling, *measured to us* as our simpleness may bear it.

And this is wrought, and shall be, by the grace of the Holy Ghost, so long till we shall die in longing, for love. (Ch. 43, p. 78.)

Hence the contemplation in faith—destined to develop into this more perfect state of illumination and finally into the Beatific Vision—seems to correspond exactly to the state to which St John of the Cross seeks to direct souls, freeing them from the hindrances that would obstruct their progress, when God is working to carry them forward and unite them to himself through pure faith and love. In fact also for St John of the Cross when this union in faith is established, the deeper communication of illuminations takes place.

This contemplative knowledge, which is the knowledge of the Spirit of Wisdom ('notitia sapientialis') carries an interior witness—God's own—to the truths of faith. This truth, though integral to the experience and pertaining to its form, is not identical with the experience: for even whilst it enlightens it remains hidden: it teaches by drawing a veil over the object of its teaching. God is not yet actually revealed as the Intelligible: nor is the creature's capacity for grasping the Intelligible as yet fulfilled. He is not yet present as Truth itself, but only in the power of His truth (*in virtute veritatis suae*).

But even so the familiar friendship of Christ with the 'interior man' is matter of intense wonderment. And on the journey to the divine union, there are afforded sweet comforts of a lesser kind—the loving kindness of God adapting itself to halting progress of man's understanding—by which many things are made clear to him—human and divine.

But since these comforts produce, of their own accord, the spiritual effects intended by God, and are not given as a substitute for ordinary faith, or for the natural powers of a mind wholly intent on God, the soul ought not—nay must not—allow itself to be distracted by them from this contemplative experience in the spirit of wisdom, or from its constant and ardent seeking after eternal union. It is during this time, when man's

by grace; for in faith, with hope and charity, our life is grounded.' (Ch. 7, p. 15.)

The 'seeking' prepares and disposes the soul for the beholding which is special shewing, and tends towards it as to its outcome and fruit: 'it is God's will that we seek him *to the* beholding of him' (= clearness of finding) (ch. 10, p. 21). Similarly, in ch. 7, it is said of the second form of contemplation: 'faith and belief with charity deserveth *the meed:* and so it is had by grace' (p. 15). But while both passages show the connection and relationship between the two forms of contemplation, both also insist on the gratuitousness of the special beholding: 'of his special grace' —'when he will' (ch. 10, p. 21); 'it is had by grace' (ch. 7, p. 15).

The 'seeking' should be the normal state of the Christian: 'the seeking is common' (ch. 10, p. 21); so too, the lower form of contemplation is 'based on faith, hope and charity', 'on which our life is grounded' (ch. 7, p. 15). Finally, the 'seeking' should not only be our 'common working' but should be enjoyed by all without exception: 'the seeking is common—that *every soul* may have with his grace,—and ought to have that discretion and teaching of the Holy Church' (ch. 10, p. 21).

(e) *Comparison between the 'beholding which is special shewing', and the 'beholding which is not shewing'*

After describing this form of infused contemplation, deprived of the extraordinary elements proper to the 'beholding which is special shewing', Julian goes on to compare the one form with the other.

She knows and points out that the 'clearness of finding' proper to the 'beholding which is shewing', being a possession, a vision, produces 'marvellous enjoying with a great sweetness and delight'. This satisfies the soul: '*pleaseth the soul*' (ch. 10, p. 21). On the other hand, in the preceding state the soul, still deprived of the 'clearness of finding', is also deprived of the marvellous 'sweetness and delight': it cannot be fully satisfied because still seeking. And this 'seeking', prompted by love, satisfies God: 'pleaseth God'.

But Julian knows that what is of value is what satisfies and pleases God, not what satisfies and pleases the soul. And this leads her to posit some sort of equality between the two states:

> The seeking, with faith, hope, and charity, *pleaseth our Lord*, and the finding *pleaseth the soul* and fulfilleth it with joy.
>
> And *thus* was I learned, to mine understanding, that the *seeking is as good as beholding*, for the time that he will suffer the soul to be in travail. (Ch. 10, p. 21.)

This equality, however, is not absolute, but is conditioned by God's will: '[the seeking] is as good as beholding, *for the time that he will* suffer the soul to be in travail'. In fact, she is well aware that when the two forms of contemplation are considered in themselves, the 'beholding which is shewing' is superior. And for this reason she hastens to add that when God pleases to grant the soul the higher form of contemplation, it should be received with grateful humility, for '[the grace of special beholding] is most worship to him and profit to thyself' (ch. 10, p. 21). When this grace is received 'with meekness and virtues, with the grace and leading of the Holy Ghost' it produces its full effect.

But once more Julian seems to wish to stress in what lies the essence of every form of contemplation: 'For a soul that only *fasteneth* it[self] on to God with very trust, *either* by seeking *or* in beholding, it is the most worship that it may do to him, as to my sight'. (Ch. 10, p. 21.)

Conclusion

By way of conclusion we may say that contemplation in its highest form (' beholding which is special shewing ') is, for Julian, a marvellous grace, to which we may aspire; but it is a grace given freely by God, and does not follow *necessarily* on the efforts of our will.

In this form of contemplation the soul has some knowledge of the nature of God, of his properties. As this knowledge is not obtained by means of our natural faculties, it cannot be expressed in words ; for all human language owes its origin to sense impressions. This infused knowledge is accompanied by an ineffable joy; which can only be understood indirectly in terms of everlasting joy. But nevertheless, this knowledge, although the loftiest that we know in this life, is no momentary anticipation of the Beatific Vision. It remains on the level of faith.

The lower form of contemplation, on the other hand, is deprived of the accessory elements, of the marvellous sweetness and ineffable joy; at least in the initial stages the soul seems in darkness, because its natural faculties, its natural desires to know and understand, are not satisfied. The reason for this dissatisfaction is that the soul is being flooded by a light of a higher order, which is imperceptible to its natural powers. However, this light is destined to penetrate ever more deeply into the soul and thus to expel progressively the initial darkness. This light we call infused grace, and it gives the soul a deeper insight into the truths of faith. In this state, the soul, deprived of the sweetness and of the ' sight ' proper to the ' shewing ', lives by faith, a faith which has become luminous by means of the infused grace.

Small wonder then, that Julian should so often speak of faith, should insist on its importance in our life, should so often exalt its beauty and grandeur:

For our faith is contraried in diverse manners by our own blindness, and our ghostly enemy, within and without; and therefore our precious Lover helpeth us *with ghostly sight* and *true teaching in sundry manners within* and *without*, whereby that we may know him.

And therefore in what manner he teacheth us, he willeth that we perceive him wisely, receive him sweetly, and keep us in him faithfully.

For *above the Faith is no goodness kept in this life*, as to my sight, and *beneath the Faith is no help of* soul; but *in the Faith, there willeth the Lord that we keep us*. (Ch. 70, p. 144.)

The higher form of contemplation ('shewing') is, as we have seen, a 'sight' but not 'face to face' as in the 'Beatific Vision'.[1] It is transitory: it is only 'given for a time'. And in fact these seasons of sights or shewings soon go, and the soul returns to its usual state in which it lives by faith. But this faith is now stronger, because it has been momentarily enlightened, and it is now enriched by its experiences which enable it to love more ardently.

And when the Shewing which is given in a time is passed and hid, then the faith keepeth [it] by grace of the Holy Ghost unto our life's end. (Ch. 7, p. 15.)

. . . our good Lord gave understanding that the Sight should pass: which blessed Shewing *the Faith keepeth*, with his good will and his grace.

For he left with me neither sign nor token whereby I might know it, but he left with me his own blessed word in true understanding, *bidding me* full mightily *that I should believe it*.

And so I do—Blessed may he be!—

I believe that he is our Saviour that shewed it, and that it is the Faith that he shewed; and therefore I believe it, rejoicing. And thereto I am bounden by all his own meaning, with the

---

[1] Compare the various elements of the 'shewing' with the description and analysis given by J. Huby of St Paul's rapture to the third heaven. 'Paul ravi au troisième ciel', in *Mystiques Paulinienne et Johannique*, pp. 115-120.

next words that follow: 'Keep thee therein, and comfort thee therewith, and trust thou thereto. . . .
and thou shalt not be overcome.' In these six words that follow, 'Take it' [etc.]—his meaning is to fasten it faithfully in our heart: *for he willeth that it dwell with us in faith to our life's end*, and after in fulness of joy, willing that we have ever stead-fast trust in his blissful behest—knowing his Goodness. (Ch. 70, pp. 143-144.)

'Shewing' and 'Faith'

'Shewing' and faith, then, are not two separate and distinct things, as though the 'shewing' revealed new truths. Shewing and faith have both the same object, viz. God, his love, his active presence in his creatures, etc.: 'The Shewing, made to whom that God will, plainly teacheth *the same*, opened and declared, with many privy points belonging to our Faith which be worshipful to know.' (Ch. 7, p. 15.)

The difference consists in the fact that the shewing confers some sort of sight in which the same truths are known 'plainly, opened and declared'. Consequently because the light is brighter the soul sees in the objects of faith details that escaped it when it had only the dim light of faith, not yet strengthened by the special grace of shewing. This is the meaning of the words quoted above: 'plainly teacheth the same, . . . with many privy points belonging to our faith'. And Julian explicitly states that these details are already part of our faith; there is no question of new revela-tions: 'And thus through the Shewing it is not other than the faith, nor less nor more.' (Ch. 7, p. 15.) [1]

---

[1] Hence we may apply to Julian Abbot Butler's words on St Augustine, when, at the conclusion of his paragraph on the 'Effects of the experience', he says: 'Here again St Augustine is in harmony with the great mystics, many of whom declare that an effect of their contemplations and unions was a clearer perception of the truths of the Catholic Faith and a deeper insight into the secret things of God—the Divine Being and Attributes, the Mysteries of

K

No new revelation

To confirm what has been said, there can be found in the book of the Revelations an experience of Julian which has bearing on this point. Having been granted this shewing, she was led by curiosity to try to take advantage of this intimate contact with God, in order to obtain information on some point not belonging to the field of faith. She tells us of her mistake, and of the misuse she thus made of God's gift. Julian's personal experience leads her to dwell more particularly on this point, and she gives some valuable teaching regarding the nature of the shewing.

This teaching, as we shall see, is in exact accord with what other masters of the spiritual life, notably St John of the Cross, say as regards the '*general*' character of the knowledge had in contemplation, i.e. without any *particular* notion.

It will be useful to quote at length Julian's description of this experience and the doctrine she was taught.

---

the Trinity and Incarnation, the nature of the soul itself, and the workings of the cosmic laws of God's governance of the Universe. Such claims are made by Ruysbroeck, St John of the Cross, St Teresa, St Ignatius, and are formulated by Fr Augustine Baker in the following passage, which like his other descriptions of the high mystic states, is certainly autobiographical : In regard of the understanding, there is a divine light communicated, not revealing or discovering any new verities, but affording a most firm clear assurance and experimental perception of those verities of Catholic religion which are the objects of our faith, which assurance the soul perceives to be divinely communicated to her. O happy evidence of our Catholic belief. No thanks to them that believe after such sight, which is more evident than anything we see with our corporal eyes ' (*Sancta Sofia*, p. 533). C. Butler, *Western Mysticism*, pp. 49-50. See also this other passage by Fr Baker: ' A soul that is newly awakened, as it were, from such a contemplation or union, coming to read the Holy Scriptures or any spiritual book, will pierce far more deeply into the verities contained in them, and will see clearer lights and feel far more perfect tastes of the divine truths therein than ever before; so that all the knowledge that she formerly had will seem unto her mere darkness and a knowledge of the outward letter only, whereas now she penetrates into the internal spirit of the writings.' (Fr Augustine Baker, *Holy Wisdom*, p. 534, n. 13.)

And when God Almighty had shewed so plenteously and so fully of his Goodness, *I desired to wit of a certain creature* that I loved, if it should continue in good living, which I hoped by the grace of God was begun.

And in this *singular* desire it seemed that *I letted myself:* for I was not taught in this time.

And then was I answered in my reason, as it were by a friendly mean:

> ' Take it *generally*, and behold the courtesy of the Lord God as he sheweth to thee: for *it is more worship to God to behold him in all than in any special thing.*'

I assented and therewith I learned that it is more worship to God to know all thing *in general*, than to take pleasure in any *special* thing.

And if I should do wisely after this teaching, I should not only be glad for nothing in special but I should not be greatly diseased for no manner of thing: for ' All shall be well '. (Ch. 35, pp. 60-61.)

It seems to me important that immediately following this account Julian gives the reason for the greater perfection contained in this ' general ' contemplation. God, she says, is infinite and includes in himself everything; and therefore when we contemplate him we comprehend, in some ways, all things in him, though during this life of faith we *do not see* every thing in detail.

> . . . : for by the same blessed Might, Wisdom, and Love, that he made all thing, to the same end our good Lord leadeth it continually, and thereto himself shall bring it; *and when it is time we shall see it.*

And the ground of this was shewed in the First [Revelation], and more openly in the Third, where it saith: ' I saw God in a Point.' (Ch. 35, p. 61.)

From these considerations it will be obvious that faith is the central point of Julian's doctrine on prayer and contemplation. Faith for Julian is a faith that is rich, illumined; it is a participation in the light of God himself, for God, in giving it to us, grants us the grace of living our life in his light—'which light is God, our endless Day':

> Our faith is a light kindly coming of our endless Day, that is our Father, God. In which light our Mother, Christ, and our good Lord, the Holy Ghost, leadeth us in this passing life. This light is measured discreetly, needfully standing to us in the night.

> The light is cause of our life; the night is cause of our pain and of all our woe: in which we deserve meed and thanks of God. For we, with mercy and grace, wilfastly know and believe our light, going therein wisely and mightily.

> And at the end of woe, suddenly our eyes shall be opened, and in clarity of light our sight shall be full: which light is God, our Maker and Holy Ghost, in Christ Jesus our Saviour.

> Thus I saw and understood that our faith is our light in our night: which light is God, our endless Day. (Ch. 83, p. 166.) [1]

Faith, being a participation in the light of God, confers on the soul that live by it a deepened perception of revealed truth, and puts it in intimate contact with this reality. Supernatural truths thus come to have a wonderful vividness, become really present to us; and Julian tells us: '. . . notwithstanding all our feeling of woe or weal, God willeth that we should *understand* and *know* by faith that we are more verily in heaven than in earth.' (Ch. 55, p. 111.)

Here again Julian is in perfect agreement with the traditional theological interpretation of infused contemplation:

Living faith and mystical contemplation

The theological principles of mystical contemplation are preeminently the theological virtues, or living faith. The proper sphere of contemplation is this living faith which is a

[1] Cf. similarity with Walter Hilton, *The Scale of Perfection*, Bk. I, ch. 9, ed. cit. p. 12.

growth, it is its most fruitful exercise contributing to its vital increase, though in a manner unforeseen and entirely gratuitous. What then, is the relationship between infused contemplation and this living faith?

The better to answer this question, one must first distinguish two aspects of the knowledge which is faith—the notional or intentional aspect, and the unitive, which means a vital and supernatural communion with the infallible testimony of God. . . .

The knowledge which is faith is capable of increase under either aspect. The notional increase gives birth to a science, a theology of revealed truths, which has varying degrees of perfection. Mystical contemplation has nothing to do with this aspect of faith or with its increase; for, of itself, it is independent of the number or the technical theological quality of notions or propositions.

The unitive increase of faith corresponds to the increase of charity. To the extent that love is enlarged in the soul, faith increases in intensity, in solidity, in trust: and to the same extent, it acquires a deeper ' affective ' penetration into things divine, and a more delicate palate for the mysteries of Revelation.

It is possible for this faith thus to develop vitally over a long period though there be no question of mystical contemplation —strictly so called. Even an intense increase in living faith by no means involves the crossing of the threshold of infused prayer. For, though mystical prayer moves within the same ambit of living faith as a growth, it is God who decides precisely the when and the how of its entry: it is he alone who gives the ' beginning of eternal life ', a special and extraordinary experience of something already present in a confused and obscure way, to the consciousness of the faithful soul.' [1]

---

[1] C. Baumgartner, *Contemplation: conclusion générale*, in DSp, II cc. 2189-2190.

6

SUMMARY OF RESULTS

WHEN writing her book of the *Revelations* Julian did not compose a systematic treatise on the spiritual life, filling it with classifications and speculative theorising. In the light of what was shown to her, she intended merely to describe with vividness and precision the characteristic and vital elements of the main stages of the soul's ascent to God, and to show how man should behave in each of them.

The titles of the various chapters in which I have examined Julian's conception of the spiritual life seem to summarize adequately these stages. My analysis shows how Julian conceives of them as progressive states of an ever increasing union between God and man. This progressive union requires the co-operation of both these agents: God is seen as the principal agent, the inspirer, the first to act (he is 'the Ground'). But man has to play his part by following the movement begun in him by God. That is to say, man has to unite his will to the will of God, so as to be ' fastened ' to him and in perfect accord ' with him in all things '. Not only the will but also the intellect plays its part, by participating in God's light communicated to it by faith: this participated light is destined to become more and more luminous as the union becomes purer and closer.

When dealing with each of these stages in particular, I intended to point out, by means of occasional references and comparisons, the harmony existing between Julian's teaching and the doctrine of the spiritual writers considered as classics.

These references and comparisons could be multiplied almost indefinitely, for Julian appears to be in full accord with traditional teaching.

However, though she follows the main stream of thought, Julian is highly personal. Her book, in spite of its brevity, is highly condensed, and by no means a mere digest of what had been said by others; it touches on an enormous number of delicate points of doctrine, and Julian often manages to express in a very concise manner what others have tried to say in many words and less accurately. Her sentences are strikingly profound and full of consequence for the spiritual life; their theological precision is astounding: this fact alone would openly point to a divine light communicated to this ' woman unlettered '. Whilst in full agreement with the classical doctrine, Julian emphasizes those aspects of it which she thinks more apt to engender love and a generous response to the divine advances. But she appears most of all to be original, and to contribute to the development of the doctrine on contemplation, when she speaks of the ' beholding which is not shewing '.

I draw particular attention to this point because from the teaching here given by Julian it is clear that according to her there exists a second type of infused contemplation, distinct from the higher type, the beholding which is *special shewing*. This form of contemplation is—particularly at the beginning —characterized by two elements: viz. the infusion from God, which is not necessarily felt or perceived; the activity of the soul, of which it is still aware, and which still has a great part.[1]

[1] Richard of St Victor (*d.* 1173) is said to be the theologian who first explicitly spoke of this type of contemplation: ' The outstanding contribution of Richard to the subject of prayer is that he plainly teaches the existence of another sort of contemplation, obtainable by the soul's own industry, aided by ordinary grace and is thus the first to bridge the gap between discursive meditation and mystical contemplative prayer. Others must have recognized the *thing*—as we know several later authorities did—but they did not recognize

The first, as we have seen, is treated accurately, but in few words, whilst the second is described more at length (cf. the amplification found in ch. 10). This more detailed treatment of the soul's own activity is only to be expected; whereas not only Julian, but all mystics alike are at a loss for words in which to describe the divine activity on the soul.

Further we may note that in ch. 10 the initial stages of this type of beholding are considered and described as part of the ' seeking '; and this term ' seeking ' would suffice by itself to indicate the active part of the soul in this contemplative union.[1]

Anyone confronted with this presentation of Julian's teaching will recognize that it touches closely on the central

---

that this, later to be called " acquired ", or " beginners " contemplation, was a definite form of prayer, and marking a critical transition stage in the spiritual life during which souls need wise guidance.' (See A Benedictine of Stanbrook Abbey, *Mediaeval Mystical Tradition and St John of the Cross*, p. 45.) However, the simple statements of Richard in this regard (cf. Beniamin Major, 1, V, c. 1-2; PL, 196, 169-170) are far from being an accurate analysis of the nature of the intermediate type of contemplation such as Julian's is.

[1] See the correspondence between this form of beholding and Fr Augustine Baker's description of the state of union which he calls ' *Active Mystic* Union ' (or ' Prayer of Aspirations '). ' Internal prayer proper to the state of active contemplation consists of certain most purely spiritual operations of the will, longing and thirsting after God, and an union with him in the supreme point of the spirit, where his most proper dwelling is.' (A. Baker, op. cit. pp. 509-510.) ' . . . and so I believe him to be, and as such I adore and love him only; I renounce all pretending to a distinct knowing of him, and content myself with such a blind believing. . . .' (Ibid. p. 512.) ' . . . Aspirations proceed from an interior impulse, indeliberately, and as it were naturally flowing from the soul, and thereby they show that there is in the interior a secret, supernatural, directing principle, to wit, God's Holy Spirit alone, teaching and moving the soul to breathe forth these Aspirations, not only in set recollections, but almost continually. Now this doth not infer that the Holy Spirit is not also the principle of all other good acts and affections of the will (for none of them have any true good in them further than they proceed from this divine principle); but in them the will doth previously and forcibly raise up itself to the producing them, in which, likewise, much of nature is mixed; and so the Holy Spirit is not so completely and perfectly the fountain of them as He is of Aspirations.' (Ibid. p. 512.)

problem with regard to the so called ' acquired ' (or ' active ',
or ' mixed ') contemplation, which has been the subject of
controversy among the theologians and spiritual writers of
the various schools since 1911.[1]

Julian's doctrine on this subject corresponds perfectly,
even at times in the use of the terms, with the opinion which
has been commonly accepted in recent years,[2] and has been
clearly exposed, e.g. by Fr Gabriele di S. Maria Maddalena,
O.C.D.[3] The pages where this great scholar resumes the
teaching of St John of the Cross on this matter can be taken
as a commentary to Julian's words on the two forms of contemplation which have been analysed in the preceding pages:

It is historically certain that during the Middle Ages—we have
in mind, e.g. Richard of St Victor—the term ' contemplation '
included those forms of prayer in which the soul's activity had
a large part to play. . . . We are willing to admit that, up to the
time of St John of the Cross, no clear and explicit distinction
existed between acquired and infused contemplation. But the
necessary and immediate deduction from this fact is not—as is
too often alleged—that the old writers were aware only of
' infused ' contemplation; rather is it that the sense of the
word was indeterminate: that it could mean either a form of
contemplation entirely infused, or else a form in which the
soul's own proper activity was engaged to a greater or a less
degree. And though this activity of the soul certainly would
not exclude the intermittent intervention of a divine illumination—a special impulse of the Holy Ghost, let us say; at the

[1] The bibliography on this subject is very ample indeed. A good summary
of the discussion has been given by several authors, especially by C. Butler,
in his ' Afterthoughts'; which appeared in the second edition of *Western
Mysticism* (reprinted 1951); by J. V. Bainvel, in his Introduction to the
11th edition of the *Des Grâces d'Oraison*, by A. Poulain (Eng. trans.:
The Graces of Interior Prayer); by P. Gabriele di S.M.M., in his various works,
especially *La contemplazione acquisita;* and most recently by C. Baumgartner,
Contemplation: conclusion générale, see DSp, II, cc. 2177 ff.

[2] Cf. Baumgartner, loc. cit.

[3] Cf. Gabriele di S. Maria Maddalena, *La contemplazione acquisita*, especially
pp. 45-49, and Julian's ch. 43, pp. 77-78, ch. 10, pp. 21-22.

same time such an intervention would not prevent this prayer, taken as a whole, from being a result of man's own effort.

It is precisely this type of contemplation, surely, of which St John of the Cross speaks: and Fr Aravalles, Fr Gratian, and the 'Instruction for Novices' as well.

Hence it would appear that it is a real fruit of meditation, though one shall find in it here and there the intervention of the Holy Spirit as he communicates his light to the soul.

In this form of contemplation the divine intervention is not directly perceived by the soul, rather it remains hidden behind the soul's own simplified activity; which alone is consciously perceived. But it is none the less real for all that: and the grace received by the soul belongs to the order of 'infused motions'.[1]

All these considerations seem to apply exactly to our study of Julian's doctrine; hence she would appear to be a fore-runner of St John of the Cross in explicitly distinguishing the two forms of contemplation and giving an accurate analysis of the second type whilst stressing the infused element. In fact we may well apply to Julian what Fr Gabriele di S. M. Maddalena himself says of St John of the Cross:

We must be grateful to St John of the Cross for having shown us so clearly that, in the soul's progress in mental prayer, there exists a form of contemplation which is more nearly within our grasp than infused contemplation strictly so called. It is true that this form of prayer is not so elevated as mystical contemplation in the full sense of that term: but it is, all the same, a type of prayer most precious to the soul which devotes itself to the contemplative life—the soul's first acquaintance with the substance of this life.

For here it begins to have truly intimate dealings with God, to achieve a truly substantial contact with him. Here occurs the first meeting of the 'bride' with her Beloved. It is true

[1] Gabriele di S. M. Maddalena, *École Thérésienne*, p. 76. What P. Gabriele says about the indeterminate nature of the word 'contemplation' reminds us that also Julian's own term 'beholding' is not restricted to that type of contemplation in which the soul is aware of God's action.

that all this is done in the obscurity of faith; but the fact remains that there is established a living contact with God.

This, then, is a form of contemplation greatly to be cherished, a most worthy object of the soul's ardent and constant striving —the goal of this first stage of the spiritual life.

It is not, of course, the final goal: and the soul must be careful not to confine its aspirations to this first degree of intimacy with God. It is however important, from the very beginning of the spiritual life, for the soul to be continually occupied in reaching out after this ' ordinary ' type of contemplation, which constitutes the best preparation for higher contemplative graces.

We say that the soul will do well constantly to reach out for this form of contemplation, precisely because there is room here for its own activity—either in the way of fervent meditation, or, in times of aridity, by the practice of loving attention.

As for the higher flight of contemplation, the soul can do nothing, apart from disposing itself to receive the same: and there can be no better preparation for it than to cooperate with God in this humbler form.[1]

The perfect correspondence between Julian's teaching and that of the Mystical Doctor constitutes the best commendation of Julian's doctrine on prayer and contemplation and of her sound advice and prudent way of directing souls who are led by God.

[1] P. Gabriele di S. M. M., *La contemplazione acquisita*, pp. 134-135.

III

THE OBJECT OF CONTEMPLATION

In Part II I have studied Julian's teaching on prayer and contemplation by considering the different stages and types of prayer by which the soul ascends towards an ever closer union with God.

Julian's doctrine remains now to be completed by considering *the object* which is attained in the various stages of prayer and contemplation. While attempting to answer this question I hope to clarify at the same time Julian's fundamental attitude towards God. By so doing I shall be able to expose the root from which springs her typical teaching as to how our spiritual life should be conceived and lived.

It has been seen that the various types of prayer and contemplation (longing, unitive prayer, beholding which is not shewing, beholding which is shewing) are not separated one from the other, but rather that they constitute a strict organic unity whereby the lower forms tend towards the special shewing as towards their end. Because of this finalistic orientation of the whole process of prayer and contemplation towards the 'special shewings', it seems obvious that an accurate analysis of Julian's 'shewing' or relevations will answer the question adumbrated at the beginning of this part, concerning the object to be attained.

I

THE 'HOMELY LOVING OF GOD' AS THE FUNDAMENTAL THEME OF THE SPECIAL SHEWINGS GRANTED TO JULIAN

A summary description of what Julian 'saw' in the Revelations

JULIAN herself summarizes the content of the Revelations in the following words, which constitute ch. 1 of her book:

The first chapter. Of the number of the Revelations particularly

This is a Revelation of Love that Jesus Christ, our endless bliss, made in Sixteen Shewings, or Revelations particular.

Of the which *the First* is of his precious crowning with thorns; and therewith was comprehended and specified the Trinity with the Incarnation, and unity betwixt God and man's soul; with many fair shewings of endless wisdom and teachings of love: in which all the Shewings that follow be grounded and oned.

The Second is the discolouring of his fair face in token of his dearworthy Passion.

The Third is that our Lord God, Almighty Wisdom, All-love, right as verily as he hath made everything that is, also verily he doeth and worketh all-thing that is done.

The Fourth is the scourging of his tender body, with plenteous shedding of his blood.

The fifth is that the Fiend is overcome by the precious Passion of Christ.

The Sixth is the worshipful thanking of our Lord God in which he rewardeth his blessed servants in Heaven.

The Seventh is often feeling of weal and woe—feeling of weal is gracious touching and lightening, with true sickerness of endless joy, the feeling of woe is temptation by heaviness and irksomeness of our fleshly living—with ghostly understanding that we are kept also sickerly in Love, in woe as in weal, by the Goodness of God.

The Eighth is the last pains of Christ, and his cruel dying.

The Ninth is of the liking which is in the Blissful Trinity of the hard Passion of Christ and his rueful dying: in which joy and liking he will[eth that] we be so solaced and mirthed with him, till when we come to the fulhead in Heaven.

The Tenth is, our Lord Jesus sheweth in love his blissful heart even cloven in two, rejoicing.

The Eleventh is an high ghostly Shewing of his dearworthy Mother.

The Twelfth is that Our Lord is most worthy Being.

The Thirteenth is that our Lord God will[eth] we have great regard to all the deeds that he hath done: in the great nobleness of all things making, and of the excellency of man's making, which is above all his works; and of the precious amends that he hath made for man's sin, turning all our blame into endless worship. Where also our Lord saith: ' Behold and see! For by the same Mighty Wisdom and Goodness I shall make well all that is not well; and thou shalt see it.' And in this he will[eth] that we keep us in the Faith and truth of Holy Church, not willing to know his secrets now, but as it [be]longeth to us in this life.

The Fourteenth is that our Lord is the Ground of our Prayer. Herein were seen two properties: the one is rightful prayer, the other is secure trust; which he will[eth should] both be alike large; and thus our prayer pleaseth him and he of his Goodness fulfilleth it.

The Fifteenth [is] that we shall suddenly be taken from all our pain and from all our woe, and of his Goodness we shall come up above, where we shall have our Lord Jesus to our meed and be fulfilled of joy and bliss in Heaven.

The Sixteenth is that the Blissful Trinity, our Maker, in Christ Jesus our Saviour, endlessly dwelleth in our soul, worshipfully ruling, and giving us all things mightily, and wisely saving and keeping for Love; and we shall not be overcome of our Enemy. (Ch. 1, pp. 1-3.)

Analysis of the special shewings, as well as Julian's own explicit statements, reveal that the 'homely loving of God' is the key to a right understanding of the Revelations

From the general summary of the Revelations left to us by Julian, and from the book itself, we can easily see that the 'Revelations' or 'shewings' were initially focused on:

The Passion of Christ; but while Julian was contemplating the scenes of the Passion, vividly and realistically set before her eyes, she was granted a much higher 'ghostly sight', whereby she enjoyed, in Christ, some partial sight of

The Godhead, because, as Julian says: 'Where Jesus appeareth, the blessed Trinity is understood, as to my sight.' (Ch. 4, p. 7.) The ghostly sight of the Divinity led Julian to penetrate into the greatness of God. In this sight her attention was drawn primarily to

The Goodness of God, viz. his tender love for man which Julian, with a very beautiful expression, calls the 'homely loving' or 'homeliness' of God.

This process—by which Julian 'sees' first the suffering Christ; in Christ the Divinity; and in the Divinity the Love and Goodness of God—is evident from the very beginning in the first Revelation.

Analysis of the elements of the 1st Revelation

1. *The suffering Christ:* 'In this suddenly I saw the red blood trickling down from under the Garland hot and freshly and right plenteously.' (Ch. 4, p. 7.)

L

2. *The Divinity* in the Passion: ' And in the same Shewing suddenly the Trinity fulfilled my heart most of joy. . . .' (Ch. 4, p. 7.) The reason of the connection between the two elements is explicitly stated: ' For where Jesus appeareth, the Blessed Trinity is understood, as to my sight.' (Ibid.)

3. *The Goodness of God, or his ' homely loving'* in the Divinity: ' In this same time our Lord shewed me a ghostly sight of his homely loving.' (Ch. 5, p. 8.) Julian takes care to underline that ' This Shewing was made to learn our soul wisely to cleave to the Goodness of God.' (Ch. 6, p. 10.)

As Julian herself tells us that in the first Revelation ' all the shewings that follow be grounded and oned' (ch. 1, p. 1), we may rightly expect that the fundamental truths with which the First Revelation is concerned, and the plan according to which it is unfolded, will be found in the ones that follow. An examination of some of the other shewings will verify this hypothesis. Let us take the eighth, ninth and tenth Revelations as being the most typical amongst those shewings in which the first object of vision is the Humanity of Christ :

Eighth Revelation

(1) *The suffering Christ:* ' Christ shewed a part of his Passion near his dying.' (Ch. 16, p. 30.)

(2) *The Divinity* in the Passion: ' For the highest point that may be seen in the Passion is to think and know *what he is* that suffered. And in this [Shewing] he brought in part to mind *the height and nobleness of the glorious Godhead*, and therewith the preciousness and the tenderness of the blissful Body, which be together oned. . . .' (Ch. 20, p. 38.)

Here again the last words give the reason for the connection between the two elements, that is to say, the Hypostatic Union.

(3) *The Goodness of God*, his tender love for men, his ' homely loving ' in the Divinity: ' And the cause why he suffereth

[it to be so] is for [that] he will *of his Goodness make us the higher with him* in his bliss.'   (Ch. 21, p. 40.)

Ninth Revelation

(1) *The suffering Christ:* ' Then said our good Lord Jesus Christ: " Art thou well paid that I suffered for thee ? " '   (Ch. 22, p. 40.)

(2) *The Divinity* in the Passion: ' In this feeling my understanding was *lifted up into Heaven*, and there I saw three heavens: . . . For the First Heaven, Christ *shewed me his Father;* in no bodily likeness, but in his property and his working.   That is to say, I saw in Christ that the Father is.'   (Ch. 22, p. 40.)

Here again the last words show the connection between the two elements, between the vision of the Humanity and the consequent sight of the Divinity: viz. the Hypostatic Union.

(3) *The Goodness of God*, his ' homely loving ' in the Divinity: ' Then said Jesus, our kind Lord: " If thou art paid, I am paid: it is a joy, a bliss, and an endless liking to me that ever suffered I passion for thee; and if I might suffer more, I would suffer more." '   (Ch. 22, p. 40.)

Tenth Revelation

(1) *The suffering Christ :* ' Then with a glad cheer our Lord looked unto his Side and beheld, rejoicing . . . he led forth the understanding of his creature by the same wound into his Side within. . . . he shewed his blissful heart even cloven in two.'   (Ch. 24, p. 44.)

(2) *The Divinity* in the suffering Christ: ' And with this sweet enjoying, he shewed unto mine understanding, in part, *the blessed Godhead*, . . .'   (Ch. 24, p. 44.)

(3) *The Goodness of God*, his ' homely loving ' in the Divinity: ' . . . stirring then the poor soul for to understand, as it may be said, that is, to think on *the endless Love* that was without beginning, and is, and shall be ever.   And with this our good Lord said full blissfully: " Lo, how that I

loved thee ", as if he had said: " My darling, . . . and for
my love enjoy now with me. . . . Lo, how I loved thee!
Behold and see that I loved thee so much ere I died for
thee, that I would die for thee; and now I have died for
thee and suffered willingly that [which] I may. . . ." '
(Ch. 24, pp. 44-45.) [1]

Also, in all the other Revelations in which the Passion of
Christ is no longer the first and direct object of the vision,
when Julian sees God, her understanding is led to consider
the same particular attribute or property: viz. God's

[1] All the quotations given above (as well as the passages cited in part I,
ch. 2, pp. 57-61) clearly show how tender is Julian's devotion to the Humanity
of Christ. In the entire literature concerning the Humanity of Christ, including the writings of St Bernard, these pages stand out for their beauty and the
immediacy of the spiritual experiences they express. ('Saint Bernard a été dans
l'Eglise le chef de file d'une expansion de la dévotion à l'Humanité du Christ '
—see A. Le Bail, O.C.R., *Bernard* (Saint) DSp., I, c. 1481. For a very accurate
study of St Bernard I refer the reader especially to J. Leclercq, O.S.B., *Etudes
sur saint Bernard et le texte de ses écrits*, Analecta Sacri Ordinis Cisterciensis, 9
(1953), pp. 1-247. One may also usefully read M.-A. Dimier, O.C.R. *Saint
Bernard, est-il allé en Angleterre ?*; Collectanea Ordinis Cisterciensis Reformati,
9 (1947), pp. 16-19.) I should like to draw attention to one particular aspect
under which Julian looks at the suffering Christ, and that is the consideration
of the joy that our Lord had in suffering for us: ' It is a joy, a bliss, and
endless liking to me that ever suffered I passion for thee; and if I might
suffer more, I would suffer more.' (Ch. 22, p. 40.) The author of *Mediaeval
Mystical Tradition and St John of the Cross* (London, 1954), p. 42, remarks that
'Already, also, in Hugh [of St Victor], we meet with that " grievous joy in
the Holy Cross " which was to be such an outstanding feature of the Franciscan
spirituality in the next age.' Whether or not Julian owes this consideration
to the reading of The Victorine or to the influence of the Franciscans it is
impossible to ascertain. (We know that the Franciscans arrived in Norwich
in 1226—cf. The Victoria History of the Counties of England, edited by
William Page, *Norfolk*, vol. 2, p. 430; Rev. D. Harford, *A Norwich Parish
500 years ago*, pp. 29-30.) We also know that ' The Franciscan school there
was sufficiently active to attract foreign students; the manuscript note-book
of an Italian Friar, Nicholas of Assisi, contains notes of lectures and disputa-
tions attended at Norwich, *c.* 1337, . . .' (W. A. Pantin, *The English Church in
the Fourteenth Century*, p. 119). However, Julian's account is so vivid and
beautiful that I am rather inclined to think that she derived her consideration
of the joyful Passion directly from the contact she had with God in the shewings.

goodness and homely loving. This is, e.g. the case in the sixteenth Revelation in which—as we shall see later—the conception of the 'homely loving' reaches its climax. The reason why we choose this shewing rather than any other is that Julian attaches to it the same comprehensive value as she has attached to the first of the Revelations:

. . . the good Lord shewed the Sixteenth [Revelation] on the the night following, as I shall say after: which Sixteenth was conclusion and confirmation to all Fifteen. (Ch. 66, p. 136.)

The main passages of this Revelation read as follows:

And then our Lord opened my ghostly eye and shewed me my soul in midst of my heart. . . .

In the midst of that City sitteth our Lord, Jesus, *God and Man*, . . .

And *the God-head* ruleth and sustaineth heaven and earth and all that is—sovereign Might, sovereign Wisdom, and sovereign Goodness—[and] the place that Jesus taketh in our Soul he shall never remove it, without end, as to my sight:

for in us is his homeliest home and *his endless dwelling*. (Ch. 67, pp. 138-139.)

So that at the end of her account of the sixteenth Revelation, she can say:

I had, in part, touching, sight, and feeling in *three properties of God, in which the strength and effect of all the Revelation standeth:* and *they were seen in every Shewing*, and most properly in the Twelfth where it saith oftentime: [I it am]. The properties are these: Life, Love, and Light.

In life is *marvellous homeliness*,

and in love is *gentle courtesy*,

and in light is *endless kind-hood*.

These properties were in *one Goodness* (ch. 83, p. 166).[1]

It is here explicitly stated by Julian that this 'marvellous homeliness', 'gentle courtesy', and 'endless kind-hood'

[1] As is obvious from the text, the three properties are unified in 'one Goodness', and the terms used to describe each one of the properties are but aspects of the 'love' or 'homely loving'.

(' one Goodness ') are the keynote of ' every shewing '; and indeed it would not be a difficult task to go through each one of the Revelations and prove that Julian's attention is always led from the sight of God to the more specific consideration of God's goodness and homely loving.[1]

We may conclude by reproducing what Julian herself states with regard to the ultimate meaning of the shewings:

> And from that time that it was shewed I desired oftentimes to witten *what was our Lord's meaning*. And fifteen years after, and more, I was answered in ghostly understanding, saying thus:
> ' Wouldst thou witten thy Lord's meaning in this thing?
> Wit it well: *Love was his meaning*.
> Who shewed it thee? *Love*.
> What shewed he thee? *Love*.
> Wherefore shewed it he? For *love*.
> Hold thee therein and thou shalt witten and know more in the same.
> *But thou shalt never know nor witten therein other thing without end.'*
> *Thus was I learned that Love was our Lord's meaning.'* (Ch. 86, p. 169.)

It would be difficult to ask for a more definite statement, or to demand a clearer answer to our question: what is the object attained by Julian in her contemplation (in her shewings)?

It is simply the love of God, his ' homely loving ': there can be no other interpretation. Nor is this Julian's own interpretation, for, as Julian says: ' Love was our Lord's meaning.'

---

[1] The value of the proofs given is increased when one considers that even in the Revelations in which Julian speaks of the most difficult and disparate subjects, the Goodness of God is indicated as the solution and explanation of every problem. This is the case of the thirteenth Revelation, where Julian asks herself with some anxiety: ' good Lord, how might all be well, for the great hurt that is come, by sin, to thy creatures?' (Ch. 29, p. 51.) The problem of sin is solved by recourse to the Goodness and Love of God: cf. ch. 31, pp. 54-55. See also chs. 25, 41-43.

2

JULIAN'S PROGRESSIVE REALIZATION OF GOD'S 'HOMELY LOVING'

WHAT remains now is to study what Julian has to say of the 'homely loving'. Already in ch. 5 she tells us: 'In this same time our Lord shewed me a ghostly sight of his homely loving' (ch. 5, p. 8), and immediately goes on to say in what this 'sight' consists:

> I saw that he is to us everything that is good and comfortable for us.
>
> He is our clothing that for love wrappeth us, claspeth us, and all becloseth us for tender love, that he may never leave us; being to us all thing that is good, as to mine understanding. (Ch. 5, p. 8.)

God's presence among creatures

'Homely loving' is thus at first conceived by Julian as being a sort of nearness, a presence of God who lovingly enfolds his creatures. The nature of the devine presence is conveyed by the 'hazel-nut' comparison:

> Also in this he shewed [me] a little thing, the quantity of an hazel-nut, in the palm of my hand; and it was round as a ball. I looked thereupon with eye of my understanding, and thought: 'What may this be?' And it was generally answered thus: 'It is all that is made.' (Ch. 5, p. 9.)

and the explanation she gives enables us to penetrate more deeply into the ever present and active love of God: 'In this Little Thing I saw three properties. The first is that

God made it: the second is that God loveth it: the third, that God keepeth it.' (Ch. 5, p. 9.)

She introduces here the terms God ' the Maker, the Keeper, the Lover ' which are a sort of formula she uses throughout her work; it is meant to recall the teaching of this Relevation and to sum up all God's loving activity among his creatures.

And in this activity there is not so much a question of nearness, as of presence, for God works in everything in order to keep it in being and in well-being: ' In which Shewing I understood six things. . . . The fifth is: he that made all thing for love, by the same love keepeth [it], and it is kept and shall be without end.' (Ch. 8, pp. 15-16.)

We find the same idea expressed even more vividly in the words spoken to her by our Lord:

> See! I am God:
> see! I am in all thing:
> see! I do all thing:
> see! I *lift never mine hands off my works*, nor ever shall, without end:
> see! I lead all thing to the end I ordained it to from without beginning, by the same Might, Wisdom, and Love whereby I made it. (Ch. 11, p. 24.)

It is clear from the two parts of this quotation that Julian is considering two aspects of the divine presence. The one is that which we commonly call Providence, whereby God is present in history and controls events. (' I lead all thing to the end I ordained it to from without beginning.') [1]   The

[1] See also in the same chapter: ' For I saw truly that God doeth all thing, be it never so little. And I saw truly that nothing is done by hap nor by adventure, but all things by the foreseeing wisdom of God: if it be hap or adventure in the sight of man, our blindness and our unforesight is the cause. For the things that are in the foreseeing wisdom of God from without beginning (which rightfully and worshipfully and continually he leadeth to the best end, as they come about), fall to us suddenly, ourselves unwitting. And

other is that of God's presence *in* every single creature whereby he gives it being and life. It is primarily this second aspect that Julian has in mind when she uses her formula ' God the Maker, the Keeper, the Lover '.

God's presence in creatures

A deeper penetration of this second aspect of God's presence in creatures leads her to say that not only is God present in every good thing, but that the goodness itself in that creature is God: ' in which Shewing I understood six things. . . . The sixth is, that God is all that is good, as to my sight, and the goodness that every thing hath, it is he.' (Ch. 8, pp. 15-16.)

And again in the following chapter she says: ' For God is all that is good, as to my sight, and God hath made all that is made, and God loveth all that he hath made: and he that loveth generally all his even-Christians for God, he loveth all that is.[1] . . . For in man is God, and God is in all.' (Ch. 9, p. 17.)

The appreciation of this active presence of God, in creatures and in events, should carry the soul to a deep and unshakeable sense of security, and so to a sense of peace and joy. Repeatedly Julian asserts this. Here are two passages that seem to show this most clearly:

---

thus by our blindness and our unforesight we say: these be haps and adventures; but to our Lord God they be not so. Wherefore me behoveth needs to grant that all thing that is done, it is well done: for our Lord God doeth all. For in this time the working of creatures was not shewed, but [the working] of our Lord God in the creature: for he is in the Mid-point of all thing, and all he doeth.' (Ch. 11, pp. 22-23.)

[1] The Shorter Version gives a slightly different reading: ' He that loves his fellow-Christians in general, loves all that is. . . . for in man is God, and so in man is all.' (Reynolds, Ch. VI, p. 16.) This reading seems preferable, because it fits more properly into the whole context: in fact it is an application of the preceding statement. However, the reading of the Longer Version does not disprove what is said above with regard to the presence of God in all things.

Then I understood thus: that if a man or woman were under the broad water, *if he might have sight of God so as God is with a man continually, he should be safe* in body and soul, and take no harm: and overpassing, he should have *more solace and comfort* than all this world can tell.[1]

For he willeth we believe that we see him continually, though that to us it seemeth but little; and in this belief he maketh us evermore to gain grace. For he will be seen and he will be sought: he will be abided and he will be trusted. (Ch. 10, p. 19.)

. . . and this may now be seen and felt in measure by the gracious *presence of our Lord* when it is [felt]: *which presence in all things* is most desired, for *it worketh marvellous sureness* in true faith, and sure hope, by greatness of charity, in dread that is sweet and delectable. (Ch. 65, p. 135.)

God's presence in man

This presence of God in his creatures is considered in a special way in man. For it is in man's soul that God places 'his homeliest home and his endless dwelling'. (Ch. 67, p. 139.) [2]

Julian sees in the soul of man a special presence, which is superior to every presence of God either in events or other creatures; it is truly a ' dwelling ':

Our Good Lord shewed himself in divers manners both in heaven [and] in earth, but I saw him take no *place* but in man's soul.

He shewed himself in earth in the sweet Incarnation and in his blissful Passion.

[1] See also the depth and beauty of the following expression: 'God is nearer to us than our own Soul ' (ch. 56, p. 114), which reminds us of St Augustine's expression: ' Tu autem eras interior intimo meo et superior summo meo ' (*Confessiones*, III, 6, 11; P.L. 32,688). ' But thou wert more inward to me, than my most inward part; and higher than my highest.'

[2] We may note the correspondence between these terms and the scriptural text of St John: ' If any one love me, he will keep my word, and my Father will love him, *and we will come to him and make our abode with him*.' (John. xiv. 23.)

And in other manner he shewed himself in earth [as in the Revelation] where I say: 'I saw God in a point.'

And in another manner he shewed himself in earth thus as it were in pilgrimage: that is to say, he is here with us, leading us, and shall be till when he hath brought us all to his bliss in heaven. He shewed him[self] divers times reigning, as it is aforesaid; *but principally in man's soul.*

He hath taken there his resting-place and his worshipful City: out of which worshipful See he shall never rise nor remove without end.' (Ch. 81, p. 163.) [1]

This chapter contains clear expressions which show the differences in the modes of God's presence in creatures, in events, and in man. It is only in man that there is question of a ' dwelling ', of a ' homeliest home ', of a ' place ', of a ' resting-place ', in which God resides and rules. The soul is as it were a throne on which God is seated.

And then our Lord opened my ghostly eye and shewed me my soul in midst of my heart.

I saw the Soul so large *as it were an endless world*, and as it were *a blissful kingdom.*

---

[1] In passing, I draw attention to the statement: ' out of which worshipful See he shall never rise nor remove without end '. Not only here, but also in ch. 67—using a similar expression—Julian teaches that God never separates himself from the soul. This has caused some critics to suggest that Julian might here exceed the limits of strict orthodoxy (cf. Hudleston, note at p. 174 and Appendix, pp. xxiii ff.). Indeed as the words stand, they could be interpreted, e.g. in the sense of the gnostics with the refutation of whose doctrine the first Epistle of St John is largely concerned (cf. especially i. 8-12; ii. 1-6). However, if due attention is paid to the immediate context as well as to the whole trend of Julian's thought, they need not necessarily bear this meaning. In fact—and this is my opinion—they can be interpreted in the sense of the very similar expressions used by other Mystics, cf. e.g. St John of the Cross, *Spiritual Canticle*, st. I, n. 7-8, ed. cit. pp. 189-190. However, a more complete answer to this difficulty can result only from a full study of Julian's doctrine on predestination—a study already in a state of advanced preparation by the Rev. J. Chown, M.S.C. Miss Kröger has dealt with this point of Julian's teaching (see op. cit. pp. 67-160), but she would appear not to have approached the highly complex problem of predestination from the really decisive point of view, viz. that of theological science.

And by the conditions that I saw therein I understood that it is *a worshipful City*.

In the midst of that City *sitteth* our Lord Jesus, *God and Man*, a fair Person of large stature, highest Bishop, solemnest King, most worshipful Lord; and I saw him clad solemnly.

And worshipfully he sitteth in the Soul, even-right in peace and rest. And the God-head ruleth and sustaineth heaven and earth and all that is—sovereign Might, sovereign Wisdom, and sovereign Goodness—[and] the place that Jesus taketh in our soul he shall never remove it, without end, as to my sight: for in us is his *homeliest home and his endless dwelling*. (Ch. 67, pp. 138-139.)

And at the end of her account of this vision of God dwelling in her soul she explains and repeats the permanence and sureness of this divine presence: ' And this was a singular joy and bliss to me that I saw him *sitting:* for the secureness of sitting sheweth endless dwelling.' (Ch. 68, p. 140.) Comparing this description with that given by St Teresa, we cannot but be struck by the likeness not only of ideas, but also of expressions and similes:

And now *let us imagine* that we have within us *a palace of priceless worth*, built entirely of gold and precious stones—a palace, in short, fit *for so great a Lord*. Imagine that it is partly your doing that *this palace* should be what it is—and this is really true, for there is no building so beautiful as a soul that is pure and full of virtues, and, the greater these virtues are, the more brilliantly do the stones shine.

Imagine that within the palace *dwells this great King*, Who has vouchsafed to become your *Father*, and Who *is seated* upon *a throne* of supreme price—namely, your heart. (St Teresa, *The Way of Perfection*, ch. xxviii, ed. cit. vol. II, p. 117.)

However, this perception of the presence of God reigning in the centre of the soul is not the final point of Julian's experience. Her personal union with God and her teaching go farther.

God's presence in man: a union which transforms

The presence of God in man is not conceived by Julian
as being a sort of static presence, as chs. 67-68 might lead us
to think; in her teaching there is a further stage, which is
described in ch. 54. In this chapter Julian recalls the
essentials of what was contained in the Revelations of 1373,
and especially in the sixteenth Revelation:

> He is with us in Heaven, very Man, in his own Person, us
> updrawing; and that was shewed in [the Shewing of] the
> ghostly Thirst.
> And he is with us in earth, us leading; and that was shewed in
> the Third [Shewing], where I saw God in a Point.
> And he is with us in our soul, endlessly dwelling, us ruling and
> keeping; and that was shewed in the Sixteenth [Shewing], as
> I shall say.   (Ch. 52, p. 104.)

Then she goes on to develop for us the doctrine of the
divine indwelling: God comes into our hearts not only to
reign within us as King, but to unite us to himself, so that
by this penetrating and vivifying presence man is wholly
plunged in God and lives with his life. The expressions
that Julian uses could scarcely be more explicit:

> Highly ought we to rejoice that God dwelleth in our soul, and
> much more highly ought we to rejoice that our soul dwelleth
> in God.
> Our soul is made to be God's dwelling-place; and the dwelling-
> place of the soul is God, which is unmade. And high under-
> standing it is, inwardly to see and know that God, which is
> our Maker, dwelleth in our soul; and an higher understanding
> it is, inwardly to see and to know that our soul, that is made,
> dwelleth in God's substance: of which substance, God, we
> are that we are.
> And I saw no difference betwixt God and our Substance: but
> as it were all God; and yet mine understanding took that our

Substance is in God: that is to say, that God is God, and our Substance is a creature in God. (Ch. 54, p. 110.)

We find much the same terms in St John of the Cross, St Teresa, and other writers who speak of 'transforming union' or 'spiritual marriage'.[1]

And the soul is like this window, whereupon is ever beating (or, to express it better, wherein is ever dwelling) the Divine light of the Being of God according to nature, which we have described. 7. In thus allowing God to work in it, the soul (having rid itself of every mist and stain of creatures which consists in having its will perfectly united with that of God, for to love is to labour to detach and strip itself for God's sake of all that is not God) is at once illumined and transformed in God, and God communicates to it His supernatural Being, in such wise that *it appears to be God Himself*, and has all that God Himself has.   And this union comes to pass when God grants the soul this supernatural favour, that all the things of *God and the soul are one in participant transformation;* and *the soul seems to be God* rather than a soul, and is indeed God by participation; *although it is true that its natural* being, *though thus transformed, is as distinct from the Being of God as it was before*, even as the window has likewise a nature distinct from that of the ray, though the ray gives it brightness.[2]

[1] It will be noticed that Julian is speaking explicitly of the supernatural union of grace which exists, in Christ, between God and all Christians, and not of that profound awareness of God's presence which is of the essence of the 'transforming union'. (Hence I have chosen to speak of *a union which transforms*, rather than of the 'transforming union'). The terms which she uses in chs. 51, 52, 58—'Spouse' and 'Wife'—('and God rejoiceth that he is our Very Spouse and our soul is his loved Wife': 'And in the knitting and the oneing he is our Very, True Spouse, and we his loved Wife and his Fair Maiden'), is reminiscent rather of St. Paul (Ephesians, ch. 5, vv. 25 ff.), than of St. John of the Cross. Perhaps we may see in the similarity of language between Julian, in her description of the nature of the union, and John of the Cross, who is speaking of the awareness of the union, the beginnings of a solution to the difficult question of the relation between this union and the mystical union properly so called.

[2] St John of the Cross, *Ascent*, Bk. II, c. 5, nn. 6-7, ed. cit. v. I, pp. 77-78.

I reproduce this particular passage from St John of the Cross, one of the many that might be brought forward,[1] because it seems to me opportune to point out the great similarity of expression and ideas that there is between Julian and this great master of the spiritual life.

We may also note that Julian shows the same soundness of doctrine and confidence in expressing herself that we find in St John of the Cross. Both of them, after making some assertion that might seem exaggerated and even perhaps pantheistic, hasten to clarify their teaching and give their words their precise meaning.

Development of this doctrine

The text quoted above is followed by a further clarification. The words that occur there recall to us the source of all this doctrine of the divine indwelling, namely our Lord's discourse at the Last Supper.

. . . the high Goodness of the Trinity is our Lord, and in him we are enclosed and he in us.

We are enclosed in the Father, and we are enclosed in the Son, and we are enclosed in the Holy Ghost. And the Father is enclosed in us, and the Son is enclosed in us, and the Holy Ghost is enclosed in us: Almightiness, All-Wisdom, All-Goodness: one God, one Lord. (Ch. 54, p. 110.) [2]

Although Julian develops this theme chiefly in ch. 54, she also treats of it elsewhere. In ch. 55 we find mention of it, with more explicit reference to our union with the life of the Blessed Trinity:

And thus was my understanding led of God to see in him and to understand, to wit and to know, that our soul is made [a]

---

[1] Cf. e.g. *Spiritual Canticle*, st. 22, nn. 3-5, ed. cit., v. II, pp. 292-294; st. 38 n. 3, pp. 369-370; st. 39, nn. 2-3, pp. 374-375; *Living Flame*, st. 3, nn. 78-79, v. III, ed. cit. pp. 184-185. See also St Teresa, *Castle*, 7 Mans, c. 2, n. 1-5, v. II, ed. cit. pp. 333-336.

[2] Cf. St John, xiv. 10-11; xiv. 20; xvii. 20-23.

trinity, like to the unmade blissful Trinity, known and loved from without beginning, and in the making oned to the Maker, as it is aforesaid.
This sight was full sweet and marvellous to behold, peaceable and restful, sure and delectable. (Ch. 55, p. 112.)

This union of ours with God is also touched on in ch. 43, where Julian, speaking of 'prayer', says that its purpose is to make us 'to be oned to God'. This phrase is brief, but rich in meaning, and after having read chs. 54-55, we can appreciate the better its power, its implication and its beauty.

Julian is speaking of the higher form of contemplation, the 'special beholding', and she says: '. . . I saw and felt that his marvellous and fulsome Goodness fulfilleth all our might; and therewith I saw that his continual working in all manner of things is done so goodly, so wisely, and so mightily, that it overpasseth all our imagining, and all that we can ween and think' (ch. 43, p. 78), and then she goes on with this simple but profound statement: 'and then we can do no more but behold him, enjoying, with an high, mighty desire to be all oned into him,—*centred to his dwelling*—and enjoy in his loving and delight in his goodness.' (Ch. 43, p. 78.)

This expression, 'centred to his dwelling', must be taken in the concrete sense of 'entering into God' [1] and so living wholly united to him. 'Dwelling' in Julian's writings always refers to the divine indwelling in us: 'for in us is his homeliest home and his endless dwelling.' (Ch. 67, p. 139.) And therefore this phrase 'entered to his dwelling' corresponds exactly to the union described in ch. 54:

We are enclosed in the Father, and we are enclosed in the Son, and we are enclosed in the Holy Ghost.

[1] I say this because a comparison of the various manuscripts shows that the best reading is that of MS. Sloane 2499, which has 'and *entred* to his wonying' (see my note at p. 109). I owe this interpretation of the manuscript reading to Sister Reynolds.

And the Father is enclosed in us, and the Son is enclosed in us, and the Holy Ghost is enclosed in us. (Ch. 54, p. 110.)

In these words Julian ends her teaching on our union with God, and nothing more beautiful could be said on the nature of this ' oneing '.

Union ' in faith '

But Julian is always concerned with telling us the means to attain our union with God, and after the words just quoted, without any preamble, she returns at once to the importance of faith:

. . . our faith is a Virtue that cometh of our kind Substance into our Sensual soul *by the Holy Ghost;* in which all our virtues come to us: for without that, no man may receive virtue.

For it is naught else but a right understanding, with true belief, and sure trust, of our Being: that we are in God, and God in us, which we see not. And *this virtue,* with all other that God hath ordained to us coming therein, *worketh in us great things.* (Ch. 54, p. 110.)

These words are the hall-mark, as it were, of Julian's teaching on prayer and contemplation.

As we saw in the chapter that dealt with the various states and degrees of contemplation, she maintains that the essence of our contemplative union with God lies in a penetrating faith; this penetration (into the revealed truths of our faith) is communicated to our souls by the infused action of God. But the awareness of this action and the ' sight ' of these truths (Shewing) is only an accessory element, and though useful to us, it is not necessary, for without it, basing ourselves on pure faith, we may still live this life of close union with God.

In the lines just quoted Julian returns to each one of these points. It is faith which brings us to penetrate revealed truths: ' a right understanding '; by faith we penetrate even

M

the highest of these truths: that 'we are in God, God in us'; even though there be no vision ('sight' or 'Shewing'): 'whom we see not'. And this penetrating faith is the work of the Holy Ghost: 'faith is a virtue that cometh . . . by the Holy Ghost'. This insistence by Julian that faith is the foundation of our union with God and of our contemplative life constitutes a proof of the depth and theological exactness of Julian's teaching, which we feel inclined to attribute rather to the direct teaching of God than to any human source.

3

A FURTHER ASPECT OF GOD'S 'HOMELY LOVING': THE CONCEPT OF GOD AS OUR MOTHER

In the previous chapter we have considered Julian's conception of the 'homely loving of God': moved by love, God 'cometh down to the lowest part of our need', he 'wrappeth us, claspeth us, and all becloseth us for tender love'; he works for us, is near to us, dwells in us and encloses us in him. It would be difficult to think of a more complete and more tender way of speaking of God's active love for us. Yet Julian seems to have had an even more penetrating insight.

By considering God *as a Mother and as the fount and origin of all motherhood*[1] she apprehended some further and touching aspects of his love. For ' The Mother's service is nearest, readiest, and surest'. (Ch. 60, p. 123.) Julian is therefore one of those

> mystics of the Middle Ages who have not hesitated to speak of the maternal aspect of Christ's love and have contemplated it in Christ himself, nay even in the Eternal Word in the bosom of the Trinity.

> In their meditations, and meditative and contemplative prayers . . . they have delighted to address our Lord as 'Mother'.[2]

Though we have to a certain extent lost familiarity with this

---

[1] Cf. ' This fair lovely word *Mother*, it is so sweet and so kind itself that it may not verily be said of none but of him; and to her that is very Mother of him and of all.' (Ch. 60, p. 125.)

[2] A. Cabassut, *Une dévotion médiévale peu connue*, RAM, 25 (1949), p. 234. In this connection I quote the following: ' The charity that is seen in Mary is nothing else but a reflection [of Christ's charity]. But this reflection has been adapted by God to human nature in such an admirable way, that—according to the plan of divine Providence—there is an aspect of Christ's love that cannot

idea, it is nevertheless, as Fr Cabassut has pointed out in his valuable article, explicitly grounded in Holy Scripture [1] and at times found in the writings of Christian antiquity.[2]

In the eleventh century the conception of God as our Mother began to appear more frequently and gave rise to a special devotion.   One of the famous texts of this period is the ' Oratio 65 ',[3] by St Anselm of Canterbury (1033-1109).

St Anselm's prayers were widely spread in the West.   Cistercians and Carthusians played a great part in this.   In other

---

be seen properly except by fixing one's attention on his Mother, just as there is an aspect of God's love which cannot be seen but by looking at Christ, God made man.' (*Sainte Marie, Mère de Dieu*, by Fr Mersch, S.J., in NRT, 67 (1940), pp. 149-150.)

[1] Cf. A. Cabassut, art. cit., pp. 236-237: ' Several times, in the Old Testament, in order to teach men how great is his love for his people, God compares himself to a mother.   He reminds the Israelites that he feels towards them as the mother feels towards the fruit of her womb.   " Listen, remote islands; pay heed to me, nations from far away.   Ere ever I was born, the Lord sent me his summons, kept me in mind already, in my mother's womb." (Isaias, xlix. 1.)   And then he declares: " What, can a woman forget her child that is still unweaned, pity no longer the son she bore in her womb?   Let her forget; I will not be forgetful of thee." (xlix. 15.)   And again: " I will console you then, like a mother caressing her son." (lxvi. 13.)   Following the same line of thought, there is in the New Testament St Matthew's well known text in which our Lord compares himself to the hen that gathers her chickens under her wings: this is a very expressive image to describe the motherly aspect of his love: " Jerusalem, Jerusalem . . . how often have I been ready to gather thy children together, as a hen gathers her chickens under her wings; and thou didst refuse it." ' (xxiii. 37.)

[2] See A. Cabassut, art. cit. pp. 237-238, where he quotes the Apocryphal Acts of St Peter composed at the beginning of the third century, and St John Chrysostom.

[3] Many writings which already in medieval times went under the name of St Anselm and hence found a large diffusion are today known to have been erroneously attributed to him.   The recent studies of Dom Wilmart have shown, however, that the ' Oratio 65 ' (PL, 158, 975-983) was indeed composed by St Anselm himself. (Cf. Dom Wilmart, *La tradition des Prières de Saint Anselme, Tables et Notes* in Revue Bénédictine, 36 (1924), pp. 52-71: *Méditations et Prières de S. Anselme*, Introd.)   His conclusions are fully accepted by the latest scholars on the subject. (Cf. Mgr P. Glorieux, *Pour revaloriser Migne. Tables Rectificatives*—Mélanges de Sciences Religeuses, 9me Année, Lille (1952), p. 62; M. Mähler, Art. ' Anselme ' in DSp., t. I, col. 693.)

words one may say that these prayers were highly esteemed and very often used in their monasteries. Often enough they were also imitated. The ' Oratio 65 ' was certainly a source of inspiration for the numerous mystical writers who came after St Anselm. The theme of the motherhood of Christ owes much to him either directly or indirectly. In fact one can retrace in all these writers the fundamental idea that Christ has given birth to us by dying on the Cross, and that the pains of his Passion have been the sufferings of our spiritual forthbringing.[1]

Hence St Anselm may rightly be called ' the originator of the devotion to our Lord, our Mother '.[2]

Fr Cabassut points out [3] that in the centuries that followed St Anselm this devotion is found, e.g. in Marguérite d'Oyngt (d. 1310), Mechtilde v. Hackeborn (d. 1298) and particularly in Julian of Norwich. The fact that this devotion was originated by St Anselm, who was a Benedictine, and found a widespread diffusion in circles influenced by the Benedictines, offers a new argument for the connection of Julian with that Order. This, however, does not mean that she simply took over an idea current at that time, for, as we shall see, Julian developed this conception into a doctrine not found before in such fulness, and made it a pillar of her teaching on the spiritual life.

The grounds on which Julian bases her consideration of God as Mother are some amongst the fundamental truths of our faith, that is to say Creation, Incarnation and Redemption, Providence, by which God gives, maintains and increases in us both natural and supernatural life.

She clearly expresses this in ch. 59: [4]

And thus is Jesus our Very Mother in kind [by virtue] of our first making; and he is our Very Mother in *Grace*, by taking our kind made. All the fair working, and all the sweet natural

---

[1] A. Cabassut, art. cit. p. 239.   [2] Ibid. p. 238.   [3] Ibid. pp. 240-241.
[4] Note that she explicitly attributes the Motherhood to the Second Person of the Blessed Trinity.

office of dearworthy Motherhood is appropriate to the Second
Person: . . .

I understood *three manners of beholding of Motherhood* in God:
the first is grounded in our kind making; the second is taking
of our kind—and there beginneth the motherhood of Grace;
the third is Motherhood of working—and therein is a forth-
spreading by the same Grace, of length and breadth and of
height and of deepness without end.[1]
And all is one Love.   (Ch. 59, pp. 122-123.) [2]

Whereas the concept of the Word of God, ' Mother in kind
of our first making,' is mentioned but not fully developed,
the idea of the *Incarnate* Word as ' Mother of Mercy', in whom
' we have our reforming and restoring ' is dwelt upon more
at length by Julian.   In fact in a like manner as a mother
brings forth her child in sufferings and pains, so too Christ
has brought us to supernatural life in the sufferings and
pains of His Passion:

We wit that all our mother's bearing is [bearing of] us to pain
and to dying: and what is this but that our Very Mother,
Jesus, he—All-Love—beareth us to joy and to endless living?
—blessed may he be!

Thus he sustaineth us within himself in love; and travailed,
unto the full time that he would suffer the sharpest throes and
the grievousest pains that ever were or ever shall be, and died
at the last.

And when he had [so] done, and so borne us to bliss, yet might
not all this make full content to his marvellous love; and that
sheweth he in these high overpassing words of love: ' If I
might suffer more, I would suffer more.'   (Ch. 60, p. 124.) [3]

---

[1] These terms re-echo St Paul's expression: ' so that, being rooted and
grounded in love, you may be able to comprehend with all the saints what is
the breadth and length and height and depth, and to know Christ's love which
surpasses knowledge, in order that you may be filled unto all the fullness of
God '.   (Eph. iii. 17-19.)

[2] Cf. also ch. 58, p. 120, where the Motherhood of God in Creation, Incarnation, Redemption and Providence is described in a similar manner.

[3] The last words of this quotation refer to ch. 22, p. 40.

A still greater emphasis, however, is laid on Christ's 'Motherhood of working'. In fact, if it is true that 'our Mother Christ' in his desire of giving life to us may say: 'If I might suffer more, I would suffer more', yet—as Julian explains—'He might no more die, but he would not stint of working.' (Ch. 60, p. 124.)

At the beginning of her description of this 'Motherhood of working', that is to say, of 'the service and the office of Motherhood in all things', Julian takes care to point out that the working of an earthly mother, though delicate and great, cannot be equal to Christ's 'working', because : 'This office none might, nor could, nor ever should do to the full, *but he alone*' (ch. 60, pp. 123-124); and even more clearly: 'And in our ghostly forthbringing he useth more tenderness of keeping, *without any likeness:* by as much as our soul is of more price in his sight.' (Ch. 61, p. 126.)

In her further description, Julian compares Christ's mother-hood of working with the offices proper to a human mother:

> The mother may give her child suck [of] her milk, *but our precious Mother, Jesus*, he may feed us with himself, and doeth it, full courteously and full tenderly, with the Blessed Sacrament that is precious food of very life; and with all the sweet Sacraments he sustaineth us full mercifully and graciously. And so meant he in this blessed word where that he said: 'I it am that Holy Church preacheth thee and teacheth thee.' That is to say: 'All the health and life of Sacraments, all the virtue and grace of my Word, all the Goodness that is ordained in Holy Church for thee, I it am.'[1]
>
> The mother may lay the child tenderly to her breast, *but our tender Mother, Jesus*, he may homely lead us into his blessed breast,

---

[1] I draw attention to the theological depth of this remark in which Julian clearly speaks of the union of Christ with his Church and of the identification of the life of Christ and the life of the Church. In this context see *The Mystical Body in the English Mystics*, by C. Pepler, O.P., Clergy Review, 23 (1943), pp. 49-59, where this doctrine is more explicitly examined.

by his sweet open side, and shew therein part of the Godhead and the joys of Heaven, with ghostly sureness of endless bliss.[1]

And that shewed he in the Tenth [Shewing], . . .

The kind loving Mother that witteth and knoweth the need of her child, she keepeth it full tenderly, as the kind and condition of Motherhood will. And as it waxeth in age, she changeth her working, but not her love.

And when it is waxen of more age, she suffereth that it be beaten in breaking down of vices, to make the child receive virtues and graces.

This working, with all that be fair and good, our Lord doeth it in them by whom it is done: thus he is our Mother in kind by the working of Grace in the lower part for love of the higher part. (Ch. 60, pp. 124-125.)

And then Julian concludes the comparison by saying:

And he willeth that we know this: for he will have all our love fastened to him. And in this I saw that all our duty that we owe, by God's bidding, to Fatherhood and Motherhood, for [reason of] God's Fatherhood and Motherhood is fulfilled in true loving of God; which blessed love Christ worketh in us. (Ch. 60, p. 125.)

I think that by this emphatic assertion Julian intends to draw attention to the impact that these considerations have on her doctrine on union with God. In fact, the preceding paragraph contains the main principles that justify and support her doctrine on full trust and optimism which she develops in the last part of her book. The validity of this claim is amply proved by the parallelism of ideas and expressions existing between the enlargement that Julian offers of her previous sentence, and the pages in which she explains how we should attain to an utter detachment from self by trusting in God's motherly love.

To show this parallelism, let us cite here the main passage in which she describes at length the delicate ' working ' of

<hr />

[1] Cf. ch. 24, p. 44.

our Mother Christ ' in our ghostly forthbringing '; and then, in the following chapter, analyse her doctrine on trust.

Christ's ' Motherhood of working ' in ' our ghostly forthbringing '

Christ ' kindleth our understanding, he directeth our ways, he easeth our conscience, he comforteth our soul, he lighteneth our heart, and giveth us, in part, knowing and believing in his blissful Godhead, with gracious mind in his sweet Manhood and his blessed Passion, with courteous marvelling in his high, overpassing Goodness; and maketh us to love all that he loveth, for his love, and to be well paid with him and all his works.

And when we fall, hastily he raiseth us by his lovely clasping and gracious touching.

And when we be thus strengthened by his sweet working, then we wilfully choose him, by his sweet grace, to be his servants and his lovers lastingly without end.

And after this *he suffereth some of us to fall more hard* and more grievously than ever we did afore, *as us thinketh*.

And *then ween we* (who be not all wise) that all were naught that we have begun. *But it is not so*.

For it *needeth us to fall*, and it *needeth us to see it. For if we never fell we should not know how feeble and how wretched we are of our self*, and also *we should not fully know that marvellous love* of our Maker.

For we shall see verily in heaven, without end, that we have greviously sinned in this life, and notwithstanding this, we shall see that *we were never hurt in his love*, nor were never the less of price in his sight. And by the assay of this falling *we shall have an high marvellous knowing of love in God*, without end.

For hard and marvellous is *that love which may not, nor will not, be broken* for trespass.

And this is one understanding of profit.

Another is *the lowness and meekness that we shall get by the sight of our falling:* for thereby *we shall highly be raised* in heaven; to which raising *we might never have come without that meekness*.

And *therefore it needeth us to see* it; and if we see it not, though we fell it should not profit us. And commonly, first we fall and later we see it: *and both of the Mercy of God.*

The mother may suffer the child to fall sometimes, and be *dis-eased* in diverse manners *for its own profit, but she may never suffer that any manner of peril come to the child for love.*

And though our earthly mother may suffer her child to perish, *our heavenly Mother, Jesus, may not suffer us* that are his children to perish: for he is All-Mighty, All-Wisdom, and All-Love; and so is none but he—blessed may he be!

But oftentimes when our falling and our wretchedness is shewed us, we are so sore adread, and *so greatly ashamed* of our self, *that scarcely we wit where we may hold us. But then willeth not our courteous Mother that we flee away,* for him were nothing lother.

But *he willeth then that we use the condition of a child:* for when it is dis-eased, or adread, *it runneth hastily* to the mother for help, with all its might.

So willeth he that we do, as a meek child *saying thus:* ' *My kind Mother,* my Gracious Mother, my dearworthy Mother, have mercy on me; I have made myself foul and unlike to thee, and I nor may nor can amend it but with thy privy help and grace.'

And if we feel us not then eased forthwith, be we sure that he useth the condition of a wise mother. *For if he see that it be more profit to us* to mourn and to weep, he suffereth it, with ruth and pity, unto the best time, *for love.* And *he willeth* then *that we use the property of a child, that evermore kindly trusteth to the love* of the mother *in weal and in woe.* (Ch. 61, pp. 126-128.)

---

[1] A very similar passage is found in the Ancrene Riwle, a book specifically written for anchoresses and still widely read in Julian's time:

" The sixth comfort is that Our Lord, when He allows us to be tempted, is playing with us as a mother with her darling child. She runs away from him and hides, and leaves him on his own, and he looks around for her, calling " Mama ! Mama ! " and crying a little, and then she runs out to him quickly, her arms outspread, and she puts them round him, and kisses him, and wipes his eyes. In the same way Our Lord sometimes leaves us alone for a while and withdraws His grace, His comfort and consolation, so that we find no pleasure in doing things well, and our heart's savour is gone. And yet, at that very moment Our Lord is not loving us any the less, but is doing this out of His great love for us." The *Ancrene Riwle,* edited by M. B. Salu, p. 102.

4

CONSEQUENCES: OPTIMISM AND TRUST. DETACHMENT FROM SELF OBTAINED BY THE PERCEPTION OF GOD'S LOVE

(' Homely loving')

JULIAN's experience and doctrine—as so far analysed and studied—are not a mere theoretical teaching, but are meant to have a very practical influence on the spiritual life of those who dispose themselves to serve God with generosity.

Julian's personal approach to God as to a Lover, and her teaching—of which the keynote is the 'homely loving' of God who is also a Mother to us—contain the main principle from which Julian derived her optimistic and serene outlook on the spiritual life, and on which she based the most typical part of her doctrine: in fact it is precisely by showing more in detail what the love of God is, and what this love expects from us, that she sets herself to teach 'good souls' how to overcome the obstacle that 'hindereth most God's lovers' and thus to attain to the full union she has spoken of before.

There is no doubt that the main obstacle to this full union is that form of attachment to self by which the soul prevents God from acting freely upon her, and taking the lead in her ascent: there is a moment in the spiritual life of God's lovers when the soul, 'under the colour of holiness', may be deceived, and still cling too much to self. Though essentially animated by the serious desire of serving God and pleasing him, the soul may still unconsciously look for the subtle satisfaction of herself, trying to have that feeling of assuredness in what she has done: in other words, giving way to spiritual pride, trust in self, and, consequently, lacking trust in God.[1]

Julian's merit and main contribution in this very important matter consists in this: that she goes straight to the essential point by laying open the most secret root of self attachment, the last one to be discovered. This teaching of Julian may be conveniently summed up under the following headings:

1. Julian says that those who ' for God's love hate sin and dispose themselves to do God's will ' may fall into a false ' dread ', viz. an excessive anxiety, due to ' spiritual blindness '. This ' doubtful dread ' contains the cause of their lack of progress and union with God.

2. Therefore this sort of dread has to be known as a temptation and rejected as such.

3. The remedy against such temptation lies in the knowledge of the effective love of God, who wishes to have the soul entirely in his hands, abandoned to his love; and simultaneously in an attitude of loving trust, by which the soul ' flees ' to our Lord.

---

[1] This consideration has been dwelt upon by many spiritual writers; in modern times it has been very clearly expressed thus by Fr de Jaegher: ' One of the many snares to be met with in the spiritual life, one which is even encountered on the very threshold of sanctity, is too great a preoccupation with self. Many generous souls, already advanced in the way of perfection, do not arrive at the summit because they are too engrossed with themselves. They think too much about themselves, analyse their feelings too minutely, reproach themselves excessively for their failings and infidelities, are too anxious about their spiritual progress. Without doubt, this comes from their zeal for perfection, and also from their love for God, but this love is not sufficiently free from self-love. How much they would gain by thinking less of self and more of God! ' (P. de Jaegher, *One with Jesus: The Life of Identification with Christ*, p. 43.)

4. Hence sin—which is the cause of the doubtful dread—
has to be seen in the light of the Love of God, in the light
of ' grace and mercy '.

This will bring the soul not to despair, but to a deep
knowledge of self and its utter incapacity in doing good
('matter of meekness that saves from presumption'),
together with a full, loving, and joyful trust in God alone,
who is the Ground of our goodness.

We shall simply follow Julian's teaching as contained in
ch. 73 and following.

Ch. 73 and following

1. ' I speak of such men and women as for God's love
hate sin and dispose themselves to do God's will: . . . '
(Ch. 73, p. 148.)   It is necessary to stress this point, because
it would be a serious mistake to apply indiscriminately to
all possible categories of men a teaching which Julian herself
intended explicitly for the particular group of those who
strive seriously after perfection.   'When we begin to hate
sin, and *amend* us by the ordinance of Holy Church, yet there
dwelleth a dread that letteth us . . .' (ch. 73, p. 149) which
is specified as being ' despair, *or doubtful dread*, . . . ' (ch. 73,
p. 148), doubtful dread, in as much as it draweth to despair
. . .' (ch. 74, p. 150).

It is due to the ' beholding of our self and of our sins
afore done.   And some of us because of our every-daily sins:
for we hold not our Covenants, nor keep we our cleanness
that our Lord setteth us in, but fall oftentimes into so much
wretchedness that shame it is to see it ' (ch. 73, p. 149).
and has as its consequence that ' the beholding of this maketh
us so sorry and so heavy, that scarcely we find any comfort '
(ibid).   After having indicated the existence of this doubtful
dread, after having described the various forms that it may
assume in different souls, and indicated the consequences,

Julian states that ' this dread we take sometime for a meek-ness, but it is a foul blindness and a weakness ' (ibid.). Because

> the cause why we are travailed with them is for unknowing of Love. . . .
>
> And of this knowing are we most blind.
>
> For some of us believe that God is Almighty and may do all, and that he is All-Wisdom and can do all; but that he is All-Love, and will do all, there we stop short. And this unknow-ing it is, that letteth most God's lovers, as to my sight. (Ch. 73, pp. 148-149.)

According to Julian, therefore, this kind of doubtful dread which is taken by the soul as ' meekness ', is nothing else but a lack of love and trust in God; it is a form of attach-ment to self. In fact it means that the soul does not find any comfort because she still relies on what *she can do* and does not admit, at least in practice, that it is only God who, in his love, can do and will do what we, of ourselves, cannot do. The knowledge of God's love in this case is still too theoretical, and does not move the soul to rely wholly upon God; she is more confident in what she can do, than in what the love of God would do if she only would give up the trust in self and the desire of feeling sure that she has done all she had to do; and this is the deepest and most hidden root of self attachment, the one that ' letteth most God's lovers '.

2. From these premises Julian draws her first very prac-tical consequence and teaching: ' And therefore it is God's will that they be known [viz. impatience, or sloth, and despair or doubtful dread], for then we shall refuse them as we do other sins.' (Ch. 73, p. 148.) Because if we do not know them ' we cannot despise it as we do another sin, that we know [as sin]: for it cometh [subtly] of Enmity, and it is against truth '. (Ch. 73, p. 149.) In fact, as Julian herself explains:

Thus is it our enemy that would put us aback with his false dread, [by reason] of our wretchedness, through pain that he threateth us with.

For it is his meaning to make us so heavy and so weary in this, that we should let out of mind the fair, blissful beholding of our Everlasting Friend. (Ch. 76, p. 155.)

' Our good Lord shewed the enmity of the Fiend: whereby I understood that all that is contrary to love and peace is of the Fiend and of his part.' (Ch. 77, pp. 155-156.) [1]

3. Hence Julian teaches the way in which this temptation should be rejected: ' He willeth that in all things we have our beholding and our enjoying in Love.' (Ch. 73, p .149.) Of which Love (as she has explained at length in the course of the Revelations), we have so many and convincing proofs. For this reason she briefly summarises here what she has taught, by recourse and reference to the most touching proof of the love of God, viz. his blessed Passion (cf. chs. 24-26):

And for help of this, full meekly our Lord shewed the patience that he had in his hard Passion; and also the joying and the liking that he hath of that Passion, for Love.

And this he shewed in example that we should gladly and wisely bear our pains, for that is great pleasing to him and endless profit to us.

And the cause why we are travailed with them is for unknowing of Love. . . . (Ch. 73, p. 148.)

As is obvious, this reference to the previous Shewings on the Passion strengthens our assertion that the whole teaching on this particular subject is grounded on Julian's basic idea of the ' homely loving '. From this idea of the Love of God she derives her more and more detailed and practical teaching, and points out that:

[1] Cf. the rules given by St Ignatius for the discernment of spirits for the souls who are progressing *de bono in melius* (Ex. Sp. nn. 315, 329): this expression obviously corresponds to the one by which Julian typifies the souls to whom she addresses her teaching.

Then this is the remedy, that we be aware of our wretchedness and flee to our Lord: for ever the more needy that we be, the more speedful it is to us to draw nigh to him.

And let us say thus in our meaning:

'I know well I have a shrewd pain; but our Lord is All-Mighty and may punish me mightily; and he is All-Wisdom and can punish me skilfully; *and he is All-Goodness and loveth me full tenderly.*'

And in this beholding it is necessary for us to abide; for it is a lovely meekness of a sinful soul, wrought by mercy and grace of the Holy Ghost, when we wilfully and gladly take the scourge and chastening of our Lord [that] himself will give us.

And it shall be full tender and full easy, *if that we will only hold us satisfied with him and with all his works.* (Ch. 77, p. 156.)

The last words indicate explicitly how easy the progress would be if the soul gave up the desire of finding satisfaction in what it does.

This place is prison and this life is penance, and in the remedy he willeth that we rejoice.

The remedy is that *our Lord is with us, keeping* and *leading* into the fulness of joy.

For this is an endless joy to us in our Lord's meaning, that he, that shall be our bliss when we are there, he is our keeper while we are here.

Our way and our heaven is true love and sure trust: and of this he gave understanding in all [the Shewings] and *especially* in *the Shewing of the Passion* where he made me mightily to choose him for my heaven.

Flee we to our Lord and we shall be comforted, touch we him and we shall be made clean, cleave we to him and we shall be secure, and safe from all manner of peril.

For our courteous *Lord willeth* that we *should be as homely* with him as heart may think or soul may desire.

But [let us] beware that we take not so recklessly this homeliness as to leave courtesy. (Ch. 77, p. 157.)

These last words show how prudent Julian is, and how balanced is her way of proceeding. Though insisting on the necessity of cleaving to God and expecting everything from him, she is too experienced and too cautious not to guard against possible misunderstanding. Therefore she says: 'I speak but little of *reverent* dread, for I hope it may be seen in this matter aforesaid.' (Ch. 76, p. 154.) By these words she refers to the previous chapter where she had classified four kinds of 'dread', the third of which was 'doubtful dread', but the fourth was:

. . . *reverent dread*: for there is no dread that fully pleaseth God in us but reverent dread.

And that is full soft, for the more it is had, the less it is felt for sweetness of love.

Love and Dread are brethren, and they are rooted in us by the Goodness of our Maker, and they shall never be taken from us without end. . . .

And though this reverent dread and love be not parted asunder, yet they are not both one, but they are two in property and in working, *and neither of them may be had without other*. Therefore I am sure, *he that loveth, he dreadeth*, though that he feel it but a little.

All dreads other than reverent dread that are proffered to us, though they come under the colour of holiness yet are not so true, and hereby may they be known asunder.

That dread that maketh us hastily to flee from all that is not good and *fall into our Lord's breast, as the Child into the Mother's bosom*, with all our intent and with all our mind, knowing our feebleness and our great need, knowing his everlasting goodness and his blissful love, only seeking to him for salvation, cleaving to [him] with sure trust: *that dread that bringeth us into this working, it is kind, gracious, good, and true*. . . .

Desire we of our Lord God to dread him reverently, to love him meekly, to trust in him mightily; for when we dread him reverently and love him meekly our trust is never in vain.

For the more that we trust, and the more mightily, the more we please and worship our Lord that we trust in. And if we fail in this reverent dread and meek love (as God forbid we should!), our trust shall soon be misruled for the time.

And therefore it needeth us much for to pray our Lord of grace *that we may have* this *reverent dread and meek love,* of his gift, in heart and in work. For without this, no man may please God. (Ch. 74, pp. 150-152.) [1]

After these preliminaries, Julian proceeds with her positive teaching, in so far as this concerns a new aspect of our life and deals more explicitly with the way in which we should consider sin.

4. For well I wot the soul that truly taketh the teaching of the Holy Ghost, it hateth more sin for vileness and horribleness than it doth all the pain that is in hell.

For the soul that beholdeth the fair kindness of our Lord Jesus, it hateth no hell but sin, as to my sight.

---

[1] ' *Love and fear of God.*—We know that, among the saints, the love of God —that drawing-power and ravishing fascination of the excellence of the divine perfections—always includes an element of reverential awe born of the contrast existing between the impurities in sinful man and the unalloyed holiness of God: St Peter admirably expressed this feeling of recoil when Christ revealed himself in the miracle of the draught of fishes: " Leave me to myself, Lord, he said; I am a sinner" (Luke, v. 8). Yet this attraction and recoil are in no way mutually exclusive: rather they belong together—the one perfecting the other. The more profoundly the Christian (who is seriously seeking perfection) appreciates the gulf that lies between man's impurity and God's holiness, the more eagerly he seeks his own purification, in order to bind himself more closely to the God who is so attractive. It is true that St John says that " love has no room for fear; and indeed, love drives out fear when it is perfect love, since fear only serves for correction. The man who is still afraid has not yet reached the full measure of love " (1 John iv. 18). But the Apostle is here speaking—as he tells us expressly—of that fear of God as a judge who punishes, and it is *this* kind of fear which perfect love drives out, not that fear of falling short of the holiness necessary for union with the infinite holiness of God.' (J. Huby, *Mystiques Paulinienne et Johannique,* pp. 215-216. See also Huby, *Le discours de Jésus après la Cène,* p. 93.)

And therefore it is God's will that we know sin, and pray busily and travail wilfully and seek teaching meekly that we fall not blindly therein; and if we fall, that we rise readily. For it is the most pain that the soul may have, to turn from God any time by sin. (Ch. 76, p. 154.)

Hence it appears that Julian is not imprudent in emphasizing the beauty and the advantages of a spiritual life based on the more perfect motive of love. She is well aware of the obstacle, which is sin, but at the same time she knows that for good souls the anxiety and preoccupation even with regard to sin may become an obstacle. Therefore, in order to help these souls, she declares the way that they should follow, by saying:

Our Lord of his mercy sheweth us our sin and our feebleness by the sweet gracious light of himself; for our sin is so vile and so horrible that he of his courtesy will not shew it to us but by the light of his grace and mercy. . . .

And thus by this gracious knowing we may see our sin profitably without despair.

For soothly we need to see it, and by the sight we shall be made *ashamed of our self* and *brought down* as anent *our pride and presumption;* for it behoveth us verily to see that of ourselves we are right naught but sin and wretchedness. . . .

And *by this meek knowing* thus through contrition and grace we shall be broken from all thing that is not our Lord.

And *then shall our blessed Saviour perfectly heal us, and one us to him.* (Ch. 78, p. 158.)

Though on the road of love, Julian does not succumb to the temptation of so over-emphasizing love that she loses sight of the dangers to which less prudent persons may be exposed, in so far as they forget the concrete actual condition of fallen man.

And hereby was I learned that though we be highly lifted up into contemplation by the special gift of our Lord, yet it behoveth us therewith to have knowing and sight of our sin and our feebleness. For without this knowing we may not have true meekness, and without this [meekness] we may not be saved. (Ch. 78, p. 159.)

This was the case of Julian herself; she had been granted the special gift of contemplation; but at the same time the conviction of her misery and wretchedness had been strengthened in the Shewings, so that she opens the next chapter by saying: ' Also I had in this [Revelation] more understanding. In that he shewed me *that I should sin*, . . . And also in this same Shewing where I saw that I should sin, there was I learned to be in dread for *unsureness of myself.*' (Ch. 79, pp. 159-160.) But ' Also our courteous Lord *in the same time* he shewed full surely and mightily the *endlessness* and the *unchangeableness of his love; . . .*' (ibid.); so that she may conclude by saying: ' And thus *in this dread* I have matter of *meekness* that saveth me *from presumption*, and *in the blessed Shewing of Love* I have matter of true comfort and of joy that *saveth me from despair*' (ibid.), and give the very practical teaching:

and then willeth he that we see our wretchedness and meekly bear it a-known.

But he willeth not that we abide thus, nor he willeth not that we busy us greatly about our accusing, nor he willeth not that we be wretched over our self; but he willeth that we hastily intend unto him.

For he standeth all aloof and abideth us sorrowfully and mournfully till when we come, and hath haste to have us to him.

For we are his joy and his delight, and he is our salvation and our life. (Ch. 79, pp. 160-161.)

By these words the main idea is repeated again: God wishes to draw the soul to himself, but he will do this only when the soul will go to him, and rely wholly upon him.

5

SUMMARY OF RESULTS

OUR analysis of the object of Julian's contemplation
has revealed that the fundamental theme both of
her special Shewings and of her teaching is the
'homely loving' of God. God is 'the Maker, the Keeper,
the Lover':

> See! I am God: see! I am in all thing: see! I do all thing:
> see! I lift never mine hands off my works, nor ever shall,
> without end: see! I lead all thing to the end I ordained it to
> from without beginning, by the same Might, Wisdom, and
> Love whereby I made it.
> How should any thing be amiss? (Ch. 11, p. 24.)

He is the loving God who proves his tender affection by
giving his life for us:

> Lo, how I loved thee! Behold and see that I loved thee so
> much ere I died for thee, that I would die for thee; and now
> I have died for thee and suffered willingly that [which] I may.
> And now is all my bitter pain and all my hard travail turned to
> endless joy and bliss to me and to thee. (Ch. 24, p. 45.)

We have found Julian's doctrine on trust and optimism to
be the outcome of this fundamental theme. It will hardly
be necessary to prove at length that all this corresponds
fully with the very deepest Christian truths and insights. On
every page of Holy Scripture, both of the Old and of the
New Testament, we find ample proofs of God's loving preoccupation with the work of his hands: all things derive
from him, they are totally his own; he keeps them in being,
governs and provides for them, and even elevates them to

the supernatural order, granting them supernatural life so that they live, by adoption, the very life of the Blessed Trinity through Jesus Christ, God and Man. But this loving preoccupation becomes still more manifest when we consider that the Word of God, in order to restore fallen man, stooped down, 'was made flesh and dwelt amongst us' and 'delivered himself for us'.

At the end of her book ('Revelations of Divine *Love*'), Julian lays open the inner meaning of all her experiences and teaching:

> And from that time that it was shewed I desired oftentimes to witten what was our Lord's meaning. And fifteen years after, and more, I was answered in ghostly understanding, saying thus:
>
> 'Wouldst thou witten thy Lord's meaning in this thing?
>
> Wit it well: Love was his meaning.
>
> Who shewed it thee? Love.
>
> What shewed he thee? Love.
>
> Wherefore shewed it he? For Love.
>
> Hold thee therein and thou shalt witten and know more in the same. But thou shalt never know nor witten therein other thing without end.'
>
> Thus was I learned that Love was our Lord's meaning. (Ch. 86, p. 169.)

Holy Scripture, and St John in particular, explains to us God's dealings with the world in the very same terms:

> *Love* appears throughout as the *motif*. In stressing love, John does not, of course, say something essentially new, since everywhere in the New Testament love appears as the dominating principle. But St John underlines this conception in a particular way and conceives it so to say, essentially as the supernatural stream of life. Nowhere does the verb ἀγαπᾶν (more rarely φιλεῖν —but without essential differences) occur so frequently as here. This love proceeds from God; in the first instance it extends to 'the Son', and then diffuses itself

upon the whole world and finds its parallel in the love of our
Lord towards his Father and towards men.[1]

As I have shown in my analysis, from the consideration of
God's love Julian derives her optimism, her trust in God
alone and her deep joy. And this conception corresponds
equally well to the teaching of Holy Scripture:

The Greek word for *joy* ($\chi\alpha\rho\acute{\alpha}$) is etymologically closely related to the word $\chi\acute{\alpha}\rho\iota\varsigma$, grace. At times one may be sub-
stituted for the other in the textual tradition (thus 2 Cor i. 15;
viii. 2; Phm. 7), which is easier to explain, since even logically
they are very closely related to one another. Joy is one of
the fundamental attitudes of the Christian religion (Rom. xii. 12;
2 Cor. i. 24; vi. 10; Phil. ii. 18; Col. i. 11; etc.) which is
essentially a ' happy furtherance of faith ' (Phil. i. 25) and a
' rejoicing in the Holy Spirit ' (1 Thess. i. 6) or ' in the Lord '
(Phil. iii. 1; iv. 4, 10); joy belongs to ' the harvest of the
Spirit ' (Gal. v. 22). According to Rom. xiv. 17 ' joy in the
Holy Spirit ' together with rightness of heart and peace belong
to the very essence of God's Kingdom, and in Rom. xv. 13 the
desire is expressed that ' God, the author of our hope ' might
fill the Christians ' with all joy and peace ', so that they may
have hope in abundance ' through the power of the Holy

[1] M. Meinertz, *Theologie des Neuen Testamentes*, vol. II, p. 287. A very
valuable and fully documented synthesis of St John's teaching on God's love
may be found in A. Šuštar, *De caritate apud S. Ioannem*, VD, 28 (1950),
pp. 110-119; 129-140; 193-213; 257-270; 321-340. The whole work
substantiates what has been said on the conformity of Julian's
doctrine with Holy Scripture. I quote a few sentences which summarize some of Šuštar's main findings: ' The theology of love of St John the
Apostle is the life and death of Christ as the concrete realization, the very
proof of the love of Christ himself: and the revelation of the Father's love—
the Father who in his love for man, sent his only son into the world to redeem
the world: it is to consider the entire economy of salvation, from the Father's
eternal decree to the consummation on the Cross as a work of love ' (p. 132).
. . . ' God's love, which was made manifest to us in Christ, is not only a
revelation, but is also a communication of love. And this is the purpose of
God's love, to bring men to himself as the sons of his own choice: and this,
not only as objects upon which God exercises his love, but also as subjects
—that is, capable of loving, precisely because God has poured out his own
love upon them ' (p. 257).

Spirit '. This spiritual attitude of joy and peace is the expression of our objective salvation which can in no way be lessened by the remorse caused by sin (2 Cor. vii. 8-11; 1 Cor. v. 2). Hence, too, our '*sure footing* in Christ' (παρρησία) which cannot be shaken (1 Tim. iii. 13; 2 Cor. iii. 12). Along with this goes παράκλησις (consolation): the Greek word more frequently means exhortation, but sometimes it also has the meaning of consolation. God himself is 'the merciful Father, the God who gives all encouragement. He it is who comforts us in all our trials' (2 Cor. i. 3; Rom. xv. 5), 'who never fails to comfort those who are brought low' (2 Cor. vii. 6), 'who has shewn such love to us, giving us unfailing comfort and welcome hope through his grace' (2 Thess. ii. 16). This supernatural comfort finds its source in the passion of the Lord. For 'the sufferings of Christ, it is true, overflow into our lives; but there is overflowing comfort too which Christ brings us' (2 Cor. i. 5, 7). Such comfort fills the faithful with joy and happiness (μακάριοι), in the same sense in which happiness and comfort are put together in the beatitudes of the Sermon on the Mount (St Matt. v. 4). This blessedness results from the remission of sins (Rom. iv. 7, 8), from a holy way of living (Rom. xiv. 22; cf. James, i. 25) and successful striving against temptations (James, i. 12), but also from suffering for Christ and Christianity (1 Peter, iii. 14; iv. 14). And since God himself may be called 'the blessed God' (1 Tim. i. 11; vi. 15), we are to look forward to a future with him 'blessed in our hope' (Tit. ii. 13). [1]

---

[1] M. Meinertz, op. cit. pp. 111-112. Let us quote the final conclusion of Fr U. Holzmeister's article referred to by M. Meinertz, V.D., 22 (1942), p. 262, since it offers a confirmation of Julian's teaching on how we should find in our misery reasons for constant joy: ' And indeed, both feelings which predominate in compunction, viz., contrition for one's own sins, and mourning over the miseries of this life, may become the object of spiritual joy. For we contemplate with deep gratitude the mercy of God by which in His goodness He has granted us forgiveness of our sins, and we advance eagerly towards the chastisements of Divine Providence, ready to suffer patiently all the miseries of this world, when, and how, and to what extent this may be pleasing to God, saying courageously with Christ: "Am I not to drink that cup which my Father himself has appointed for me?" (John

We find then in Julian's doctrine a perfect correspondence with the guiding ideas of Holy Scripture.[1] We would also like to show that Julian's deep insight into God's active presence and loving work for his creatures is in close harmony with the experiences and teachings of the classic masters of the spiritual life.

Whilst dogmatic theologians have developed the content of Revelation with the methods proper to their science, there have always been in the Church privileged souls who were granted, by a special grace, a more direct insight into and vivid consciousness of the same revealed truths. The mystics not only know that God loves his creatures and is actively present in them, but they are aware of his divine indwelling: they ' see ', ' find ', ' experience ' God in his works and most particularly in their own souls.

In the course of this study I have often given references to parallels existing in this respect between the experiences and teachings of Julian and those of some great mystics. However, I think it would be particularly apt to quote here, from the abundant literature on this subject, a few passages from the writings of St Ignatius of Loyola, who, as is known,

---

xviii. 11). The mourning which Christ called blessed may therefore very well go together with a continual joy, not only because it necessarily precedes it and thus introduces it most conveniently, but also because it may become the object itself of this holy joyfulness.'

[1] This close dependence of Julian's writings from Holy Scripture is also one of Sister Reynolds's conclusions: ' By far the most important single influence is the Bible, both Old and New Testaments. This scriptural element is present in three forms: as more or less direct quotation; as the source of concepts adopted and expanded by Julian; and as the unconscious borrowings of a mind steeped in the language and thought of the Bible.' (Sister Reynolds in LSE, pp. 20-21, and the numerous illustrations and scriptural references at pp. 21-22.) In reference to Julian's use of Scripture we may also note an article by Sister M. Dulcidia, *Dame Julian and St Paul*—Cross and Crown, 7 (1955), pp. 100-106. Though some of the citations given in this article may be added to those already quoted by Sister Reynolds and by me, I think that Sister Dulcidia's thesis is scarcely borne out by the text of the Revelations.

habitually 'found God in all things' and centred his whole spiritual teaching on 'trying to find God in all things', 'procurar en todas cosas . . . hallar a Dios'.[1]

> The second point is to consider how God dwells in the creatures; in the elements, giving them being; in the plants, giving them growth; in the animals, giving them sensation; in men, giving them understanding; and so in me, giving me being, life, sensation, and causing me to understand; likewise making of me a temple, seeing that I am created in the likeness and image of his divine Majesty; and then to reflect on myself, . . .

> The third is to consider how God works and labours on my behalf in all created things on the face of the earth, i.e. *habet se ad modum laborantis* (acts as one who labours), as in the heavens, elements, plants, fruits, flocks, etc., giving them being, preserving them, giving them growth and sensation, etc.; then to reflect on myself.

> The fourth point is to contemplate how all good things and gifts descend from above, as, for example, my limited power comes from the Supreme and Infinite Power on high; and in the same way justice, goodness, pity, mercy, etc., just as the rays descend from the sun, and the waters from the fountain. Then to end by reflecting on myself, as has been said above.[2]

> For if men, so to speak, go out of themselves with the intention of entering totally into our Lord and Creator, they become aware, with holy consolation and continual recollection, how our eternal highest Good dwells in all things that have been created, giving being to all and preserving them by his infinite being and presence; and so I believe also of you, that you find spiritual consolation in many things: whosoever loves God with his whole soul will be helped in his devotion by everything, so that he merits ever more and is taken into an ever closer union of love with his Creator and Lord. In this,

---

[1] Cf. Monumenta Historica Societatis Jesu, *Monumenta Ignatiana*, Series I, 3, p. 502.

[2] St Ignatius of Loyola, *Contemplation for obtaining love*, Ex. Spir., nn. 235-237

however, it is, as you say, quite true that the creature not rarely hinders the work of God in its soul.[1]

*   *   *   *

As our scholastics, considering their labours, cannot prolong their prayers, let them have recourse to the exercise of seeking God's presence in everything, in their conversations, their walks, in all that they see, taste, hear, and whatever else they do. For it is true that the Divine Majesty is in all things by his presence, his power, and his essence. Now this way of meditating, of rising to God our Lord through all creatures is easier than that which raises us to the consideration of divine things that are more abstract and require a greater effort in making them present to us. It is an excellent exercise which disposes the soul for great visits from our Lord even in a short prayer.[2]

If we compare these citations with Julian's texts quoted above (cf. especially Part III, ch. 3), it is at once clear how closely her teaching corresponds to the doctrine of this great master of the spiritual life.

We know well that many spiritual writers have derived from the same premises (God's Providence and loving activity) a clear and sound doctrine on abandonment to God, a doctrine which is destined to bring to the soul a deep peace.[3]

[1] MHSI, Mon. Ign., I, 1, pp. 339-340.

[2] Mon. Ign., I, 3, p. 510. For further developments and bibliography on St Ignatius' teaching on this subject, cf. e.g.: K. Truhlar, La découverte de Dieu chez S. Ignace de Loyola, RAM, 24 (1948), pp. 313-337; H. Rahner, Ignatius von Loyola, Geistliche Briefe, Benziger, Einsiedeln Köln, Einführung, especially pp. 53 ff. E. Przywara, Deus semper maior, Theologie der Exerzitien, vol. III, c. 'Liebe', pp. 363-407, Nachwort, Gott in allen Dingen, pp. 409-428.

[3] For fuller information and bibliographical data on 'abandonment', see M. Viller, Abandon, DSp., I, cc. 2-25. See also the second part of the article 'Le faux abandon', by P. Pourrat, ibid. cc. 25-49, from which may easily be gathered how far Julian's doctrine is removed from less prudent ideas.

Even when this abandonment is conceived not merely as a progressive resignation, but more positively as a growing conformity to the will of God, there often seems implicit in it the idea that such perfect trust is only possible after a long and painful process of ' conformation '. But for Julian this perfect trust is divinely offered to every good soul immediately it is ' turned unto the will of God '; and its keynote is joy rather than resignation—' rejoycing in God's love ' and joy. It is in the shadow of this love and filled with this joy that the soul advances to a complete forgetting of self by ' fleeing to God as the child into his mother's breast '. And this very positive concept of conformity to the divine will derives directly from the particular aspect under which she ' saw ' God's goodness, that is to say the motherly and homely loving of God.

In modern times we may find a similar teaching in St Francis of Sales, in St Jeanne de Chantal, and more particularly in St Teresa of Lisieux:

St Francis of Sales conceives of abandonment more or less as the spirit of the child: this particularly in the directions given to St Jeanne de Chantal during her retreat of 1616: *Instruction XII. On Simplicity*, and in one of his booklets: *The Exercise of Perfect Abandonment of Self into the Hands of God*, which bears the date of Holy Thursday, 1616—and was also intended for the nuns of the Visitation.

Abandonment is the entire surrender of oneself ' to the mercy of the eternal love ', without turning back to self, after the manner of small children who take a simple pleasure in the presence of their parents, without any desire of analysing its cause or effects. The soul which completely surrenders itself to that solicitude which the supremely wise Providence of the Creator has for it, will accept without disquiet all the various vicissitudes which will befall it; it will be worried not at all by its own daily imperfections.

Throughout the ages this ' way of the child ' has found its followers. But it has been held in special honour in recent years. On one of the last days of her life, St Teresa of the Infant Jesus was asked by her sister, Mother Agnes of Jesus: ' which is the way to perfection you most recommend to souls ? ' ' My dear Mother '—she answered—' it is the way of spiritual childhood, that is to say the road of confidence and total surrender ' (Mgr Laveille, *Sainte Thérèse de l'Enfant Jésus*, ch.14, p. 377, Lisieux, 1926). The way of the spiritual childhood is not a complicated one, in fact it is very simple indeed. But it postulates a degree of detachment from self which is very seldom found: it postulates extraordinary humility and a signal obedience, constant mortification and a remorseless victory over self which has no end. ' You should not think ' —so St Teresa said to one of her novices—' that this way is a way in which one may rest.' [1]

It is of set purpose that I conclude these considerations on Julian's teaching on optimism and joyful trust with this quotation, because the remarks here contained clearly show the inner value of this doctrine. As I said before (cf. Part III, ch. 4) it is by this attitude of trustful love that the soul allows God to take the lead in bringing it to full detachment from self.

[1] M. Viller, art. cit., cc. 21-22.

GENERAL CONCLUSION

THOUGH the *Revelations of Divine Love* is not a technical treatise, it contains nevertheless a definite doctrine on prayer and contemplation, which is admirable in the theological precision of its concepts and expressions.

Accurate analysis of its content reveals first of all a clear and sound distinction between accidental and essential elements of the spiritual life.

The accidental elements (sickness and sights), though 'profitable', are considered as alternative means to be used only in so far as they help the soul to advance in the ascent towards God, and to an ever closer union with him (essence of the spiritual life).

Prayer and contemplation, which constitute the essential elements in so far as they establish this union, have been the direct object of this present investigation. It would appear superfluous to repeat here a detailed exposition of the findings, for I have taken care to provide a synthesis at the end of each part. Nevertheless, I wish to underline that Julian's doctrine, though in perfect harmony with the classical teaching, is not a mere summary of what had been said by the great masters of the spiritual life, but it is a clear and personal exposition, not overburdened by speculations, but meant to advise on the attitudes to be taken in the various stages of the spiritual ascent. It is also original inasmuch as it contains a clear description of a form of infused contemplation which is not the 'special beholding'.

As for the way in which Julian tries to direct souls, so that they may attain to this close union with God, she insists that the object of contemplation should be God in his Goodness, in his 'homely loving', his active, tender, motherly love.

Thus Julian leads the soul to fix its attention on God, who, in his motherly love, is the giver of life, the source of our 'yearnings' to be 'fastened' and 'oned' to him.

As God is the chief agent in this process of unification, he wishes to retain the lead; and only when the soul has abandoned the most hidden forms of presumption and trust in its own efforts, and has adopted 'the property of a child, that evermore kindly trusteth to the love of the mother in weal and in woe' will it be able to receive the communication of divine life more abundantly, and correspond to God's graces.

Complete trust in God and, consequently, optimism and joy, are the spiritual atmosphere in which 'good souls' ('Christ's lovers') should live.

In the course of this study I have already stressed the fact that Julian's spiritual doctrine is in full conformity with Catholic truths, especially with regard to the points in which Julian is most personal; and I have spoken of her teaching on the infused form of contemplation 'beholding which is not special shewing', and her insistence on an optimistic trust in God's love. With regard to the former I have underlined the similarity with St John of the Cross; and with regard to the latter, the deep understanding of Holy Scripture (St John the Evangelist in particular). This dependence on and conformity with the sources of Christian belief—Scripture and Tradition—constitute the best grounds for approval and recommendation of the *Revelations of Divine Love*.

These conclusions also throw light on the question of the origin of Julian's Shewings.

Obviously I cannot pretend to give a decisive answer to this question which, of its very nature, must be beyond the competence of the individual theologian. But having made a careful investigation into the effects of these extraordinary

experiences, as well as examination of the theological soundness of the doctrine based upon them, [1] I am in a position to
advance a suggestion: viz. that, at the very least, Julian's
doctrine on prayer and contemplation does not contain
anything that would exclude or even dissuade from a divine
origin.

For my part, I should be inclined to go farther and maintain that the attitude of sincere humility, obedience in faith
and prudence, as well as the astounding theological accuracy
of this ' woman unlettered ', point to the divine origin of
the Shewings. By applying, then, the same criteria to
Julian's further experiences and lights I should be inclined
to assert that the ' lightings and touchings ' ' often renewed '
during her life came indeed—as Julian hoped they did—
from God, and hence that she should be ranked among the
true mystics of the Church.

It is for all these reasons that the book of the Revelations
is an important document in the history of the spiritual life.
But it is my view that its essential value is in the fact that
the prayerful reading of the *Revelations of Divine Love* will
stir the soul to a more ardent longing for God.

And this, after all, was Julian's only purpose in recording
her Revelations:

> . . . and truly charity urgeth me to tell you of it,
> for I would that God were known and my fellow-Christians
> helped (as I would be myself), to the more hating of sin and
> loving of God. . . .
> Then shall ye soon forget me that am a wretch, and act so that
> I hinder you not, and behold Jesus who is Teacher of all.' [2]

[1] That these are the criteria to be followed in this matter has been clearly
exposed by Benedict XIVth in his classic work: *De Servorum Dei beatificatione
et Beatorum canonizatione* (Prati, 1840), T. 3, L. 3, Cap. 53, pp. 600 ff.

[2] Reynolds, ch. VI, p. 17.

BIBLIOGRAPHY

Manuscripts

British Museum, Additional MS. 37790.
British Museum, Sloane MS. 2499.
British Museum, Sloane MS. 3705.
Westminster Cathedral Library (not yet numbered).
Bibliothèque Nationale, Paris, Fonds Anglais No. 40.

Editions

XVI Revelations of Divine Love, Shewed to a devout Servant of our Lord called ' Mother Juliana ', an Anchorete of Norwich: who lived in the Dayes of King Edward the Third. Published by R. F. Serenus Cressy, Benedictine, 1670 (reprinted London, 1907). [From the Paris MS.]

Sixteen Revelations of Divine Love, shewed to a devout servant of our Lord called Mother Juliana of Norwich, edited by G. H. Parker (Leicester, 1843). [From the Paris MS.]

Revelations of Divine Love, shewed to a devout Anchoress, by name Mother Julian of Norwich, with a Preface by H. Collins (London, 1877). [From the Sloane MS. 2499.]

Revelations of Divine Love, recorded by Julian, Anchoress at Norwich, Anno Domini 1373. Edited by Grace Warrack (London, 1901, 14th edn. 1952). [From the Sloane MS. 2499.]

XVI Revelations of Divine Love, shewed to Mother Juliana of Norwich, 1373, with a Preface by George Tyrrell, S.J. (London, 1902, reprinted 1920). [From the Paris MS.]

Comfortable Words for Christ's Lovers, being the Visions and Voices vouchsafed to Lady Julian Recluse at Norwich in 1373, Transcribed and edited from the recently discovered Manuscript (Brit. Mus. Add. MS. 37790), by the Rev. Dundas Harford, M.A. (London, 1911, reprinted 1912), referred to as Harford.

The Shewings of the Lady Julian, Recluse at Norwich, 1373 (previously
   entitled: *Comfortable Words for Christ's Lovers*). Transcribed and partly modernized from the earliest known
   manuscript (Brit. Mus. Add. MS. 37790), by the Rev.
   Dundas Harford, M.A. (London, 1925).
*Revelations of Divine Love, Shewed to a devout Ankress, by name Julian
   of Norwich*, edited from the manuscripts by Dom Roger
   Hudleston, O.S.B. (London, 1927). [From the Sloane MS.
   2499.] Second edition, 1952, referred to as Hudleston.
*An Edition of MS. Sloane 2499 of Sixteen Revelations of Divine Love
   by Julian of Norwich*, by Sister Anna Maria Reynolds, C.P.,
   unpublished M.A. thesis, Leeds University (1947).
*A Critical Edition of Sixteen Revelations of Divine Love by Julian of
   Norwich*, by Sister Anna Maria Reynolds, C.P., in prepara-
   tion, under the auspices of Leeds University.
*A Cathedral Manuscript: I. Excerpts from the Revelations of Divine
   Love by Julian of Norwich as they appear in a manuscript belonging
   to the Cathedral Library*, by B. Foucard, in Westminster
   Cathedral Chronicle, 50 (1956), pp. 41-43.
*A Shewing of God's Love: The Shorter Version of 'Sixteen Revelations
   of Divine Love' by Julian of Norwich*. Edited and partially
   modernized from the 15th century MS. by Anna Maria
   Reynolds (London, 1958), referred to as Reynolds.

Excerpts

'*Amen, amen*' (London, 1906).
*The Shewing of a Vision, being Extracts from 'Revelations of Divine
   Love' shewed to a devout Anchoress by name Julian of Norwich*, by
   G. Congrave, M.A. (London, 1915).
'*All shall be well.*' Selections from the writings of the Lady
   Julian of Norwich, A.D. 1373 (London, no date).

Translations

*Julienne de Norwich. Mystique anglaise du XIVe s. Révélations de
   l'Amour de Dieu*. Traduites par un Bénédictin de Farn-
   borough [G. Meunier] (Paris, 1910, 2ème éd. 1925).

Juliana von Norwich, Offenbarungen der göttlichen Liebe. Übersetzung von Dr G. Gerlach, in: ' Dokumente der Religion ', herausgegeben von Otto Karrer (Paderborn, 1926).

Giuliana di Norwich. Rivelazioni dell'amore divino. Introduzione, traduzione e note. Traduzione di Maria De Luca (Torino, 1932).

Studies on Julian

BAKER, A. E.   *Prophets for a Day of Judgment.*   London, 1944.

BULLETT, G.   *The English Mystics.*   London, 1950.

CHAMBERS, F.   *Juliana of Norwich, An Appreciation and an Anthology.*   London, 1955.

The Wisdom of Mother Julian, An Anthology.   London-Oxford, 1951.

COLEMAN, T. W.   *English Mystics of the Fourteenth Century.*   London, 1938.   Referred to as *English Mystics.*

DRANE, F. W.   *Masters of the Spiritual Life.*   London, 1916.

DULCIDIA, SISTER M., S.S.N.D.   *Dame Julian and St Paul,* in Cross and Crown, 7 (1955), pp. 100-106.

English Way, The, edited by Maisie Ward.   London, New York, 1933.

FLOOD, R. H.   *A Description of St Julian's Church, Norwich, and an Account of Dame Julian's connection with it.*   Norwich, 1936.

GARDNER, E. G.   *Juliana of Norwich,* in The Catholic Encyclopedia.   New York, 1907 ff., vol. 8, p. 557.

HODGSON, G. E.   *English Mystics.*   London, 1923.

INGE, W. R.   *Studies of English Mystics,* St Margaret's Lectures 1905.   London, 1907.

KARRER, O.   *Juliana von Norwich, O.S.B., Reklusin,* in Lexikon für Theologie und Kirche, 2. Aufl., Freiburg im Breisgau, 1930 ff., vol. V, c. 713.

KIRCHBERGER, C.   *The Coasts of the Country, An Anthology of Prayer drawn from the Early English Spiritual Writers,* with an introduction by Godfrey Anstruther, O.P.   Chicago, London, 1952.

KNOWLES, D.   *The English Mystics.*   London, 1927.   Referred to as *English Mystics.*

KRÖGER, C.   *Die Mystikerin Lady Julian von Norwich*, Dissertation
zur Erlangung des Doktorgrades der Philosophischen
Fakultät der Universität Hamburg, 1952 (unpublished).

LAWLOR, J. J.   *A Note on the Revelations of Julian of Norwich*, in
Review of English Studies, New Series II (1951), pp. 255-258.

MARY BENVENUTA, O.P.   *Juliana of Norwich*, in The Dublin
Review, 176 (1925), pp. 81-94.

*Meditations on the Litany of the Sacred Heart of Jesus, culled by F. A.
Forbes from the writings of Juliana of Norwich.*   London, 1951.

PEPLER, C., O.P.   *Life of the Spirit*, 3 (1949), pp. 450-454, 486-493,
545-550; 4 (1949), pp. 10-19, 56-64, 149-156, 217-224, 249-
255, 393-402.

The Mystical Body in the English Mystics, in The Clergy Review,
23 (1943), pp. 49-59.

RENAUDIN, P. *Quatre Mystiques Anglais.* Paris, 1945. Referred to as *Quatre Mystiques Anglais.*

REYNOLDS, SISTER ANNA MARIA, C.P.   *Some Literary Influences in
the Revelations of Julian of Norwich*, in Leeds Studies in English
and Kindred Languages (1952), pp. 18-28.   Referred to as
LSE.

STEUART, R. H. J., S.J.   *Diversity in Holiness.*   London, 1936.

THOULESS, R. M.   *The Lady Julian of Norwich, A Psychological
Study.*   S.P.C.K., London, 1924.   Referred to as *The Lady
Julian.*

TYRRELL, G.   *The Faith of the Millions.*   London, 1901.
Referred to as *The Faith.*

WATKIN, E. I.   *Poets and Mystics.*   London, 1953.   Referred to
as *Poets and Mystics.*

Dame Julian of Norwich, in The English Way, edited by Maisie
Ward.   London, New York, 1933, pp. 128-158.

WHITWELL, R.   *Words from the Mystics.*   Chichester, 1931-1935
(vol. IV: *Revelations of Divine Love to Julian of Norwich.*
As abridged and transcribed by R. Whitwell.)

General Bibliography

BENEDICTINE OF STANBROOK, A.   *Mediaeval Mystical Tradition and
Saint John of the Cross.*   London, 1954.

ALVAREZ DE PAZ, J., S.J. *De Inquisitione Pacis sive Studio Orationis.* Lugduni, 1617.

Ancrene Riwle, The, The Corpus MS.: Ancrene Wisse, translated into Modern English by M. B. Salu. With a preface by Professor J. R. R. Tolkien, and an Introduction and Appendix by Dom Gerard Sitwell. London, 1955.

Ancrene Riwle, The English Text of the, edited from Cotton MS. Nero A. XIV, by Mabel Day, D.Lit., EETS. OS. 225, 1952.

ANTONIUS A SPIRITU SANCTO, O.C.D. *Directorium Mysticum.* Parisiis, 1904.

ATTWATER, D. *A Dictionary of Saints.* London, 1948.

AXTERS, ST, O.P. *La spiritualité des Pays-Bas.* Louvain-Paris, 1948.

BAINVEL, J.-V., S.J. *Naturel et Surnaturel, Elévation, Déchéance. Etat présent de l'Humanité.* Paris, 1903 (4 ème éd. 1911).
Introduction to the 11th edition of Poulain, A., S.J. *Grâces d'Oraison.* Paris, 1931, pp. xxiv-xciv.

BAKER, A., O.S.B. *Holy Wisdom or Directions for the Prayer of Contemplation,* edited from the Douay edition of 1657 by the Right Rev. Abbot Sweeny, D.D., O.S.B. London (no date; about 1876).

BAUMGARTNER, C., S.J. *Contemplation: Conclusion générale,* in DSp., II, cc. 2171-2193.

BEA, A., S.J. *De Inspiratione et Inerrantia S. Scripturae. Ad usum auditorum.* Romae, 1947.

BEECHING, H. C.—JAMES, M. R. *The Library of the Cathedral Church of Norwich,* communicated by the Very Rev. H. C. Beeching, D.D., D.Litt., Dean of Norwich. With an appendix of Priory Manuscripts now in English Libraries, by Montague Rhodes James, Esq., Litt.D., F.B.A., Provost of King's College, Cambridge, in Norfolk and Norwich Archaeological Society, Original Papers, 19 (1917), pp. 67 ff., 174.

BENEDICTUS XIV. *De Servorum Dei beatificatione et Beatorum canonizatione.* Prati, 1840.

BERLIÈRE, U., O.S.B. *L'Ordre Monastique.* Paris, 1912 (3rd edn. 1924).

BERNHART, J. *Heiligkeit und Krankheit*, in GL, 23 (1954), pp. 172-195.

BESSE, J. M. *Anachorètes*, in DTC, I, cc. 1134-1140.

BLOMEFIELD, F. Parkin Charles. *An Essay towards a Topographical History of the County of Norfolk.* London, 1805-1810.

BROWNE, H., S.J. *Darkness or Light.* St. Louis, 1925.

BUTLER, A. *The Lives of the Saints*, vol. V (May). London, 1936.

BUTLER, C., O.S.B. *Western Mysticism, The teaching of SS. Augustine, Gregory and Bernard on contemplation and the contemplative life.* London, 1928 (2nd edn. with Afterthoughts, 1926—reprinted, 1951). Referred to as *Western Mysticism.*

Benedictine Monachism. London, 1919 (2nd edn. 1927).

CABASSUT, A., O.S.B. *Une dévotion médiévale peu connue*, in RAM, 25 (1949), pp. 234-245.

CHAMBERS, R. W. *On the Continuity of English Prose from Alfred to More and his School.* London, 1932.

CHAPMAN, J. *Mysticism (Christian, Roman Catholic)*, in Encyclopaedia of Religion and Ethics, edited by James Hastings. Edinburgh, 1908 ff., vol. 9, pp. 90-101.

CLAY, R. M. *The Hermits and Anchorites of England.* London, 1914.

Cloud of Unknowing, The, edited by Dr P. Hodgson, EETS. OS. 218. 1944.

Cloud of Unknowing and other treatises by a 14th Century English Mystic, The, edited by J. McCann, O.S.B. London, 1924 (reprinted 1952).

DALBIEZ, R. *La controverse de la contemplation acquise*, in Technique et Contemplation, Etudes Carmélitaines. Bruges, 1949, pp. 81-145.

DARWIN, F. D. S. *The Medieval Recluse.* London (no date).

DE GUIBERT, J., S.J. *Theologia Spiritualis Ascetica et Mystica.* Romae, 1952. English Translation: *The Theology of the Spiritual Life.* London, 1954.

Une définition des grâces mystiques, in RSR, 18 (1928), pp. 269-280.

Trois définitions de théologie mystique, in RAM, 3 (1922), pp. 162-179.

A propos de la contemplation mystique: problèmes actuels et question de méthode, in RAM, 1 (1920), pp. 329-351.

DE JAEGHER, P., S.J. *An Anthology of Mysticism.* London, 1935.

One with Jesus: The Life of Identification with Christ. London, 1929 (3rd edn. 1955).

DE LA PUENTE, L., S.J. *Meditations upon the Mysteries of our Holie Faith.* St Omers, 1619.

DE LA TAILLE, M., S.J. *L'Oraison contemplative*, in RSR, 10 (1919), pp. 273-292 (also published separately, Paris, 1921).

Théories Mystiques. A propos d'un livre récent [*Western Mysticism*, by C. Butler], in RSR, 18 (1928), pp. 297-325.

DE PUNIET, P. J., O.S.B. *Saint Benoît. La doctrine spirituelle*, in DSp., I, cc. 1388-1409.

DE TONQUÉDEC, J., S.J. *Apparitions*, in DSp, I, cc. 801-809.

DIMIER, M.-A., O.C.R. *Saint Bernard, est-il allé en Angleterre?* in Collectanea Ordinis Cisterciensis Reformati, 9 (1947), pp. 16-19.

English Writings of Richard Rolle, The, edited by H. E. Allen. Oxford, 1931.

ETUDES CARMÉLITAINES. *Nuit Mystique, Nature et Grâce, Sainteté et Folie.* Bruges, 1938.

GARDEIL, A., O.P. *La structure de l'âme et l'expérience mystique.* Paris, 1927.

GABRIELE DI S. MARIA MADDALENA, O.C.D. *Visioni e Rivelazioni nella vita spirituale.* Firenze, 1941. English Translation: *Visions and Revelations in the Spiritual Life.* Westminster, Maryland, 1950.

La contemplazione acquisita. Firenze, 1938.

L'orazione di raccoglimento e l'orazione di quiete in S. Teresa di Gesù, in Vita Cristiana, 9 (1955), pp. 263-283.

Ecole Thérésienne, et problèmes mystiques contemporaines, Traduit par le P. Etienne de S. Marie. Paris, 1936.

Conferenze Spirituali, Conferenza III: Genesi della contemplazione acquisita (estratto dalla Rivista: Vita Cristiana, 6 (1934), pp. 559-596). Firenze, 1934.

GARRIGOU-LAGRANGE, R., O.P. *Les trois âges de la vie intérieure.* Paris, 1938.

GOUGAUD, L. *Etudes sur la reclusion religieuse,* in Revue Mabillon, 13 (1923), pp. 26-39, 77-102.

La vie érémitique au moyen-âge, in RAM, 1 (1920), pp. 209-240, 313-328.

Ermites et reclus. Ligugé, 1928.

HARFORD, D., M.A. *A Norwich Parish 500 years ago.* Norwich, 1905.

HERTLING, L., S.J. *Theologia Ascetica,* 2a ed. Roma, 1944.

HILTON, WALTER. *The Scale of Perfection,* edited by G. Sitwell, O.S.B. London, 1953.

HOLZMEISTER, U., S.J. ' *Gaudete in Domino* ' et ' *beati qui lugent* ', in VD, 22 (1942), pp. 257-262.

HUBY, J. S. J. *Mystiques Paulinienne et Johannique.* Paris, 1946.

JAEGEN, J. *La vie mystique* (Trad. de l'allemand). Paris, 1936.

JAMES, M. R. *See* Beeching, H. C.—James, M. R.

JOHN OF THE CROSS (SAINT). *The Complete Works of Saint John of the Cross, Doctor of the Church,* translated and edited by E. Allison Peers from the critical edition of P. Silverio de Santa Teresa, C.D., 3 vols. London, 1935 (new edn., 1953).

JOSEPHUS A SPIRITU SANCTO, O.C.D. *Enucleatio Mysticae Theologiae S. Dionysii Areopagitae,* ed. crit. Romae, 1927.

MARGERY KEMPE, THE BOOK OF, vol. I, edited by S. B. Meech and H. E. Allen, EETS, OS. 212. 1940.

KNOWLES, D. *The Monastic Order in England.* Cambridge, 1940 (reprinted 1950).

The Religious Orders in England. Cambridge, 1948 (reprinted 1950).

The Religious Houses in Medieval England. London, 1940.

LANZ, A., S.J. *Lineamenti di Ascetica e Mistica.* Milano, 1953.

LE BAIL, A., O.C.R. *Bernard (Saint),* in DSp, I, cc. 1454-1499.

LECLERCQ, J., O.S.B. *Contemplation et vie contemplatives du VIe au XIIe siècle,* in DSp, II, cc. 1929-1948.

Etudes sur Saint Bernard et le texte de ses écrits, in Analecta Sacri Ordinis Cisterciensis, 9 (1953), pp. 1-247.

LECLERQ, H. *Reclus,* in DACL, XIV, cc. 2149-2159.

LEDRUS, M., S.J. *Introductio in doctrinam theologicam Sancti Joannis a Cruce de Contemplatione.* Romae, 1955.

LÉPÉE, M. *Saint Thérèse Mystique.* Paris, 1951.

LHERMITTE, J. *Mystiques et faux mystiques.* Paris, 1952.

MÄHLER, M., O.S.B. *Anselm,* in DSp, I, cc. 689-696.

MARÉCHAL, J., S.J. *Etudes sur la Psychologie des Mystiques,* 2me éd. Paris, 1938. English Translation: *Studies in the Psychology of the Mystics.* London, 1927.

MARMION, C., O.S.B. *Le Christ, idéal du moine.* Maredsous-Paris, 1923.

MEINERTZ, M. *Theologie des Neuen Testamentes,* vol. II. Bonn, 1950.

MONUMENTA HISTORICA SOCIETATIS JESU, *a Patribus eiusdem Societatis edita.* Madrid, 1894 ff. Romae, 1932 ff., Monumenta Ignatiana, Series Prima.

OLIGER, L., O.F.M. *Regulae tres Reclusorum et Eremitarum Angliae saec. XIII-XIV,* in Antonianum, 3 (1928), pp. 151-190 ; 299-320.

Regula Reclusorum Angliae et Quaestiones tres de vita solitaria, in Antonianum, 9 (1934), pp. 37-84; 243-268.

PANTIN, W. A. *The English Church in the Fourteenth Century.* Cambridge, 1955.

PHILIPPE, P., O.P. *La contemplation au XIIIᵉ siècle,* in DSp, II, cc. 1966-1988.

PHILIPPUS A SS. TRINITATE, O.C.D. *Summa Theologiae Mysticae.* Lugduni, 1656 (re-edited, Friburgi Brisgoviae, 1874).

PINARD DE LA BOULLAYE, H., S.J. *La spiritualité ignatienne.* Paris, 1949.

Conversion, in DSp, II, cc. 2224-2265.

POULAIN, A., S.J. *Des grâces d'Oraison,* Paris, 1901 (llème éd., 1931). English Translation: *The Graces of Interior Prayer.* London, 1950.

POURRAT, P. *La Spiritualité Chrétienne.* I: Dès origines au moyen âge, Paris, 1918. II: Le moyen âge, 1921; III-IV: Les temps modernes, 1925-1928.

Le faux Abandon, in DSp, I, cc. 25-49.

POWER, E. *Medieval English Nunneries.* Cambridge, 1922.

PRZYWARA, E. *Deus semper major, Theologie der Exerzitien*, vol. III. Herder, Freiburg im Breisgau, 1940.

RAHNER, H., S.J. *Ignatius von Loyla. Geistliche Briefe.* Übertragen und eingeleitet von Otto Karrer. Neu durchgesehen und vermehrt von Hugo Rahner. Einführung von Hugo Rahner. Einsiedeln Köln, 1942.

RAHNER, K., S.J. *Über Visionen und verwandte Erscheinungen*, in GL, 21 (1948), pp. 179-213.

Le début d'une doctrine des cinq sens spirituels, in RAM, 13 (1932), pp. 113-145.

ROLLE, RICHARD. See *The English Writings of Richard Rolle.*

RYE, W. *Carrow Abbey, otherwise Carrow Priory: near Norwich . . . ; its foundation, buildings, officers and inmates.* Norwich, 1889.

RYELANDT, I., O.S.B. *Essai sur la physionomie morale de saint Benoît.* Coll. Pax, Paris, 1924.

SAUDREAU, A. *L'Oraison d'après Saint François de Sales.* Paris, 1927.

L'Oraison d'après Sainte Jeanne de Chantal. Saint-Maximin, Paris-Liège, 1925.

Les degrés de la vie spirituelle, 6th edn. Angers, 1935 (first published, 1896).

L'Etat Mystique. Sa Nature-Ses Phases et les Faits extraordinaires de la vie spirituelle, 2nd edn. Paris-Arras-Angers, 1921.

SCHRAM, D., O.S.B. *Institutiones theologiae Mysticae.* Augsburg, 1777 (re-edited: Paris, 1868).

STAEHLIN, C. M., S.J. *Apariciones, Ensayo critico.* Madrid, 1954.

Mystische Täuschungen. Zur Beurteilung einiger mystischer Phänomene, in GL, 27 (1954), pp. 276-290.

STEUART, R. H. J., S.J. *The mystical doctrine of St John of the Cross* (an abridgement made by C. H. with an introduction by R. H. J. Steuart, S.J.). London, 1948.

ŠUŠTAR, A. *De caritate apud S. Ioannem*, in VD, 28 (1950), pp. 110-119, 129-140, 193-213, 257-270, 321-340.

TERESA OF AVILA (SAINT). *The Complete Works of Saint Teresa of Jesus*, translated and edited by E. Allison Peers, from the critical edition of P. Silverio de Santa Teresa, C.D., 3 vols. London, 1944-1946.

THURSTON, H., S.J. *The Physical Phenomena of Mysticism*, edited by J. H. Crehan, S.J. London, 1952.

TRUHLAR, K., S.J. *Lumière de la contemplation dans la nuit mystique*, in NRT, 71 (1949), pp. 1063-1071.

La découverte de Dieu chez S. Ignace de Loyola, in RAM, 24 (1948), pp. 313-337.

De Experientia Mystica. Romae, 1951.

UNDERHILL, E. *The Mystic Way, A Psychological study in Christian Origins*. London-Toronto, 1913.

The Mystics of the Church. London (no date).

Mysticism, A study in the nature and development of man's spiritual consciousness. London, 1912 (12th edn. 1930).

The Mirror of Simple Souls, in Fortnightly Review, 89 (1911), pp. 345-354.

VALGORNERA, T. a, O.P. *Mystica Theologia Divi Thomae*. Torino, 1911.

VERNET, F. *Anglaise, Ecossaise, Irlandaise (Spiritualité)*, in DSp, I, cc. 625-659.

Victoria History of the Counties of England, The, edited by William Page, F.S.A., 'Norfolk', v. 2. London, 1906.

VILLER, M., S.J. *Abandon*, in DSp, I, cc. 2-25.

WATKIN, E. I. *The Bow in the Clouds. An Essay towards the integration of experience*. London, 1954.

WILMART, A., O.S.B. *Méditations et prières de Saint Anselm*. Coll. Pax, Paris, 1923.

La tradition des prières de Saint Anselm, Tables et Notes, in Revue Bénédictine, 36 (1924), pp. 52-71.

WHITWELL, R. *Words from the Mystics*. Chichester, 1931-1935 (vol. IV: *Revelations of Divine Love to Julian of Norwich*, as abridged and transcribed by Richard Whitwell).

LIST OF CITATIONS FROM AND REFERENCES TO THE TEXT OF THE SHORTER VERSION

(Reynolds edition, Longmans Green, London, 1958)

Reynolds	Molinari
Ch. I	pp. 13-14, 15, 16, 17, 18, 27, 49
II	21-22, 29
III	30, 50
IV	74
VI	5, 28, 52, 54-55, 73, 159, 198
XIII	74

LIST OF CITATIONS FROM AND
REFERENCES TO THE TEXT OF THE
LONGER VERSION

(Hudleston edition, Burns & Oates, London, 1952)

Hudleston	*Molinari*
Ch. I	pp. 50, 149-151
II	5, 7, 10, 16, 30, 55, 73
III	122
IV	34, 38, 41, 42, 45-46, 47, 48, 50, 86, 87, 151, 152
V	38, 46, 69, 75, 77, 84, 85, 86, 87, 88, 89, 90, 91, 92, 94, 95, 99, 152, 157, 158
VI	75, 84, 86, 87, 90, 92, 94, 95, 100, 152
VII	34-35, 75, 77, 87, 119, 120, 121, 122, 130, 131, 134, 135
VIII	90, 91, 158, 159
IX	33-34, 41, 53, 67, 111, 159
X	51, 55, 75, 77, 104, 108, 109, 111, 115, 116, 117, 119, 121, 122-123, 124, 127, 130, 131, 132, 142, 143, 160
XI	158, 159, 187
XII	35, 62
XIII	68
XVI	35-36, 152
XX	152
XXI	152-153
XXII	37, 48, 67-68, 153, 173
XXIII	48
XXIV	41, 48, 110, 153-154, 174, 181, 187
XXV	39, 40, 56, 68, 156, 181
XXVI	69, 181
XXVII	81
XXVIII	81
XXIX	156
XXX	53
XXXI	156
XXXII	53
XXXIII	53
XXXIV	53, 53-54
XXXV	136-137
XXXIX	75, 76, 78, 79-80, 81, 83, 84, 94
XL	75, 76, 78, 79-80, 83, 84, 94

Hudleston	*Molinari*
Ch. XLI	pp. 74, 75, 76, 77, 84, 94, 96, 98, 99, 101, 104, 108, 119, 121, 123-127
XLII	74, 75, 76, 77, 84, 94, 96, 97, 101, 102, 103, 108, 119, 121, 123
XLIII	18, 65, 74, 75, 76, 77, 84, 94, 96, 97, 98, 99, 100, 101, 103, 104, 106, 107, 109-110, 111, 119, 121, 123, 127-128, 129-130, 143, 166
XLVI	53, 75
LI	6, 7, 10, 42, 43-45, 47, 66, 164
LII	163, 164
LIV	75, 163, 164, 165, 166, 167
LV	138, 165, 166
LVI	160
LVIII	164, 172
LIX	172
LX	169, 172-173, 173-174
LXI	53, 173, 175-176
LXII	53
LXIV	74
LXV	5, 72, 73, 160
LXVI	5, 51, 52, 53, 155
LXVII	40, 155, 160, 161, 162, 163, 166
LXVIII	75, 162, 163
LXX	133-134, 135
LXXI	74
LXXII	18
LXXIII	41, 65, 67, 73, 75, 179, 180, 181
LXXIV	179, 183-184
LXXVI	181, 183, 184-185
LXXVII	181, 182
LXXVIII	74, 185, 186
LXXIX	186
LXXXI	160-161
LXXXIII	110, 138, 155
LXXXVI	6, 50, 156, 188

INDEX

Acts of Peter (Apocryphal), 170
Agnes of Jesus, 195
Ancrene Riwle, 8, 176
Anselm of Canterbury, St, 9, 170-171
Antonius a S. Spiritu, O.C.D., 60
Aravalles, Fr, 144
Attwater, D., 12
Augustine of Hippo, St, 60, 85, 109, 116, 135, 160

Bainvel, J.-V., S.J., 57, 143
Baker, A., O.S.B., 136, 142
Baumgartner, C., S.J., 114-115, 139, 143
Bea, A., S.J., 60
Benedict of Nursia, St, 8, 9, 80, 90, 92-93
Benedict XIV, Pope, 198
Benedictine of Stanbrook, A, 116, 142, 154
Benet Biscop, 9
Bernard of Clairvaux, St, 9, 109, 112-113, 116, 154
Blomefield, F., 10
Bullett, G., 91
Butler, C., O.S.B., 9, 57, 93, 109, 113, 116, 117, 134-136, 143

Cabassut, A., O.S.B., 169-171
Catherine of Siena, St, 80
Chambers, R. W., 41
Chown, J., M.S.C., 161
Clay, R. M., 8
Cloud of Unknowing, The, v, 81, 84, 111
Coleman, T. W., 5, 9, 23
Crehan, J. H., S.J., 57
Cressy, S., O.S.B., v

Darwin, F. D., 8
De Guibert, J., S.J., 57, 58, 60-63
De Jaegher, P., S.J., 178

De la Puente, L., S.J., 15
De Puniet, P., O.S.B., 92-93
De la Taille, M., S.J., 57
De Tonquédec, J., S.J., 60
Dimier, M.-A., O.C.R., 154
Dulcidia, Sr M., S.N.D., 191

Edward, St, 7
Epistle of Privy Counsel, 81

Francis of Sales, St, 100, 194

Gabriele di S. Maria Maddalena, O.C.D., 57, 59, 68, 143-145
Garrigou-Lagrange, R., O.P., 75, 80
Geist und Leben, Editor of, 26
Glorieux, P., 170
Gougaud, L., 8
Gratian, Fr, 144
Gregory the Great, St, 9, 90, 93, 109, 116, 117

Hadewijch, 116
Harford, D., 4, 89, 154
Hilton, Walter, v, 4, 80, 82-83, 138
Holzmeister, U., S.J., 190-191
Huby, J., S.J., 134, 184
Hudleston, R., O.S.B., 5, 6, 7, 8, 10, 11, 12, 16, 18, 28, 30, 73, 74, 89, 161
Hugh of St Victor, 104, 154

Ignatius of Loyola, St, 26, 91, 135, 181, 191-193
Inge, W. R., 23
Isidore of Seville, St, 60

Jeanne de Chantal, St, 100, 194
John Chrysostom, St, 170
John of the Cross, St, 18, 26, 58, 59, 60, 82, 113, 115, 126, 128, 134, 143-145, 161, 164-165, 197
Joseph a Jesu Maria, 113

Josephus a Spiritu Sancto, O.C.D., 60
Julian, St, 7, 8

King, C., S.J., vii
Knowles, D., 9, 10, 23
Kröger, C., 4, 5, 63, 161

Le Bail, A., O.C.R., 154
Leclercq, J., O.S.B., 154
Leclerq, H., 8
Ledrus, M., S.J., vii, 58, 128-129
Lépée, M., 59
Lhermitte, J., 57

Mähler, M., 170
Maréchal, J., S.J., 105-106
Margery Kempe, 11, 12, 28
Marguérite d'Oyngt, Blessed, 171
Marmion, C., O.S.B., 93
McCann, J., O.S.B., 81, 111
Mechtilde von Hackeborn, St, 171
Meinertz, M., 189-191
Mersch, E., S.J., 170

Nicholas of Assisi, 154

Oliger, L., 8

Page, W., 154
Pantin, W. A., 154
Pepler, C., O.P., 23, 173
Philippe, P., O.P., 116
Philippus a SS. Trinitate, O.C.D., 59,
    60
Pinard de la Boullaye, H., S.J., 75
Poulain, A., S.J., 57, 60, 82, 109, 143
Pourrat, P., 193
Power, E., 10
Przywara, E., 193

Rahner, H., S.J., 193
Rahner, K., S.J., 63, 109
Renaudin, P., 5, 10, 23, 29, 31, 73
Reynolds, Sr A. M., C.P., vii, 3, 5, 6,
    7, 10, 14, 22, 41, 49, 52, 55, 73, 74,
    85, 89, 90, 159, 166, 191, 198
Richard of St Victor, 141-142, 143
Rolle, Richard, v, 4
Ruysbroeck, J., Blessed, 135
Rye, W., 8
Ryelandt, I., O.S.B., 93

Saudreau, A., 100
Schram, D., O.S.B., 60
Sitwell, G., O.S.B., 80
Staehlin, C. M., S.J., 26, 57
Suso, H., Blessed, 80
Šuštar, A., 189

Tauler, J., 80
Teresa of Avila, St, 40, 53, 59, 63, 68,
    74, 113, 135, 162, 164, 165
Teresa of Lisieux, St, 194, 195
Thomas of Aquinas, St, 60, 115
Thomas Gallus, 116
Thouless, R., 5, 23, 74, 100
Thurston, H., S.J., 57
Truhlar, K., S.J., 82, 109, 193
Tyrrell, G., 23, 27, 89, 115

Underhill, E., 4, 5, 60

Valgornera, T. a, O.P. 60
Viller, M., S.J., 191, 194-195

Walsh, J., S.J., vii
Warrack, G., 6, 23, 75, 89, 98
Watkin, E. I., 63, 84, 100
Wilfrid, St, 9
Wilmart, A., O.S.B., 170